THE HOUSE OF LORDS

STUDIES IN MODERN HISTORY

General editors: John Morrill and David Cannadine

This series, intended primarily for students, will tackle significant historical issues in concise volumes which are both stimulating and scholarly. The authors combine a broad approach, explaining the current state of our knowledge in the area, with their own research and judgements; and the topics chosen range widely in subject, period and place.

Titles already published

THE HOUSE OF LORDS
in British Politics and Society 1815–1911

E.A. Smith

Longman
London and New York

LONGMAN GROUP UK LIMITED,
Longman House, Burnt Mill,
Harlow, Essex CM20 2JE, England
and Associated Companies throughout the world.

*Published in the United States of America
by Longman Publishing, New York*

© Longman Group UK Limited 1992

First published 1992

ISBN 0-582-09539-5 CSD
ISBN 0-582-09538-7 PPR

British Library Cataloguing-in-Publication Data
A catalogue record for this book is available from the British Library

Library of Congress Cataloguing in Publication Data
Smith, E.A.
    The House of Lords in British politics and society, 1815–1911 /
E.A. Smith.
        p.   cm. — (Studies in modern history)
    Includes bibliographical references and index.
    ISBN 0–582–09539–5. — ISBN 0–582–09538–7 (pbk.)
    1. Great Britain. Parliament. House of Lords—History.   2. Great
Britain—Politics and government—19th century.   3. Great Britain—
Politics and government—1901–1910.   I. Title.   II. Series:
Studies in modern history (Longman (Firm))
    JN621.S65   1992
328.41′017′09—dc20
                                                                92-12203
                                                                    CIP

Set by 5B
in Bembo
Produced by Longman Singapore Publishers (Pte) Ltd.
Printed in Singapore

Contents

Preface

In the century between the battle of Waterloo and the outbreak of the First World War Britain moved from being a mainly rural society, governed by a landed aristocracy of rank and title, to an urban and industrialized democracy dominated by a wealthy middle class. Three major Reform Acts in 1832, 1867 and 1884–5 extended the right to vote to virtually all adult males, and changed the nature and boundaries of constituencies to give predominance to the middle and lower classes of the people living in the towns, who were no longer required to defer to the political authority of the landlords but were able to elect representatives of their own interests. The House of Commons thus became more directly responsible to the mass of the nation rather than reflecting the wishes of aristocratic patrons, and its political role changed accordingly. In the eighteenth century, Parliament was seen as a check on the power of a royal executive whose members, appointed by the monarch, were the individual servants of the Crown. By 1914, the House of Commons had become the focus of political power and, through the virtually all-embracing two-party system, the source of governmental authority. The monarch had all but retired from political activity except at rare moments of crisis, and the Cabinet, appointed at the wish of the Prime Minister, who was in turn chosen by the leaders of the majority party in the House of Commons, had assumed the direction of executive power.

In Parliament, the House of Commons had become the dominant House. The House of Lords still included all the (male) titled nobility of England and the United Kingdom, with representatives of the separate Scots and Irish peerages and the archbishops and most bishops of the Anglican Church. None of its members, however, sat by virtue of popular election and instead of being the superior branch of the national legislature it now appeared to be the voice of a propertied minority. Its political power had shrunk to the ability only to delay or suggest amendments to bills passed by what was now only in a titular sense the Lower House. As Walter Bagehot had forecast in his work on *The English Constitution* in 1867, the monarchy and the House of Lords had become merely part of the 'dignified' or ornamental element in the constitution, while the Cabinet and the Commons together monopolized the 'efficient' power of government.

The story of this development in relation to the House of Lords and the peerage who composed it is the theme of this book. It is a subject which has been curiously neglected by historians during the twentieth century, as though the apparent destruction of the power of the House of Lords in the Parliament Act of 1911 had removed it from serious consideration as a part of the nation's political life. Historians of eighteenth-century England, though well aware of the importance of the peerage in the politics of that period, were more interested in the character and personnel of the House of Commons. Its superior financial powers and greater frequency of meetings after 1689 meant that the Commons assumed a greater public importance, while the increased competition for seats which this produced made it a magnet for men of consequence, and thus a study of its composition offered a view of the balance of interests and the structure of society. This was the major preoccupation of Sir Lewis Namier and his 'History of Parliament' teams who dominated the eighteenth-century historiographical scene in the mid-twentieth century. They ignored the House of Lords, though they painstakingly itemized and catalogued the influence wielded by the peerage over the composition of the Lower House. They acknowledged the reality of aristocratic power, but saw its expression through the House of Commons rather than as a function of the House of Lords.

Only one major historian in the first half of the twentieth century devoted his principal efforts to the history of the House of Lords. This was A.S. Turberville, whose volumes on the House in the reigns of William III and Anne and in the eighteenth century appeared in 1913 and 1927 respectively. At the time of his death in 1945 he was engaged on a third volume, to carry the story to the end of the nineteenth century, but the work was incomplete. Turberville's manuscript was edited and published by R.J. White in 1958 as *The House of Lords in the Age of Reform*, but it did not deal substantially with the period after 1837 and it lacked coherence as a political narrative. It contains a number of valuable chapters, especially on the Reform Act crisis of 1830–2 and its effects, and several useful statistical appendices, but Turberville wrote little on the period after Victoria's accession.

Otherwise, interest in the aristocracy and the House of Lords flagged until some thirty years after the Second World War. Social historians became more engrossed in working-class and radical history, following the inspirational work of E.P. Thompson and his disciples, until the later 1970s when 'radical' history began to pass out of fashion as the external political climate changed. Economic historians had maintained a more consistent interest in the eighteenth- and nineteenth-century aristocracy because of their continuing importance in the national economy, and historians such as David Spring, F.M.L. Thompson and J.V. Beckett, among others, published much on the social and economic role and power base of the aristocracy in general, but they have not examined the political activities of the House of Lords itself in any comparable detail.

The revival of interest in the House of Lords since 1689 was led by two historians in the late 1970s and early 1980s. In 1978 Michael McCahill published *Order and Equipoise: the Peerage and the House of Lords, 1783–1806* and in 1982 John Cannon chose as his theme for the Wiles lectures at Queen's University, Belfast, an examination of the importance of the titled aristocracy in the society, economy and politics of the 'Aristocratic Century' between 1700 and 1800, published under that title in 1984. Both works illuminated the role of the nobility in British life and politics, but no further work has since tackled the history of the House of Lords after the beginning of the nineteenth century. There have been several doctoral theses dealing in detail with restricted periods during the century, and established historians such as Norman Gash, Corinne Weston and David Large, social historians and sociologists such as W.L. Arnstein, T.H. Hollingsworth and W.D. Rubinstein have published articles of great value on special topics. J.C. Sainty and members of the staff of the House of Lords Record Office have made available in print essential materials on the personnel and work of the House. Most recently, David Cannadine's book *The Decline and Fall of the British Aristocracy* has dealt authoritatively and comprehensively with the peerage in the period after 1880.

I have drawn on all of this work and this volume seeks to bring together those parts of it which throw light on the history of the House of Lords and its members and to present a coherent account of its fortunes during the century after the end of the Napoleonic Wars, which released the energies of the British nation for peaceful economic development culminating in the world economic dominance of mid- and later Victorian Britain.

The book is divided into three parts. Part One considers the physical environment and the forms of business in the House during the whole century. Part Two concentrates on the period before the 1880s, the time when the Lords adjusted, successfully on the whole, to the changing conditions of political life between the First and the Third Reform Acts. These central chapters illustrate the social and political composition of the House and its activities in relation to the Commons and the public at large. Part Three surveys the changes brought about in response to the economic, social and political developments which ended the mid-Victorian 'age of equipoise' after 1880. These changes gave rise to a number of attempts to make the House of Lords more acceptable as a continuing element in the political life of the nation, ending, after the failure of proposed reforms, in the Parliament Act of 1911 which left the House unchanged in its composition but modified its constitutional powers. The survival and, in some ways, the recovery of the House of Lords in the period down to the 1970s is the subject of the Conclusion.

The theme of the book is survival and adaptation. It is a study, in an almost Darwinian sense, of the evolution of a political animal in response to changes in the environment in which it had to operate. That it has survived, and in some senses successfully, is a tribute both to the innate conservatism of the British nation, which has shown its preference for evolutionary rather than revolutionary change, and to the wisdom, on the whole, of those statesmen who guided the House to act within the limits of what the country would accept. The history of the nineteenth-century House of Lords epitomizes the history of the society in which and as an integral part of which it acted. Its evolution and adaptation is as significant as the provisions of the Reform Acts in defining the character of Victorian and Edwardian society and politics.

Acknowledgements

I am most grateful to the Leverhulme Trust for the award of a research grant in 1986 to cover the expenses incurred in the preparation of this book. I am also grateful to the following owners of MSS for permission to use and to quote from their collections: the duke of Devonshire (the Chatsworth papers); the duke of Newcastle (Newcastle papers, Nottingham University Library); the duke of Sutherland (Sutherland papers, Staffordshire Record Office); Lord Hatherton (Hatherton papers, Staffordshire Record Office). I should also like to thank the custodians of those collections for their courteous assistance, and the writers of unpublished doctoral theses for permission to make use of their work. My debt to other scholars who have written on aspects of the subject will be apparent from the list of their works in the Bibliography. I am deeply grateful to Mrs Elizabeth Berry for her unfailingly efficient secretarial services. I am particularly grateful to Professor David Cannadine for his helpful criticisms and suggestions on the first draft of the book, though for what I have written I remain solely responsible.

My thanks are due above all to my wife, whose encouragement, wise criticism and occasional approval contributed more than I can express to the writing of this book. Without her it could not have been written as it is.

It is not true that England is governed by an aristocracy in the common acceptation of the term. England is governed by an aristocratic principle.

Benjamin Disraeli, *Lord George Bentinck*

For Virginia

Introduction

On 6 February 1649, a week after the execution of King Charles I, the House of Commons resolved 'That the House of Peers in Parliament is useless and dangerous, and ought to be abolished'.[1] England thereafter was governed with the aid of a single-chamber legislature until 1657, when the Humble Petition and Advice requested Lord Protector Cromwell to call future Parliaments of two Houses, the members of the 'Other House' being nominated by the Lord Protector and approved by the Commons. In 1658 Richard Cromwell's House of Commons agreed to the summoning of peers 'who have been faithful to the parliament', but that Parliament was replaced a few weeks later by the 'Rump', the remnant of the House of Commons in the Long Parliament, which was dissolved in turn in March 1659. In April 1660, however, the restoration of Charles II to his throne was heralded by a meeting of the House of Lords, consisting of ten peers to whom 'divers Lords' who had inherited their titles since 1649 were added two days later. On that same day the king's letter from Breda was read, announcing that 'you are again acknowledged to have that authority and jurisdiction which hath always belonged to you by your birth, and the fundamental laws of the land'. On 1 May the Lords passed a resolution, which was echoed by the Commons, 'That, according to the ancient and fundamental laws of this kingdom, the government is, & ought to be, by King, Lords, and Commons'. The hereditary peerage of England was restored to the political position it had held before 1649 and the House of Lords has remained since that day an essential part of the constitution, in both judicial and legislative capacities. No one has again voted to abolish it, though on occasions it may have appeared useless or dangerous.[2]

1

The Lords in the eighteenth century were seen as having two functions: to support the Crown as hereditary counsellors of the monarch, but also to provide a 'check and balance' to the constitution by mediating between king and Commons. The theory of the 'mild and mixed constitution' thinly disguised the reality of executive authority. By the exercise of influence and prerogative, kings even as supposedly weak as the first two Georges ensured that the ministers of their personal choice and preference would command the majority support in both Houses necessary to enable them to govern in the king's name. Executive influence ensured the existence of a substantial Court and Administration group in the Commons which was at the disposal of any minister of whom the king approved.[3] In the Upper House, the royal control of the conferment of peerages and promotions and of patronage in the form of honours, offices and pensions merely emphasized the close connections between the court and the peerage which provided ballast to the constitution as a blend of monarchy and aristocracy.

Of the two, it was a question which was supreme. As long as England remained a basically rural society, in which the ownership of great landed property conferred leadership at national and local levels, the institution which contained and embodied the interests of the greatest landowners had great political as well as social authority. The Glorious Revolution of 1688–9 subordinated the independence of the monarchy to aristocratic dominance, while a large proportion of the House of Commons was returned by the direct control or indirect influence of the peerage, whose sons, brothers, nephews and cousins made up a large proportion of its membership. It was indeed an 'Aristocratic Century'.[4] The personal preferences of monarchs, particularly of George III, continued to have weight in the choice of ministers, but government was firmly in the hands of a select circle of landowning families of whom the titled peerage were the acknowledged leaders.

The responsibilities of that government were sufficiently limited to allow its tasks to be carried out on a largely non-professional basis. Departments were run by political chieftains almost as personal empires; foreign affairs and diplomacy were the especial field of the nobility, whose rank enabled them to speak on equal terms with the leaders of other nations. Subordinate offices were filled by patronage, to provide for younger sons and brothers who did not inherit family estates, rather than with the intention to recruit a skilled bureaucracy. Only in the Treasury and other financial and economic departments like the Board of Trade was a degree of trained professional competence or experience required. In national, as in local government, the service of a social elite, fulfilling its obligations to the country which accepted its primacy, provided all that was considered necessary for the effective running of the machine.

Legislation too was in the hands of men of the same class and background, and as far as official or public legislation was concerned, like government it was kept to the minimum necessary for the smooth running of affairs. Eighteenth-century Parliaments were not so much partners in the work of governmental administration as sounding-boards for private, local and special interests who wished to promote their objectives by legislative means – to enclose land, to set up trusts to administer roads and canals, to protect game, or to divorce wives. The ties between Parliament and the localities were stronger than those between it and the central executive and its atmosphere was more that of a club for aristocrats and country gentlemen than of an institution of government. Select committees were few. Parliament did not make it its regular business to enquire into social or economic questions or to formulate policies or create administrative machinery to deal with them. Nor did it seek to publicize its proceedings: before 1771 the reporting of debates could be, and often was, punished as a breach of privilege. Neither peers nor members of the Commons saw themselves as delegates of, or even responsible for their words and actions to, any wider constituency. The 'independence of Parliament' meant not just, as originally, independence of the Crown, but independence of the mass of the people.

This situation began to change in the later years of the eighteenth century. The reasons were partly economic. The great expansion of domestic industry, of trade and colonization and exploitation of the world overseas created new wealth and new interests, which began to demand representation so that government and legislation might cater for them. The sphere of governmental activity widened as a consequence and so did its financial needs. Governments began to be seen as having a role in the regulation of economic and social questions, as 'holding the ring' in the national interest between conflicting pressures. Law and order, always a primary duty of central as well as local government, also became a more pressing concern, reflecting the growth of population and of towns, where the informal mechanisms of traditional social control no longer applied, or applied with less effect. The role of the state was expanding precisely when concern about social tensions was becoming more marked, especially in the period of the French Revolutionary and Napoleonic Wars when economic dislocation and social discontent were related to foreign war or the preaching of subversive political doctrines. Often against their wills, governments and parliaments found themselves obliged to take up a range of issues which it was too dangerous to ignore, and to develop expertise and professional management in order to deal with them.

Government was thus beginning to pass out of the hands of the aristocracy or landed elite; but the overall control was not given up readily or quickly. Britain avoided revolution in the years of turmoil in Europe after 1789 largely because her institutions and her social elite were adaptable and flexible enough to adjust to new responsibilities. As new men with professional backgrounds and awareness of the new 'science' of political economy, such as Peel or Brougham, took up the management of affairs and leadership of causes in the Commons, the membership of the House of Lords also reflected these changes. The increase in the titled nobility after 1784 has often been commented upon: the most recent investigator of the process has shown that, while the possession of wealth deriving from landed property remained a necessary formal qualification for entry to the House of Lords, a large proportion – in fact exactly a half – of new peers created between 1801 and 1830 were politicians, professional men and distinguished servants of the state in the armed forces or diplomatic service. Their claim to admission was based on past service to the country rather than mere landownership.[5]

Yet the significance of these changes is open to qualification. The notion that by or around 1830 England was passing out of her *ancien régime* phase into a new era of rational, utilitarian and professional government and ultimately of democracy does not allow for the ability and the will of the old elite to perpetuate its dominance. In Ireland in 1829 the political effects of Catholic Emancipation were much moderated by the accompanying measure to raise the qualification for the county franchise so as to perpetuate aristocratic influence. In Britain, Grey's Reform Acts of 1832 were designed as much to strengthen aristocratic dominance and make it acceptable to those admitted to a mere share of its power as to broaden the base of political life. The ecclesiastical reforms of the 1830s did much to restore the prestige and authority of the churches and the strength of Christianity as a social and moral discipline. British society was still a deferential society. Loyalism in the 1790s had strengthened the hold of traditional values and hierarchical ideas; the democrats and radicals found themselves discarded and rejected in the 1830s and 1840s as well as in the 1790s. Contemporary commentators observed that the peerage and the aristocracy in general still exercised a great influence not only in material terms of power and wealth, but as an accepted part of society.[6] This book will demonstrate how, through what seemed at times to be an era of fundamental social, political and ideological change, the House of Lords proved adaptable and influential enough not only to avoid succumbing to the tide of rational 'improvement' but even to continue to be accepted as performing an essential role in British government and society.

REFERENCES

1. *The Parliamentary History of England* (1808), III, 1284–5.
2. *Ibid.*, 1503–4, 1541–3, 1545–7, 1563, 1583–4; IV, 9, 11, 15–16, 24–5.
3. L.B. Namier, 'Monarchy and the party system', in his *Crossroads of Power* (1962), pp. 213–34.
4. J. Cannon, *Aristocratic Century* (Cambridge, 1984), *passim*.
5. M.W. McCahill, *Order and Equipoise: The Peerage and the House of Lords, 1783–1806* (1978).
6. See W.L. Arnstein, 'The survival of the Victorian Aristocracy', in F.C. Jaher (ed.), *The Rich, the Well-Born and the Powerful* (Urbana, Ill., 1973), pp. 203–57 and P. Mandler, *Aristocratic Government in the Age of Reform* (Oxford, 1990) for studies of the continued influence of the aristocracy after 1832.

PART ONE
The House of Lords and its Proceedings

CHAPTER ONE

The Chamber and its Ceremonials

PRELUDE

On Wednesday 12 July 1815, three weeks after the final defeat of Napoleon's army at Waterloo, the Prince Regent rode in state through St James's Park to his palace of Westminster to prorogue the session of Parliament. It was a fine, sunny day; the temperature of 74°F brought out larger crowds than usual in recent years, when the regent's personal unpopularity and the gloom of wartime conditions and taxation had created a mood of indifference or hostility on his rare public appearances. He rode in the state coach drawn by eight cream-coloured horses with an escort of cavalry, and his arrival at the royal entrance to the House of Lords was announced by a salute of cannon. At 2 p.m. he entered the Lords' Chamber, where two of his brothers, the dukes of York and of Kent, the Lord Chancellor, Lord Eldon, and thirty-two other peers in full robes with a number of peeresses and other ladies in full dress awaited him. As the regent took his place on the royal throne, Black Rod was despatched to summon the Speaker and members of the House of Commons to attend his royal presence. They entered the chamber and clustered behind the Speaker at the bar of the House, beyond which only peers could proceed. The Speaker then addressed the regent, assuring him of the continued loyalty of his faithful Commons, summarizing the work of the session and presenting to him a bill to grant supplies of £6 million together with six other public and four private bills for the ceremony of the Royal Assent. The historic words 'le roy le veult' having been pronounced for the public bills, and 'soit fait comme il est desiré' for the private, the regent addressed the assembled Houses. After referring briefly to the unfortunate continuance of his father's illness, he spoke of 'the splendid success with which it has pleased Divine Providence to bless His Majesty's Arms, and those of his Allies', which had 'added fresh lustre to the characters of those great Commanders [Wellington and Blücher], and has exalted the Military Reputation of this Country beyond all former Example . . .'. He followed with the customary thanks for the grant of supplies from the Commons and a brief mention of the other achievements of the parliamentary session, which he then instructed the Lord Chancellor by his side to close by prorogation until 22 August. He then retired, disrobed and returned to Carlton House.

In the evening, those present at the ceremony, together with the general public, could have gone to Vauxhall Gardens where, 'Under the Patronage of his Royal Highness the Prince Regent', there took place a 'GRAND GALA, and brilliant EXHIBITION OF FIREWORKS by Signora Hengler'. Alternatively, they could patronize Sadlers Wells, where there were to be staged 'a new Dance, called THE PLOUGH BOY . . . Mrs Sloman will sing a new song, written by Mr C. Dibdin, called "Waterloo, or Wellington for ever"' and a new pantomime produced by Dibdin called *Harlequin Brilliant*, the cast, besides the eponymous title role, including 'Prince Puzzywuzzy (afterwards Pantaloon)', Genius of Constancy, Genius of Riches, British Lieutenant, Clown (played by Mr Grimaldi), Columbine Sparkle and others. The whole was adorned by 'New Scenery: a Dock Yard, with a Ship Launch on real Water, and a grand allegorical national scenic transformation'.[1]

The day symbolized, in a sense, the continuity rather than the transformation of the national scene. The traditional ceremony of prorogation commemorated the medieval origins of the parliamentary constitution, with King, Lords and Commons gathered together to exercise the legislative function of Parliament of which they each formed a part. The House of Lords in which the ceremony took place was perhaps no longer the dominant, though it was the senior, of the two Houses, but it still retained its place in the constitution and thus symbolized, on this day more than ever, the successful emergence of Britain and her traditional constitution from the threats of revolution and republican democracy which were finally laid to rest on the field of Waterloo. The next sixty-five years were to test the durability of that constitution and of the role of the House of Lords within it: their survival was to provide another example of their ability to adjust to new circumstances by a process of peaceful evolution that transformed the working of a political system while leaving its outward appearance hardly changed.

THE CHAMBER

The chamber in which the House of Lords met at the beginning of this period was the former Court of Requests in the Palace of Westminster. Until 1800, the Lords used a smaller room, the Parliament Chamber, but the Union with Ireland which added twenty-eight representative peers and four bishops to their numbers made larger quarters necessary. In any case, the Lords had been complaining for some time about the stuffiness of their chamber, and the dilapidated state of the whole palace had been causing concern since 1789, when an architect's report showed that the buildings immediately to the east of the chamber were in danger of collapse. In 1792 it was suggested that the Court of Requests might be fitted up for the Lords and in 1794–5 Sir John Soane drew up extensive plans for improvements and refurbishment, only to be defeated by lack of money in wartime and by political favouritism towards his rival James Wyatt. Wyatt's new buildings around the new Lords' Chamber in 1801 were generally agreed to be a disaster, both visually and technically. Externally, they were faced with stucco – in which Wyatt had a proprietary interest – and provided with brick and stucco battlements, cast iron window frames and lath and plaster oriels, described by one observer as 'a piazza or Gothic arcade embattled on the top', and likened by the *Gentleman's Magazine* to 'the appearance of a cotton mill'. One observer thought it looked like a prison, and another a gentlemen's lavatory.[2]

Inside, the chamber was at least more spacious than the former House. It measured 80 feet long, 40 feet wide, and 30 feet high, and was lit by three semi-circular windows, 6 feet high, on each side. Beneath the windows hung the famous 'Armada' tapestries presented to Queen Elizabeth I by the States of Holland to commemorate the dispersion of the Spanish invasion fleet in 1588.[3] At the southern end stood the royal throne, fitted up in 1820 as part of the further alterations designed by Soane in the fashionable Gothic style. Soane's additions also included a new royal entrance, in the design of which, and of the throne, George IV took a hand, a royal gallery, library, committee rooms and offices. The former Lords' Chamber was demolished in 1823 as part of these changes.

The throne, 'a splendid and costly piece of furniture', with a canopy of crimson velvet supported by gilded columns ornamented with oak leaves and acorns, stood on a platform 3 feet above the floor and was approached by three carpeted steps. Before it was a brass rail and at the sides and on the steps members of the Commons, peers' eldest sons and other distinguished visitors were allowed to stand to hear the debates.

At the opposite end was the bar of the House, marking the legal boundary of the chamber, where members of the Commons appeared to deliver messages to the Upper House, to hear the royal speeches, or to witness the proceedings. There was room for about 150 persons to stand at the bar: 'during very interesting debates' wrote James Grant, 'the space at the bar and the space on either side of the throne exhibited a living mass of human beings'.[4] A large fireplace to the right of the throne provided heat for their lordships, though when the House was crowded with spectators it could hardly have been necessary. It was removed in 1831 to make room for additional benches for peers attending the Reform Bill debates.

The House was presided over by the Lord Chancellor or his deputy from the Woolsack, then as now an upholstered seat without back or sides, some 6 feet long, $2\frac{1}{2}$ feet wide, and 20 in. high, covered with a crimson cloth. At right angles, two other woolsacks of similar size were provided for the judges, King's Counsel and Masters in Chancery, and beyond them the clerks sat at the table of the House to record its proceedings. On the table were two boxes for the reception of petitions and other documents presented to the House and 'ordered to lie on the table'.[5]

The installation of a new chancellor was an occasion of some ceremony. In 1827, for example, Lyndhurst's appointment was notified to the House by the duke of Clarence, and the new chancellor carried his patent to the foot of the throne to be read by the clerk. The Attorney and Solicitor Generals, the Lord Chief Justice and 'a whole row of barristers' attended. The passages were so crowded, Colchester reported, that the ex-chancellor, Lord Eldon, had difficulty in getting through to the House.[6]

> The appearance of the House was singular. There were 164 Lords present. The steps of the throne were crowded with men; and twenty or thirty ladies on the sides of the throne. The ex-Ministers took their seats on the cross bench; the new Ministers took theirs in the usual front row above the fireplace.

The peers sat on benches on three sides of the table and woolsacks, those supporting the current administration generally on the right of the throne, the opposition peers on the left, and those unconnected with either, or the overflow from either side, on the cross-benches facing the throne. The bishops were provided with four benches to the right of the throne. Ministers sat on the front bench facing the judges' woolsack and the opposition front bench faced them. The four tiers of benches were supposedly reserved for dukes, marquesses, earls, and viscounts and barons respectively, but by this time these distinctions were no longer generally observed and peers sat on any tier they chose.[7]

By the mid-nineteenth century, peers tended to take their places as dictated by their political preferences. The 8th duke of Argyll, entering the House as holder of the English barony of Sundridge in 1847, noted that 'parties are less rigidly separated in the Lords than in the Commons' and, not wishing to identify himself with either of the major parties, took his seat immediately behind Lord Derby, for whom he had a personal admiration, only to discover that 'the cordiality of his reception . . . convinced me that he put an interpretation upon my doing this which I by no means intended'. He moved to the cross-benches, but 'I felt at once that it would be impossible to speak with any comfort from that position, which is the worst in the House. I therefore settled on what is called the "Dukes' bench", next the woolsack, on the left of the throne. That is the bench on which I have sat all my life, except, of course, when in office.'[8]

Members of the public – 'strangers' in parliamentary language – were admitted to watch the proceedings of the House only by order of a peer, except for reporters who by the early nineteenth century had acquired the customary right to sit at the front of the gallery for the public. Further temporary galleries were erected in 1820 at a cost of £921. 11s. 3d. and improved ventilation was provided for the debates on the Bill of Pains and Penalties, by which George IV's ministers sought to prove the queen's infidelity and divorce her – the so-called 'Queen's trial' which created the greatest public sensation witnessed in the House of Lords during this period. The Lords admired Soane's galleries as 'highly ornamental'. The illustration by Haydon of Lord Grey speaking during the proceedings is perhaps the best known depiction of the old House of Lords. A small gallery was left after the 'trial' to accommodate the public and additional ones were erected in 1829 for the Catholic Emancipation debates. Before the gallery was erected, strangers and reporters had to stand at the bar.

In about 1832, part of the gallery was divided off and allotted to ladies. It accommodated only about twenty, and Lady Holland called it the 'hen coop'. Before that time they had had to take their chance below the bar on chairs temporarily provided behind a red baize curtain, or behind the throne, or squeeze into the roof space above the chamber to view the proceedings from 'the ventilator' where they could not be seen by their lordships. Indeed, they had to meet a degree of masculine disapproval of their presence at all. Charles

Greville noted in 1829 that 'It is only since last year that the steps of the throne have been crowded with ladies; formerly one or two got in, who skulked behind the throne, or were hid in Tyrwhitt's box, but now they fill the whole space, and put themselves in front with their large bonnets, without either fear or shame'. Ellenborough, however, noted with approval the presence of 'some of the prettiest girls in London' – a relief, since he had noticed the attendance on the debate on the address at the start of the session of seventy or eighty 'all ugly'. Colchester too objected to Tyrwhitt, Black Rod, in 1824 at 'the droves of ladies who came and took chairs by the side of the Throne to hear debates, quite unprecedented'. Tyrwhitt replied that 'the chancellor had sent his two daughters there on Monday last, and Lord Liverpool had desired particular accommodation for two ladies of his family tomorrow, and so nobody could be refused'.[9]

There was some dispute as to who had the authority to admit ladies on the first and last days of the session. Colchester again reported in 1824 that Lord Gwydir, as Lord Great Chamberlain, 'claimed the sole right to issue tickets of admission for ladies' on those days. 'The *first* day is allowed', he wrote, 'because, until the King, by his speech, has opened a session, everybody, Peers, Commoners, and all, are deemed to be assembled in his palace to learn his pleasure. But on the *last*, the Peers, being assembled as a house, claim the right of introducing strangers.' The Lord Chamberlain's claim for the last day of the 1824 session was disputed by Lord Arden, who 'claimed the right of introducing two ladies *without* the tickets of the Great Chamberlain, and if obstructed, declared his intention of moving the House'. He seems to have won.[10]

The Reform Bill debates in 1831 attracted a large audience of ladies: 'There was a delightful re-union below our Bar, from 70 to 90 ladies each night', wrote Lord Clanricarde; 'These were attended by amorous MPs and Heirs apparent and were as thick as a Birthday Squeeze.' Ladies even attended the morning sessions when appeals were being heard. Greville noted on 16 August 1834 that there were 'not much more than half a dozen Peers in the House', but many ladies to hear Lord Chancellor Brougham 'in presence of the ladies, attired in his golden robes (and especially before Mrs Petre, to whom he makes love), give a judgement in some case in which a picture of Nell Gwynne was concerned, and he was very proud of the *delicacy* of his judgement.' Harriet Gower paid her first visit to the House of Lords in 1831: 'I should have had a delicious evening', she wrote, '. . . but for the atmosphere unsweet and the excessive heat, which gave me a violent headache. I went at $^1/_2$ past 3 . . . and staid till 11

– a long time, but nothing to some of the ladies who go every night and stay to the end.'[11]

THE REBUILDING OF THE CHAMBER

Relatively plain and undistinguished as the old House of Lords was, the fire of 1834 relegated their lordships to even less attractive quarters. On the night of 16 October the House caught fire from the heat of the old Exchequer tallies which were being burnt in two stoves under the floor. The greater part of the palace of Westminster was engulfed in the blaze, Wyatt's jerry-built additions being gleefully observed by A.W. Pugin as they collapsed:

> Oh, it was a glorious sight to see his composition mullions and cement pinnacles and battlements flying and cracking while his 2s.6d. turrets were smoking like so many manufacturing chimnies till the heat shivered them into a thousand pieces.[12]

The two chambers were destroyed, though the outer walls of the Lords' House still stood amid the smouldering debris of the roof. The king offered the use of Buckingham Palace, and a move to St James's Palace was briefly considered, but it was soon decided to rebuild on the same site. The Commons, meanwhile, were given the old House of Lords which was reroofed, and the Lords were placed in the repaired Painted Chamber, a small narrow room previously used for conferences of the two Houses. Macaulay wrote in 1833 that it received its name from 'an old mildewed daub of a woman in the niche of one of the windows'. Lady Sarah Lyttelton wrote in 1839, when she attended the queen at a prorogation ceremony, that it was 'a shabby, poky, little place enough, compared to the old burnt down one' and Greville described it as 'a wretched dog-hole'. It was so narrow, he remarked, 'that the Lords can almost whisper to each other across it'. Lord Duncannon complained that there was scarcely room to pass from the bar to the woolsack. Smirke, the architect, reported that the walls, though $4^1/_2$ feet to 5 feet thick, were so weak that it was unsafe to cut any thickness away to enlarge the chamber, which measured about 80 feet by 26 feet. There were three rows of seats at floor level and a single row of seats in a narrow gallery on either side. Brougham remarked on the stuffy atmosphere, and perhaps the uncooperative attitude of the Lords towards Melbourne's administration after 1835 may have had something to do with the physical and psychological effects of close confinement in such a narrow space, as well as with party differences. 'The Lords will be very sulky in such a place,' Greville prophesied.[13]

The temporary chambers were ready for occupation in February 1835, but it was to be twelve years before the Lords were able to occupy the new House that was built for them, and 1852 before both chambers were in full use. After some debate and indecision, and under intense pressure from the press, it was determined to hold a competition for the design of a new palace of Westminster, which should be worthy of the Parliament of a powerful and wealthy imperial nation and which should symbolize the progress of moral improvement, the arts and technology in the new age heralded by the Great Reform Act. Charles Barry's design, in perpendicular Gothic, was chosen from ninety-seven entries. Gothic was not only the fashionable style of the day, but it was believed to be a peculiarly English style, and symbolized the free institutions of ancient Anglo-Saxon times which were regarded as the origin of English constitutional liberties. It was also favoured because it would harmonize with Westminster Hall (which fortunately escaped the fire) and the nearby abbey. It was, however, a controversial choice from the start and by the time the palace was sufficiently completed for occupation in the 1850s, architectural taste had changed and it was criticized as a stylistic travesty, constructed at enormous expense. Nevertheless, as the modern historian of the building has shown, it was a remarkable building not only incorporating many new technical developments, making it the most advanced as well as the largest project of its day, but also proving astonishingly well fitted to its purpose, and capable of continued modification to suit the developing needs of future times.[14]

To the Lords, however, suffering the heat, stuffiness and general inconvenience of their temporary premises, it was what seemed the inordinate delay in providing new quarters which made the chief impression. In 1843 the Lords set up a committee on the building which examined Barry closely, and induced him to give assurances that their chamber might be ready for occupation for the 1844 session, though it was still without a roof. The committee's report was not officially notified to the government and Barry made no attempt to carry out his promise. In 1844–5 a new Lords committee censured him not only for delay but for making unauthorized alterations to his plans: Brougham testily remarked that Barry was 'not only a dilatory man, but the name of delay itself', and that his promises were 'not worth the paper they were written on'. It was decided to press ahead with the Lords' Chamber as a priority, leaving the Commons, who were housed in comparative comfort in the old House of Lords, to wait another five years. With the assistance of Pugin in the design of the interior furnishings and decorations, the new chamber was ready for occupation, though not fully completed, in March 1847.[15]

Whether from relief at their release from confinement in the Painted Chamber or from genuine admiration of the new House, their lordships entered their new quarters with considerable acclamation of its merits. Brougham now declared that it was

the most magnificent building that he had ever seen in any part of the world, doing the greatest possible honour to the very skilful, learned, and ingenious architect, both in the interior and the exterior of the splendid palace which was to be devoted to the two branches of the legislature. If anything could mitigate his dislike of Gothic architecture, it was what he had seen that day.

Complaints, however, were already being voiced. At the first sitting in the new chamber, on 15 April 1847, the reporter noted that 'the attendance of Peers and of strangers was so considerable, and the noise arising from their remarks and conversation was so great, that little of what passed could be distinctly heard'.[16] Six weeks before, the indefatigable Joseph Hume, who had led the fight to hold the open competition for the design to avoid suspicion of a 'job', drew attention to the inadequate space below the bar for the Speaker and members of the Commons when they were summoned to the Lords on ceremonial occasions. He maintained that less than one twentieth of the Commons – hardly thirty members – could find room to stand comfortably below the bar, and demanded that those responsible be called to account. Viscount Morpeth, Chief Commissioner of Woods and Forests, reminded the Commons that 'the new House was a room for the transaction of business' and that it should not be of an inconvenient size for that primary purpose, but pointed out that MPs were intended to have their own gallery from which to observe the Lords' proceedings. The unrepentant Hume followed up with criticism of 'the ephemeral gaudy appearance' of the building and remarked that 'he had hoped they [the Commons] would have had a House without the frippery, but exhibiting all the taste of the period of Louis Quatorze'. He asked whether additional money proposed to provide for the costs of the building was to be spent on additional gilding for the House of Lords or to complete the House of Commons. Other members joined him some weeks later in complaining of the delay in completing the Commons' chamber, Sir John Bowring demanding to know

by what mysterious influence the Lords had succeeded in getting into their apartment. . . . He would ask if the Upper House was to be lodged in all its splendour, whilst the House of Commons was looking on? Very active influence, it was said, had been used on behalf of the Lords, which had succeeded in introducing them to their most splendid apartment – his hon. friend said gorgeous, and everybody would admit that it was so.[17]

The Lords themselves complained of difficulty in hearing the speeches in the new House and in 1849 appointed a select committee to consider improvements. Barry's proposal for an alteration to the gallery was adopted, which satisfied the reporters, but members complained that they could not hear distinctly unless silence was preserved both below the bar and on the steps of the throne. It was ordered that part of the space at the foot of the throne should be railed off and that Black Rod should enforce silence below the bar. Standing order 18, which directed lords who wished to converse during a debate to go below the bar, was amended to direct them to retire elsewhere. It was also ordered that the galleries on either side of the throne be reserved for 'Foreign Ladies of Distinction', peeresses and peers' unmarried daughters. Wives of peers' eldest sons and married daughters of peers and peeresses were to occupy the box which was used on state occasions by peers' eldest sons.[18]

Three years later another select committee was appointed to consider improvements to the lighting of the chamber and robing room. It recommended the removal of the existing stained glass windows to the Royal Gallery and their replacement by lighter ones, and improvements to the gas lighting. Despite the alterations to the chamber complaints continued: in 1867 Carnarvon and Malmesbury complained of the difficulty of hearing, but that 'there was not the slightest hope of success without pulling the House to pieces'.[19] More serious, and equally intractable, was the problem during the heat of the summer of the stench from the Thames, which was virtually an open sewer for London. 'The air from the Thames is pestilential', wrote Granville in 1858, 'and must soon put an end to the session. There are questions as to moving the seat of the legislature to St James's Palace and Marlborough House.'[20] Even the tipping of large quantities of lime into the river failed to quell the nuisance; one Italian lady, returning one night from a dinner at Greenwich, 'sniffed the air with delight, saying it reminded her of her "dear Venice"'.[21]

Nevertheless, the general opinion was, as Bowring said, favourable to the new House of Lords and its surroundings. *The Builder* described the Royal Gallery as 'a noble apartment' and the furnishings of the Lords' Chamber as 'of the finest quality, richly and elaborately carved throughout'.[22] The building exhibited the happy collaboration, in artistic style at least, between Barry as architect and Pugin as interior designer, and it came at the moment when the high Victorian Gothic style was at its peak. The richness of the decoration, the elaborate symbolism of the ornamentation, struck the Victorian imagination and made the chamber a model for great public buildings not only elsewhere in Britain but all over the world.

The Lords' Chamber was a double cube, 91 feet long and 45 feet in breadth and height. Five rows of seats on each side, covered in red morocco leather, accommodated 235 peers. The throne, raised on a dais with three steps, was covered by a canopy 18 feet 6in. wide, and the oak chair itself, 'of beautiful design and execution, carved and gilt, richly studded with emeralds and chrystals: the back and arms are covered with velvet, embroidered with the royal arms, etc.'. The roof of the chamber was of iron, divided by moulded beams, coloured in rich blue bordered with red and gold and blazoned with the royal badges of the kingdom and carved and gilded emblems of royalty. Six traceried windows of stained glass lit each side of the chamber, with three arched openings at the ends. The piers between the windows were occupied by canopied niches intended to receive bronze statues of barons and others present at the signing of Magna Carta. Under the niches, gilt angels held shields blazoned with the arms of the barons. The walls behind the arches were decorated with frescoes. The gallery was supported by tracery bearing the arms of sovereigns and Lord Chancellors since the reign of Edward III. The general effect was of magnificent opulence, a fitting stage for the display of the monarchical constitution which had evolved from medieval times and which still in Victorian England represented the greatness of the nation. The royal ceremony of prorogation took place for the first time in the new chamber on 5 September 1848.

CEREMONIALS IN THE HOUSE

The Lords' Chamber had great ceremonial significance as the place where the sovereign met his or her subjects in the assembled Parliament and exercised his or her constitutional prerogatives in relation to legislation. It was, as it still is, the scene for the state opening of Parliament, the giving of the royal assent to acts of Parliament, and the prorogation or dissolution of Parliament in person or by commission.

In the early nineteenth century the opening of the parliamentary session was a spectacle of imposing magnificence.[23] Peers, peeresses and their sons and daughters assembled, peers and peeresses in full state robes, the others in full dress, from mid-day to await the ceremony which usually took place at 2.15 p.m.[24] The number of ladies even exceeded that of peers, usually amounting to 200 or 300, stationing themselves along the side galleries and on the rows of benches on either side of the floor, excepting only the government front bench. Peers, foreign ambassadors and other foreign dignitaries filled the rest of the chamber, together with the bishops in full canonicals. The galleries were closed to the general public, being occupied by peers and their distinguished guests. The new royal entrance and gallery were used for George IV's first state opening ceremony in 1820, and in 1822 the Life Guards in their new ceremonial uniforms lined the royal route through the Painted Chamber to the Lords' Chamber. The rooms and passages, reported *The Times*,[25] had all been

> new matted, painted, and fitted up for the occasion in suitable style. These apartments were all filled, through the kind attention of the Lord Great Chamberlain to the wishes of the public, with spectators. . . . Means were likewise taken to prevent any but Members of the House of Commons from filling the lobby and passages between it and the House of Lords, through which the Speaker and Members were to proceed . . . to attend their Lordships' bar. . . . The House of Lords began to be filled at an early hour: before one o'clock all the benches, except the cross-benches and the front side benches on the floor, were occupied with ladies in full dress.

Considerable public interest was also aroused at William IV's first visit to prorogue Parliament in July 1830, a month after his accession, when *The Times* again reported that the number of ladies present was greater than ever known, and 'the whole of the peers' benches, except part of the front rows, and that part allocated to the Foreign Ministers, were crowded as closely as ladies could be placed, and yet numbers of peeresses and other ladies of distinction were obliged to take their places below that part reserved for the sons of peers, and were there accommodated with chairs'. The usual brilliance of the ladies' dresses and jewellery was absent because of the court mourning for the late king: 'no other than jet ornaments were worn, . . . except by Mrs Manners Sutton, the lady of the Speaker, who wore a few brilliants intermixed with jet, in her hair and ears.' Three months later, at the state opening of the new Parliament, the peers and ladies were in full robes and presented 'an imposing spectacle'.[26]

The monarch's arrival was heralded by the firing of cannon and by a fanfare of trumpets on his entering the chamber and taking his seat on the throne while the House rose to its feet and all peers uncovered their heads. The members of the House of Commons were summoned with traditional ceremonial by Black Rod and, led by the Speaker, processed to the bar of the House. After the reading of the 'gracious speech' opening the session and the retirement of the sovereign, if it was the start of a new Parliament the Lord Chancellor, followed by the peers present, took the oath and declarations prescribed, and the Lord Chancellor reported the speech from the throne. The House formally appointed a Committee of Privileges and adjourned to the day set for debating the address in reply to the speech, usually five or six days after the state opening.

The close of a parliamentary session was a much quieter affair. By the 1850s it was customary for the royal assent to bills passed during the session to be signified by commissioners. George IV and William IV often attended to read the prorogation speech, but the announcement of the prorogation itself was made by the Lord Chancellor. Prorogations were usually less spectacular than state openings, when all the traditional ceremonial was observed. The most famous exception in this period was in April 1831, when the Whig ministry requested a dissolution after their defeat on an amendment to the first Reform Bill. William IV consented only with great reluctance, owing to the short space of time since the last election, less than a year before, and because of the excited state of the country. At first he refused to go to prorogue in person, but changed his mind on hearing that the opposition peers were trying to prevent the prorogation from taking place. Hurriedly summoning his regalia and attendants, he declared that if the state coach was not ready he would go in a hackney carriage. His arrival in the Lords' Chamber interrupted a disorderly scene:

> The insolent tones and gestures of the noble lords – the excitement, breaking down the conventional usages, not to say civilities of life, astonished the spectators, and affected the few ladies who were present with visible alarm. In a word, nothing like the scene . . . was ever before witnessed within the walls of Parliament.[27]

The immense popularity which William received as a consequence of this overt support of his ministers and their Reform Bill resulted in enormous public ovations, and on his next appearance in the Lords to open the new Parliament in June 1831 the enthusiasm

> extended itself even to the well-dressed crowd assembled to witness the passing of His Majesty through the Painted Chamber and the lobbies which lead to the body of the House of Lords. Loud huzzas

and clapping of hands greeted the King as he proceeded through these chambers, – a thing, we believe, quite unusual.[28]

Monarchs varied in the degree of their conscientiousness in attending these ceremonies. George IV opened parliamentary sessions in person only three times between November 1814 and 1819 when he was Prince Regent, though his absences were usually ascribed to 'indisposition', but he scored rather better at prorogations, attending all five down to July 1819. No doubt the hostile public demonstrations which often marked his appearance in the streets of his capital were something of a deterrent. In 1817, indeed, his coach was attacked and stoned, leading Parliament to express its fears of popular revolution by suspending habeas corpus. His record was more variable as king: he opened Parliament in person four times, and prorogued only two sessions out of eleven. William IV by contrast spoilt a 100 per cent record of attendances at both ceremonies only at the very end of his reign, when he was unable to go to the prorogation in January 1837 because of his sister's illness. Melbourne protested that his absence amounted to a breach of the constitution, as the first occasion when a monarch had failed to attend for any reason other than illness or infirmity.[29] The royal attendance was not only a constitutional duty, but signified the monarch's support of the ministers of the day by identifying him with the government's legislative policy in the royal speech. Colchester was told by Black Rod in 1825 that George IV complained of 'the peremptory tone in which the Ministers require him to open the session "in person",. . . although he is inwardly suffering from the gout and rheumatism'. He declared that his gout totally prevented his attendance and, furthermore, that he disliked the proposed speech and refused to deliver it as it was at present. 'The King is, moreover,' wrote Colchester, 'disabled by the state of his mouth, and the recent loss of the few teeth which held the false teeth; and there is not time enough now to make a proper supply for this defect.' Parliament was opened on the following day by commission.[30]

At the start of her reign, Victoria was as conscientious as her predecessor, and was the focus of considerable public interest and curiosity. The *Hansard* reporter, on Victoria's first attendance to prorogue her predecessor's last Parliament in July 1837, a month after her accession, wrote that 'though out of the line of our duty, we may record that her Majesty's youth and sex invested the scene with extraordinary interest'. She was very nervous, but Melbourne told her she had done well. Her first state opening of a new Parliament, on 20 November 1837, was attended by large crowds, her progress 'enthusiastically cheered by a great multitude of persons who lined the streets'. The young queen was accompanied by her mother, the duchess of Kent, and attended by her Mistress of the Robes, the duchess of Sutherland, her Lady in Waiting, Lady Barham, the Master of the Horse and other Household officers.

The painter Benjamin Haydon watched her pass the Royal Gallery towards the House: 'Her appearance was singular', he wrote: 'Her large eye, open nostril, closed mouth, small form, grave demeanour, and intellectual look, surrounded by nobles, ministers, ambassadors, peeresses, statesmen, and guards, has something awful and peculiar.' As she sat on the throne, on her right stood the earl of Shaftesbury with the cap of maintenance, the Lord Chancellor, the Earl Marshal and the duke of Somerset, bearing the crown on a cushion. On her left were the Prime Minister, Lord Melbourne, holding the sword of state, and members of the Household. The duchesses of Kent and Sutherland stood behind the throne and the queen's uncles, the dukes of Cambridge and of Sussex, at the foot. The House was

> resplendent with beauty and fashion. . . . The gallery was nearly filled with elegantly dressed women. Silks and velvets, of all the hues of the rainbow, shone on every side. Feathers were almost universally worn. . . . The *corps diplomatique*, in their different varieties of costume, also mustered in great force, and added considerably to the picturesqueness of the scene. . . . Her Majesty was attired in her state robes; her head was ornamented with a circlet of diamonds. She also wore a splendid diamond necklace, and a superbly brilliant stomacher of the same costly materials.[31]

In January 1840, when the queen was expected to announce her engagement to Prince Albert, 'the almost endless diversity of colours which glowed on every side gave to the house the gay and vivid appearance of a well-stocked and fancifully arranged parterre. Ostrich feathers were generally worn, and added much to the striking beauty and animation of the scene.'[32]

Victoria never lost her nervousness at the state ceremony, but it was usually noted that she read her speeches clearly and well. Attending the prorogation in August 1839 as one of the Ladies of the Bedchamber, Lady Sarah Lyttelton wrote that

> her speech was most beautifully read. Her voice is, when so raised and *sostenuto*, quite that of a child, a gushing sort of richness, with the most sensible, cultivated, and *gentlemanlike* accent and emphasis. She raised her head, and uttered, 'Gentlemen of the House of Commons!' with a little air of grandeur that was very pretty. She was frightened, but no one could have guessed it; *we* knew it by the crimson colour of her face and neck, and a little trembling. The effect of the whole is to my

taste spoilt by the shoals of ladies and the very few peers who have room. It looks like a mere pageant, and would be much finer if she (child as she looks) were speaking evidently to a crowd of grey-haired senators and sturdy statesmen.[33]

Despite her dislike of public show and ceremonial, Victoria dutifully continued to attend state openings and prorogations regularly. Her first absence occurred in October 1841, when she was barely a month short of the birth of the prince of Wales, but afterwards she omitted only seven out of twenty-seven occasions until 1854, six in years when she was again pregnant or had recently borne a child, the other when she was preparing to visit Ireland in August 1849. In August 1840 Prince Albert accompanied her to the House of Lords for the first time, and he continued to do so until his death. In February 1845, Haydon noted that the queen was

peculiarly nervous. She hurried everything; was scarcely ten minutes in the House, when she came out again; officers, heralds, and attendants, all obliged to scamper here and there to get into their places. One of the mace-men nearly knocked Lord Lyndhurst on the head, and he, lame as he was, scrambled with the rest to be in time. In the Robing-room the doors were hardly shut when they were opened again, and out they all fought their way, the queen and Prince Albert following. The Duke looked old and bent; Lord Lyndhurst like a superannuated Mephistopheles; Lord Wharncliffe had lost his teeth; the Duke of Beaufort alone kept up the character of the order. All the women looked old and ugly except that sweet, feminine Duchess of Buccleuch.

After 1854 (not, as the queen told Mr Gladstone in 1871, after 1852) she never again attended a prorogation, disliking the ceremony, though she continued to open the sessions in person, with only one more exception, when she was pregnant in 1857, until Albert's death in December 1861. From that time, she retreated into seclusion, emerging to open Parliament on only seven occasions between 1861 and her death in January 1901.[34]

Her absence from public duties was adversely commented on in the press during the first years of her bereavement, but the queen refused to submit herself to what she felt to be the ordeal of public ceremony without Albert's support at her side. In February 1866 she steeled herself to the task, but in her widow's mourning and without the usual pageantry. 'Discarding the crown she adopted the black cap of Mary Queen of Scots. Her long veil and dress were black, her crimson robes were draped over the throne like a discarded skin.' She even declined to read her speech in person, likening the experience to a public execution. 'Utterly expressionless, she stared in front of her as if she did not hear a word.' On this occasion Albert's absence was to a small degree mitigated by the presence of the prince of Wales on the queen's right. In February 1867 she again opened the session, at the special request of Lord Derby and in view of the importance of the government's Reform Bill, but she afterwards regretted doing so, citing the lukewarmness of her reception and objecting to the crowds shouting for reform as she passed. On all subsequent occasions the precedent of 1866 was followed and the old pageantry was omitted. The people had grown accustomed since the 1820s to the spectacle of this particular royal occasion, and for the queen, dressed in black, and without the splendour of the procession, to drive by in a closed carriage aroused feelings of resentment. 'It is impossible', wrote *The Times* in 1864, 'for a recluse to occupy the British throne without a gradual weakening of that authority which the sovereign has been accustomed to exert.' In 1870 she refused to open Parliament on the excuse that she would catch cold wearing a low-cut dress, but when in 1872 Gladstone suggested that she should wear ermine up to her neck, she protested that the House of Lords was too hot. On those occasions when she did attend, the press was suspicious of her motives. In 1866 it was said that she only did so because she wanted the Commons to vote a dowry for her daughter Helena and in 1871 a dowry for Princess Louise and an allowance for Prince Arthur: she only attended, it was said, with her 'begging bowl'. When Gladstone asked her to prorogue in person in 1871 to give thanks for Prince Arthur's allowance she refused on the grounds that she had never done so since 1852, and went off to Balmoral instead. Her political partisanship came into play during Disraeli's premiership, when she showed her appreciation of him by opening Parliament three times in six years, but she refused to show the same support for Gladstone. Only once, in 1886, did Victoria ever enter the palace of Westminster again.[35]

The accession of King Edward VII in 1901, like that of George IV, marked the revival of the traditional grand ceremonial at the state opening of Parliament. Like his distant predecessor, the new king had a taste for pageantry, while the jubilees of 1887 and 1897 had reawakened the enthusiasm of his subjects after decades of Victorian drabness, at a time when the glories of British imperialism, if somewhat tarnished by the South African war, shone brighter than ever. When the king and queen rode to open Parliament for the first time on 14 February 1901, *The Times* noted that 'the chamber was thronged by a vast assemblage of peers in their robes and peeresses in mourning attire', while on the processional route from Buckingham Palace 'immense crowds of people had gathered, long before the hour fixed for the starting of the procession'. Their majesties 'were greeted with a roar of cheers . . . along the whole route' from 'vast and orderly crowds that thronged the line of the procession and swarmed about every point of vantage'. The only quibble was that the crowd in the Lords' Chamber was so large, because of the number of peeresses who came, that members of the House of Commons had great difficulty in finding room to stand where they could see or even hear the royal speech, and there was 'an unseemly scramble' when Black Rod summoned them. 'It is not creditable to Parliament', *The Times* soberly declared, 'that the only point in the proceedings at which the dignity of the King's reception by his faithful lieges was marred by any lack of order was within the precincts of the palace where the legislature is installed.'[36]

Nevertheless, the reporter rhapsodized over the splendour of 'the Gentlemen-at-Arms in their rich uniforms, the heralds and pursuivants in their tabards, the high officers of State in their robes of dignity, so seldom worn, the "gilded chamber" filled with peeresses and peers' and the 'dignified and impressive' tones of the monarch reading his speech. The only other feature which detracted from the occasion was the 'most temperately and respectfully worded' protest of the Roman Catholic peers against the wording of the declaration against transubstantiation, the invocation of the Virgin Mary and the sacrifice of the mass which the king had had to make on the previous day in order to abjure their religion. They took exception to the words 'superstitious and idolatrous', which were part of the oath, and in consequence the wording has been subsequently revised to make it less objectionable to Roman Catholics.

The revival of the full ceremonial of the state opening by Edward VII restored to the chamber one of its chief, and its most spectacular, public functions. He opened every session in person until his death in 1910, and his son and successive monarchs have since maintained the tradition almost without a break. Edwardian state openings were lavish, with the chamber filled by a 'throng resplendent in robes of state, crimson, scarlet, and gold, ermine and miniver' and the peeresses 'in costumes of the most delicate hues, soft blues and greens, the glaucous colour of young corn, lilac, pale gold, or the dainty admixture of colour in a flowered device', set off by diamonds and 'some, indeed, wearing dresses sown with gems, glittered with a hundred colours'. In 1905, 'white – in nodding plumes, in shimmering silks and satins – was the dominant hue; and the impression second to that was the sparkle of countless diamonds'.[37] The wealth of the old aristocracy and the brash magnificence of the new plutocracy added to the peerage since the 1880s symbolized the grandeur and pride of an order whose real power was fast disappearing. The pomp and circumstance of royal ceremonial was a reminder of a past greatness that the First World War was shortly to bring to an end.

REFERENCES

1. *The Times*, 12 and 13 July 1815; *Journals of the House of Lords*, 12 July 1815.
2. *The Times*, 23 Oct. 1806; *Gentleman's Magazine* 1806, II, 1127; Hansard, *Parliamentary Debates*, IX (1808), 863–5; for a full account of the buildings and alterations see J. Mordaunt Crook and M.H. Port, *The King's Works* VI, 1782–1851 (1973).
3. For a description of the interior of the Lords' Chamber see J. Grant, *Random Recollections of the House of Lords* (2nd edn., 1836), pp. 1–8. The Armada tapestries were burnt in the fire of 1834.
4. *Ibid.*, p. 4.
5. Petitions were required to be presented in respectful terms. The Duke of Wellington returned some to their originators in 1834 because they did not contain the word 'humble': *The Prime Minister's Papers: Wellington, Political Correspondence*, I, 1833–4, ed. J. Brooke and J. Gandy (1975), p. 599.
6. *Diary & Correspondence of Charles Abbot, Lord Colchester*, ed. Lord Colchester (1861), III, pp. 492–3 (2 May 1827).
7. Ministers and officers in the Royal Household· were expected to wear court dress in the early years of this period. The duke of Devonshire, attending in 1827 in his new office of Lord Chamberlain to present the king's answer to addresses for papers, carried his wand of office but appeared in morning coat and boots. When a Lord of the Bedchamber remonstrated, he replied 'Oh, that is so much trouble'. Colchester, *Diary*, III, p. 498.
8. *Autobiography and Memoirs of George Douglas, 8th Duke of Argyll*, ed. Dowager Duchess of Argyll (1906), I, p. 301.
9. C.C.F. Greville, *Journal of the Reigns of George IV and William IV*, ed. H. Reeve (1874), I, p. 199; *A Political Diary, 1828–30, by Edward Law, Lord Ellenborough* ed. Lord Silchester (1881) I, p. 336; II, p. 8; Colchester, *Diary*, III, p. 329 (2 June 1824).
10. *Ibid.*, p. 336.
11. Anita Leslie, *Mrs Fitzherbert* (1960), p. 225; *The Greville Diary*, ed. P.W. Wilson (1927), I, p. 478; *Three Howard Sisters*, ed. Lady Leconfield and John Gore (1955), p. 212.
12. Quoted in M.H. Port (ed.), *The Houses of Parliament* (1976), p. 55.
13. *Letters of T.B. Macaulay*, ed. T. Pinney (Cambridge, 1974–81), II, p. 259; *Correspondence of Sarah Spencer, Lady Lyttelton, 1782–1870*, ed. Mrs Hugh Wyndham (1912), p. 287; Greville, *Journal*, I, pp. 199, 205; Crook and Port, *King's Works*, p. 575; Hansard, 3rd ser., XXIX, 5.
14. Port, *The Houses of Parliament*, Introduction.
15. *Ibid.*, pp. 135, 140; Hansard, 3rd series, LXXXI, 120–2, 203–6.
16. *Ibid.*, XC, 513; XLI, 810. Bets were laid that Brougham would be the

first to speak in the new chamber, but as he hurried to the House to do so the wheel of his carriage fell off and Campbell beat him to it – giving rise to the rumour that he had bribed a man to take the linch-pin out of the wheel: *Life of John, Lord Campbell*, ed. Hon. Mrs Hardcastle (1881), II, p. 222.

17. Hansard, 3rd series, XCI, 271–3, 539–40; XCII, 332–4.
18. *Journals of the House of Lords*, LXXXI, 241, 561–2, 585.
19. *Ibid.*, LXXXV, 24, 56–7; Hansard, 3rd series, CLXXXVIII, 263–4 (20 June 1867).
20. Lord Edmond Fitzmaurice, *Life of . . . second Earl Granville* (1905), I, p. 310 (25 June 1856).
21. Lord Malmesbury, *Memoirs of an Ex-Minister* (1854), II, p. 125 (27 June 1858).
22. Quoted in *Gentleman's Magazine* (1847), XVII, 523–5. One of the advanced features of the building was that the wood carving was carried out by machinery, and only finished by hand.
23. See my article, E.A. Smith, 'The pageant of monarchy', *The Historian*, 31 (1991), 13–16.
24. Peers who had previously taken their seats and sworn the oaths appeared in the king's presence fully robed, but 'none such came robed, unless they have previously taken their seats', or unless they intended on that occasion to do so: Colchester, *Diary*, III, p. 365.
25. 6 February 1822.
26. 24 July 1830.
27. 23 April 1830.
28. 22 June 1831.
29. Sir Sydney Lee, *Queen Victoria* (1904), p. 356.
30. Colchester, *Diary*, III, pp. 360–3 (22 Jan. and 2, 3 Feb. 1825).
31. *Autobiography and Memoirs of Benjamin Robert Haydon 1786–1846*, ed. A.P.D. Penrose (1927), p. 493; Hansard, XXXVIII, 1919 (17 July 1837); XXXIX, 12–13 (20 Nov. 1837): E. Longford, *Victoria R.I.* (1964), p. 71; *The Times*, 21 Nov. 1837.
32. *Ibid.*, 17 Jan. 1840.
33. *Correspondence of Sarah Spencer, Lady Lyttelton, 1782–187*, ed. Mrs Hugh Wyndham, 1912, II, pp. 287–8. Lady Cowper wrote of Victoria opening the session in February 1839 that 'the Queen's delivery [was] very clear and distinct, and a beautiful toned voice': *Lady Palmerston and her Times*, ed. Mabell, Countess Airlie (1922), II, pp. 1–2.
34. Haydon, *Autobiography*, pp. 592–3; Lee, *Queen Victoria*, p. 247.
35. Longford, *Victoria R.I.*, pp. 348, 351, 376, 381.
36. *The Times*, 15 Feb. 1901.
37. *Ibid.*, 3 Feb. 1904, 15 Feb. 1905.

CHAPTER TWO
The Business of the House of Lords

The House of Lords had, as it still has, a dual function. In legislation it is one of the three 'estates of the realm' by each of which bills have to be accepted before passing into statute. It is also the supreme court of appeal in civil and criminal law, saving only the ultimate jurisdiction of the Privy Council. The business of the House therefore falls into two distinct categories and, indeed, it was during this period that the two functions became more clearly separated, legislative matters remaining the concern of the whole House while judicial questions were hived off to a small group of 'law lords', the lay peers ceasing to attend for such business.

JUDICIAL BUSINESS

The judicial business of the House of Lords consisted mainly in the hearing of appeals from the lower courts. The Union with Ireland in 1801 increased the number of such appeals from Ireland, while at about the same time a change in the Scottish legal system also led to a considerable increase.[1] In 1823 the Prime Minister declared that the number of appeals from English courts averaged 5 per year, from Ireland 8 or 9, and from Scotland 40. The numbers could not be dealt with by the Lord Chancellor alone, since he had also to attend to the daily business of his own Court of Chancery, and the backlog mounted rapidly. In 1813 a bill was introduced to allow the appointment of a Vice-Chancellor, and it was agreed to set aside three mornings per week, from 10 a.m. to 3 p.m., for hearing appeals, but by 1823 the delays had become so scandalous that further steps were required. Liverpool asserted in the debate that there were presently 570 appeals awaiting determination.[2]

A committee of their lordships was appointed to study the problem and it suggested that, in the absence of any alternative method of dealing with the major problem of the Scottish appeals, three steps should be taken. These were: the extension of the appeals sittings to five half-days; a ballot of lay peers to ensure that on every occasion two would be present in addition to the chancellor or his deputy in order to make a quorum of the House; and the appointment of a Deputy Speaker who would be empowered to take the place of the Lord Chancellor and so enable him to give more time to the Chancery court. Liverpool pointed out that it was already the established practice for the king to appoint one or more persons to serve as Deputy Speaker, and that currently the Chief Baron of the Exchequer and the Chief Justice of King's Bench were so designated. It was not, Liverpool asserted, necessary for the deputy to be a peer, since standing orders allowed him to give an opinion to the House if required to do so. Strong objections were, however, expressed by some lords against the principle of a commoner presiding in the House, though Lord Redesdale pointed out that this was already established practice. The only innovation, he declared, was the requirement of the attendance of at least two lay peers for each day on which appeals were heard.[3]

After short experience of the new system, some lords voiced objections, particularly to the enforcement of attendance on lay peers to consider technical legal matters beyond their competence. Lord King protested that in a few days he was to be required to attend on an appeal of which he knew nothing, which had been going on for some days and might continue afterwards, but he and his fellow lay peers attended for only one day each. How were they to vote, if at all, at the end of the appeal?

> Was he to take a hint from some one of the big wigs which their lordships occasionally saw rising a few inches above the bar? Or was he to be directed by that equilateral triangular hat which lay there? [Looking towards the woolsack.] Or might he vote, as was done in some cases, without hearing anything on the subject, by proxy?

A week later, Lord Calthorpe declared that the new system was objectionable because the highest court in the land should not decide cases in the absence of the highest legal officer, as well as because the lay lords, who might be the only members of the House present, attended only on particular days and did not hear the whole case. Liverpool defended the system on the grounds that, 'whether three Lords or thirty were present, the decision which they came to was the decision of the House, and was as complete as if every noble Lord was in his place when it was made'. The system was merely designed to ensure that the House was quorate whenever a case was to be heard.[4]

Nevertheless, it can hardly be doubted that it was a legal fiction that the House of Lords, as a House, actually dealt with its judicial business. Lord Holland declared that the system was derogatory, and raised a further point about the relative status of legal and lay peers: it was

> the first time the House had been laid prostrate at the feet of learned lords, and the first time it had been announced that all the other peers were mere cyphers, attending to make up a House. . . . He protested against the principle of calling on individual members to discharge the duty which was common to all their lordships. . . . He knew of no distinction between learned and unlearned lords: they were all peers in parliament, whether they sat on a woolsack or on a bench.[5]

Yet it was difficult to see how else the problem could have been resolved when the House of Lords had to carry out two such different functions. As a legislative body, its deliberations were those of an assembly of men with widely different experience and expertise, representing in some degree the interests of the whole nation, but in its judicial capacity it had to master the technicalities of the law and display the highest professional competence, which resided in only a few of its members. If the House was unwilling to delegate its legal responsibilities to those professionally qualified, the lay members would have to try to perform duties for which they were unfitted, to the likely disadvantage of appellants and suitors. As it was, the fact that the great majority of appeals originated in Scotland, where the law and legal system were very different, made the judgement of those appeals very difficult. In 1827, when the matter was again discussed, on the proposal to appoint the Master of the Rolls, a commoner, as Deputy Speaker, Lord Chancellor Lyndhurst pointed out that there were currently 70 Scottish and 40 English and Irish appeals before the House. The proposal was that the Scottish appeals should be heard on two days a week by Lord Gifford, the Chief Baron of the Exchequer, who was qualified in Scots law, English and Irish similarly on two days by the chancellor and one day by the Master of the Rolls.[6] This brought up Holland once more, to repeat his objection to the idea of two sorts of peers: 'They were all "peers", and that one word showed that they were all equal. It was the duty of every man in that House, as a lord of Parliament, to sit and assist in the hearing of appeals.' Even the Lord Chancellor was only *primus inter pares*: he 'did not possess any additional power, as Lord Chancellor, in the decision of appeals; and when he spoke upon any subject under discussion, he was obliged to quit his seat, and to speak only as a peer'.[7]

From the early nineteenth century, therefore, an increasing differentiation took place between those who came to be known as the 'law lords', in whom the judicial functions of the House grew to be exclusively concentrated, and the majority of the peers. The last interventions of lay peers in judicial matters came in the 1830s and 1840s. In 1834 twelve judges were summoned to assist in determining a writ of error, but no law lord was present and some lay peers had to be recruited, and the earl of Abingdon was voted on to the Woolsack. This was the last time that non-professional peers wholly constituted a house for hearing appeals. In 1844 Daniel O'Connell appealed to the House of Lords against a conviction in the Irish courts, and though the majority of the law lords concurred with the lower court, a large number of lay peers attended and voted to reverse the verdict. Lord Wharncliffe, who was President of the Council, warned them that they ought not to vote on a question of this kind: 'if noble lords unlearned in the law should interfere to decide such questions by their votes instead of leaving them to the decision of the law lords, I very much fear that the authority of this House as a court of justice would be greatly impaired' – as, indeed, would the impartiality of the law itself. This was the last occasion on which non-professional peers attempted to vote in an appeal case.[8]

The problem of dealing efficiently with appeals remained. During the middle years of the century there was repeated criticism of the quality of the decisions made by the law lords, and the fact that they were generally old men in the twilight of their careers also meant a heavy mortality among them. The problem was to find men of sufficient calibre and experience who were willing to give up lucrative offices or practice in the law, and who were also rich enough to be given hereditary titles which their descendants could support. The queen herself appears to have suggested in 1855 the creation of peerages for life only, for which there were precedents in the remote past. The choice fell upon Sir James Parke, a former Baron of the Exchequer, who was created in 1856 by letters patent Baron Wensleydale for his life only.[9] The proposal was, however, clumsily presented by the government and fears were aroused that it was intended to set a precedent for the conferment of numbers of life peerages in order to bring about a reform of the House and to fill it with nominees of the government, so undermining its constitutional independence (and, perhaps, its Conservative character). It was also argued that it would create two different classes of peerages, discriminating against eminent lawyers who might no longer receive hereditary titles – an argument which mobilized the legal peers in the House, led by the aged Lyndhurst, to oppose it. Some even saw the hidden hand of Prince Albert, who was believed to wish to convert the House into something like a continental Assembly of Notables and to introduce men of science and letters into it. Bearing in mind these considerations the Committee of Privileges resolved that, while the Crown had the right to create peerages for life only, the right to sit and vote was to be determined by the House itself, and in this case it was refused.

The government resolved the immediate issue by making Parke an hereditary peer, which, as he was rich, old and had no son, it could well have done in the first place. The Lords then agreed to pass a bill allowing up to four life peers, drawn from the legal profession, to sit in the House to assist in the hearing of appeals, but even this compromise measure was rejected by the Commons. A preference was expressed for a more radical solution, to take away the Lords' powers of appellate jurisdiction and transfer them to a new Supreme Court of Appeal, or to the judicial committee of the Privy Council. In the absence of any firm government majority it proved impossible to reach agreement and the question was shelved.

In 1869 Russell revived the proposal to create life peerages. He proposed that there should be a maximum of twenty-eight life peers eligible to sit at any one time (equivalent to the number of Irish representative peers and of English bishops, who were the other members sitting for life only), chosen from Scottish or Irish peers, persons who had sat more than ten years in the Lower House, distinguished officers in the services, Chief Justices in any of the superior Courts of Law or Equity in the three kingdoms, or who had been puisne judges for two years and retired, persons who had been Attorney General, or Queen's Advocate in Scotland, men distinguished in science, letters, or art, and persons distinguished in the service of the Crown for at least five years. The debates focused more on the appropriateness or otherwise of those categories than on the principle of peerages for life, though Derby stressed the overriding importance of property and independence and doubted whether distinction in the arts, literature and science was a suitable qualification for the peerage. Further objections were voiced by Lord Malmesbury, who had returned from Italy expressly to oppose it. He declared it to be a greater alteration to the constitution than the Reform Acts and that the hereditary principle was 'the very essence of a peerage. . . . Here all are equal in social position, in political rights, and in that great privilege of handing down our names and title to our posterity.' He further asserted that it would place a dangerous weapon in the hands of ministers if they had the power to make poor men life peers. The bill was eventually defeated on the third reading by 76 to 106.[10]

In 1873 the alternative solution was attempted. The Supreme Court of Judicature Act set up a Court of Appeal, to which the Lords' power of appellate jurisdiction in England was transferred. Second thoughts prevailed, however, before the act came into operation, and after further hesitations the Appellate Jurisdiction Act was passed in 1876. This restored the position of the House of Lords as the supreme court of appeal, but it made provision for life peerages to be granted to at least three salaried Lords of Appeal in Ordinary, who had to be professionally qualified and experienced in the law courts and who would sit, with the Lord Chancellor and a number of other legal dignitaries, to hear appeals. Even so, there was no prohibition against any peer attending appeal proceedings, so that the judicial power of the House as a whole was not diminished. In practice, from that time the law lords have exclusively dealt with appeals.[11]

Other kinds of legal business remained, however, in the hands of the House as a whole. These included the trial of peers themselves on criminal charges, an example in this period being the case against Lord Cardigan for fighting a duel in 1841, though there are other cases of peers standing trial in the ordinary courts for minor offences. Cases concerning the privileges of peers, or claims to peerages and titles of honour, were also dealt with by the Lords, though by reference from the Crown rather than directly by inherent right of jurisdiction.[12] The Lords appointed a Committee of Privileges at the start of each session. It usually consisted in the 1820s of about eighty members and it adjudicated on all claims to peerage titles, as well as on breaches of the privilege of the House.[13] The Lords also exercised the right to determine disputed elections of representative peers of Scotland and Ireland, and the right to determine cases on writs of error until their abolition in 1875. The practice of impeachment by the Commons before the House of Lords fell out of use after Melville's case in 1805.

LEGISLATION

In matters of legislation the Lords had equal status in point of constitutional law with the Commons, but since the early eighteenth century certain conventions had grown up which tended, in some respects, to differentiate them. The best known is the convention that the Lords would not interfere with the details of financial measures sent up from the Commons. The sole right of the House of Commons to grant or refuse supply dated from medieval times and was confirmed by their resolution in 1678[14]

> That all Aids and Supplies, and Aids to his Majesty in Parliament, are the sole gift of the Commons: And all Bills for Granting of any such Aids and Supplies ought to begin with the Commons: And that it is the undoubted and sole Right of the Commons, to direct, limit, and appoint, in such Bills, the Ends, Purposes, Considerations, Conditions, Limitations, and Qualifications of such Grants; which ought not to be changed or altered by the House of Lords.

The Lords never explicitly acknowledged this claim but in practice they 'acquiesced grudgingly', though defending their right to reject outright any 'money bill' to protect themselves against any attempt by the Lower House to tack non-financial measures on to a money bill and so deprive the Lords of their legislative power in other matters. The only breach of this convention in this period occurred over the repeal of the paper duties in 1860, but a crisis was averted by the government's caution. In 1909 the Lords rejected Lloyd George's 'People's Budget' and in 1911 the Parliament Act formally took away the Lords' power to legislate on financial measures.[15]

In a few respects, chiefly proposed legislation affecting or concerning the rights of peers, there were precedents to suggest that bills on these matters ought to be introduced first into the Upper House, but where this occurred it seems to have been more a matter of courtesy than of right. Bills of pains and penalties were 'usually' introduced first into the Lords: this was the case with the Bill against Queen Caroline in 1820, the only instance of such a bill in this period.[16]

In the consideration of bills, whether public or private, and whether originating in the upper chamber or sent up from the Commons, the Lords' procedures were similar to those of the other House, but unlike the Commons they remained largely unchanged throughout the period. Any peer could put down a motion or introduce a bill at any time without (as in the Commons) having to ask leave to do so, though by standing order in 1852 precedence was given to (mostly) government bills on two days a week. Each bill was given the usual three readings, the first, as in the Commons, conventionally being formal and unopposed, the second being reserved for discussion of the principles and substance of the bill followed by a reference to a committee, either of the whole House in matters of major importance, or a select committee of usually between ten and twenty peers meeting in a room away from the chamber, where the detailed clauses were discussed and amendments considered. The bill was then reported to the whole House for any amendments inserted by the committee to be approved or rejected. The third reading was again formal, with the question being put without debate and the bill passed either for the royal assent, or, if it originated in the Lords, to be sent down to the Commons for consideration, or if amendments had been inserted by the Lords, for the Commons to consider them. In that case, the bill was returned again to the Lords after the Commons had accepted or rejected the amendments. If there was still a disagreement between the Houses, a conference of representatives of each was summoned, to be held in the Painted Chamber before 1834 and afterwards in a room elsewhere. The Lords sat covered at a table, while the Commons' representatives stood, and 'a conversational discourse' ensued between them. If agreement was not reached the bill was lost.[17]

The ceremony of the royal assent always took place in the Lords' Chamber. Occasionally the monarch attended in person – Queen Victoria attended in December 1837 to give assent to the Civil List Bill and a number of others – but this was now unusual, except when the ceremony was combined with the prorogation when bills passed towards the close of the session might be dealt with. Otherwise it was usual for commissioners to indicate the royal pleasure whenever a batch of bills was ready to be passed.

As in the Commons, the day's business in the Upper House, which usually began at 5 p.m., started with prayers, read by the junior bishop. In several respects, however, the Lords' procedures differed from those of the Commons. There was no elected Speaker, the Lord Chancellor presiding *ex-officio*, and his powers were less extensive than those of his counterpart in the Lower House. Their lordships' procedures were more egalitarian: Melbourne told Hatherton in August 1835 that 'It is not at all an aristocratic assembly in itself. Nothing can exceed the spirit of equality and of familiarity that reigns in it.'[18] Members did not address the Lord Chancellor as Speaker, but their lordships collectively, and the Lord Chancellor did not decide whom to call on to speak. In case of conflict the House would decide whom to hear. In important debates, the party whips would agree beforehand on a list of speakers. The Lord Chancellor also had no power to call the House to order. His duties were confined to putting the question. He himself, however, could speak at any time in a debate, leaving the woolsack to do so and taking his place at the head of the duke's bench as one of their lordships. It was customary for one or two individuals to be named as Deputy Speakers in case of the Lord Chancellor's absence. These need not be peers; they were often judges, and in 1835 the Master of the Rolls, Sir William Pepys, a member of the House of Commons, presided while Lord Denman was away at county assizes.

When the House went into committee on a bill the Lord Chancellor gave up his seat to the Chairman of Committees, or occasionally to another peer appointed *ad hoc* by the House. The office of Chairman of Committees was established in 1800 and though it was renewed each session it was customary for one individual to continue in the post for several years. From 1814 to 1851 the earl of Shaftesbury held the position, followed by Lord Redesdale who served until 1886. The procedure in committee was more informal. Peers were able, for example, to speak as often as they wished in committee, whereas in a first, second, or third reading debate no peer was allowed to speak more than once in each stage, unless to reply to a debate or in explanation. On occasion the Lords discussed questions without a formal motion before them – these were known as 'conversations' and the formal rules did not apply.

The quorum for debates in the Lords was the chancellor or his representative, two other temporal peers and (for other than judicial business) one bishop, and indeed at most sittings throughout the session the business was so formal or so unimportant that only a handful of peers would be present. Lord Forbes, writing in 1891 of his experience of the Lords since 1874, remarked on the paucity of attendance and scarcity of business for large periods of the session, while the major bills were still under consideration in the Commons, and on the smallness of many select committees, meetings consisting of as few as five peers.[19] In 1835 concern at what was seen as the 'scandalous' attendance of peers at committees led to a meeting of fifteen leading peers of both parties. They agreed to require that any peer who moved for the appointment of a select committee should obtain the names of eleven other peers, who would engage to attend the meetings, but they agreed also to lower the quorum from five to three. The system of referring lesser bills to select committees was, Hatherton wrote, 'excellent in itself, but by taking the discussion of them out of the [whole] House, it gives the public the notion that it has nothing to do'. The active members of the Upper House did spend a considerable part of their time in committees rather than in the House itself, where, except for major debates, attendance was generally light. The committees dealt mostly with private and local business and the chief function of the Chairman of Committees was to supervise private legislation in detail. Hatherton complained of

Shaftesbury in that office that he 'has neither manners nor wit to carry off anything', that he used the influence of his office in the service of his party and that 'the only good that he has done during his long reign is that he has introduced some uniformity of principle with regard to private legislation'.[20]

Nor were committees always impartially selected. Hatherton himself admitted in 1845 that in the Standing Orders Committee he had been 'occupied a good deal in conjunction with the Great Western people in framing a list of "objectionable" peers whom they do not wish placed on the Select Committee to try their Bill – I gave it to Lord Bessborough who will select the Committee. I find I have thus rendered them great service', he innocently added, 'by keeping off parties who were interested or pledged, or liable to influence.'[21]

The unevenness of the legislative business of the Lords was an insoluble problem. Most important bills were necessarily introduced first in the Commons, so that for a large proportion of each session the Lords had very little to do while they were awaiting the arrival of business from the Lower House. For much of the time the Lords met at 5 p.m. but had finished their business by 7 p.m. Lord Campbell alleged that 'A noble lord did not rise to speak after seven o'clock without an apology. "My Lords, at this *late hour of the evening*. . ."'.[22] Towards the end of the session, as numbers of important bills arrived from the Commons, the Lords complained of overwork and long sittings. Melbourne grumbled in July 1836 that 'business has not come into the House of Lords from the House of Commons till now in the heat of the Dog Days, when it is setting in in overwhelming quantity'. Melbourne, remarked Hatherton, was always 'bothered . . . in June and July when the Bills come up by dozens from the House of Commons, and the unpleasant things that had been delayed will admit of no longer delay'. Lord Londonderry, who chose to speak for one and a quarter hours in late July on a petition regarding the surplus revenues of the see of Durham, experienced the consequences: Melbourne and Duncannon, on the government front bench, were 'fast asleep the whole time, while the Dukes of Wellington and Cumberland were asleep behind him; and three out of seven Bishops equally happy'.[23]

In July 1860 Derby moved for a select committee to study the problem. He pointed out that the session had so far lasted twenty-six weeks, in which time 34 bills had received the royal assent, and 13 others had passed through both Houses and awaited the royal assent. Almost all, however, were 'measures of the most absolute and complete routine', hardly even of 'second-rate importance'. This was the normal state of affairs for the past ten or twelve years. Since

1848, the average number of bills receiving the royal assent up to the end of July was 61: the average from the end of July to the end of August was also 61, as more important measures arrived from the Commons. As he spoke, there were 5 bills standing for third reading, 8 for committee, 25 for second reading in the House of Lords, while 22 or 23 bills sent down from the Lords to the Commons had not yet passed or even reached the committee stage in the Lower House, where there were several other bills also in various stages. In all there were 77 bills in the Commons, of which only 19 had previously passed the Lords, so that there was a prospect of 58 further bills coming to the House before the end of the session. Bills coming up at that late stage were 'frequently passed with extravagant haste, and without the least consideration'. He suggested that a select committee should try to find a solution.

Granville agreed that the problem was serious, and that it was of long standing, going back at least fifty years. The subject was debated again in both Houses at the beginning of the 1861 session, but despite lengthy debates and the appointment of committees in both Houses no remedy was found.[24]

In 1867 Lord Lyveden originated a debate on the business of the House, in which he declared that the general public's impression that the Lords did very little was a misapprehension. The problem, he again suggested, lay in the unevenness of business through the session. Since most legislation originated in the Commons, and much of it was financial or had financial aspects, the Lords had little to do in the early part of the session:

> It was no doubt startling to read in the newspapers that the House met at five o'clock and adjourned at half-past five, leading to the inference that the Lords have done nothing, forgetting that they have nothing to do by no fault of their own. . . . [Even so] Unless a division is expected, which is seldom, the attendance diminishes at seven, and altogether disappears at eight.

He suggested the adoption of a quorum, as in the House of Commons, the replacement of the current system of voluntary attendance at committees on private bills by a rota system, and the abolition of proxy voting. Other Lords, led by the Prime Minister Lord Derby, defended the existing procedures. Derby pointed out that debates were generally shorter than in the Commons:

> I am happy to say that the *cacoethes loquendi* does not prevail in this House to the extent that it does in the other House of Parliament. There are not so many of your Lordships who are anxious to give your opinions upon every subject which is brought under

discussion, neither are there so many, I am happy to say, who suggest Amendment after Amendment in Committee. Were we to follow the example of the other House we should find that passing one Bill through Committee would probably absorb the greater portion of the Session. . . .

Redesdale and Carnarvon defended the proxy system, and Shaftesbury proposed a committee to consider the possibility of meeting at 4 p.m., instead of 5 p.m. and other procedural changes. Lyveden withdrew his motion.[25]

SPEAKING IN THE HOUSE

The House of Lords was not, in general, a stimulating place in which to speak. The major debates and the best orators of the time were usually in the House of Commons, where the audiences were usually larger and more responsive, and where members made their reputations by their skill in speaking. By contrast, the atmosphere of the Lords was dull and lacking in stimulation. Lord Grey, whose political reputation was built upon his oratory in the Commons, after his first speech there in 1808, told his wife that 'with just light enough to make darkness visible, it was like speaking in a vault by the glimmering of a sepulchral lamp to the dead. It is impossible I should ever do anything there worth thinking of.'[26] Fifty years later Robert Lowe, also recently arrived in the Lords as Viscount Sherbrooke, likened it to 'addressing dead men by torchlight'.[27] In 1876 the duke of Somerset facetiously suggested that the proceedings might be livened up if 'instead of the common air which they pump through the floor for our benefit, they should send up a little laughing gas; the effect would, no doubt, be surprising'.[28]

These conditions, however, threw into higher relief the speeches of rare individuals such as Derby, leader of the Conservative peers from 1846 to 1867. He had been called 'the Rupert of debate' in his days in the Commons. Lansdowne and Granville, who were successively leaders of the Liberal peers from 1842 to 1891, were also capable of effective if less brilliant oratory, and others who were respected for their powers included Ellenborough, one of Derby's chief lieutenants, and Lyndhurst, Lord Chancellor in Wellington's administration and a potent force in the Lords even at the age of 84 in 1856. Contests between Derby and Granville in the 1850s were likened to those of Roman gladiators, and were as eagerly watched.[29] Rarely, however, were debates in the House less than decorous in tone. In the debates on the second Reform Bill in 1867, Granville protested that Derby was using the Lords to renege on a compromise agreed between the parties in the Commons and, as Granville's biographer wrote, words like 'dodge', 'trumpery' and 'falsehood' were

> hurtled through the usually placid air, and several persons were heard addressing the House at the same time. One peer used language which . . . seemed to imply that the Lord Privy Seal was at least capable of knocking down Lord Russell, if it came to a fight, as he was much the taller and bigger of the two.

Derby declared that he had never heard 'so much personal virulence and so many misrepresentations' and the venerable Lord Harrowby deplored that the debate breached the 'gentlemanly habits' usual in the chamber: it ended with Granville leading the Liberal peers out in protest. There was another stormy scene in July 1884, when Granville and Cairns rose together and each refused to give way and 'cheered on by his excited supporters, continued to hold the floor' until the House divided on which was to be heard, and Granville won by 27 to 26.[30]

On 'great days', the House of Lords could still attract large audiences to hear debates whose quality could be well above the average of the House of Commons. Debates in the evenings were often attended by ladies and gentlemen in dinner dress, and ladies in their fine jewellery. The galleries were full for Stanley's motion of censure on Palmerston's foreign policy in June 1850, and several ladies had to sit on the floor of the House or go home. There was a diversion when Count Bunsen, the stout Prussian Minister, was noticed sitting in the ladies' gallery and refused to move when Brougham told him he had no right to be there, and 'all the more intolerable, as he is now keeping the room of *two* peeresses'. He was finally ejected by Black Rod and left the House in a fury with his wife and daughter.[31] Five years later, for the debate on Ellenborough's motion on the conduct of the Crimean War, the number of ladies present, as Malmesbury noted, 'created great displeasure among the Peers. Lord Ellenborough said it had made him nervous; and Lord Lyndhurst positively refused to speak, saying that the House looked like a Casino and not like a place where business is transacted.' Redesdale also objected to the overflow of ladies into the House and Malmesbury feared that 'this invasion will . . . lead to more stringent and less agreeable arrangements in future'. In 1858 he again recorded a crowded house for an opposition motion of censure. 'There were only two seats left in the gallery when I arrived, all filled with ladies. The steps of the Throne, the Peers' and

Strangers' galleries crammed, and all so attentive to the debate that every word was heard.' Not only the galleries were crowded: over 200 peers voted in the division. Again in 1860 for the debate on the paper duties, 'I never saw any place so crowded as the Peers' benches, the ladies' gallery and the steps of the Throne, while the bar and the strangers' gallery were crammed.'[32]

These were rare excitements. For most of the time, complaints at the non-attendance of peers, even of those recently ennobled in order to give greater strength to their parties, were frequent. Hatherton, who had recent experience of the stricter whipping system in the Commons, commented on several occasions about the difficulty of getting lords to attend. The business of the House was clearly less onerous than in the Commons, where larger attendances of members and, after the 1830s, a more intense degree of party conflict and the competition for office and distinction were making the sessions longer and more taxing. In the Lords, a House of forty or fifty peers was considered large, except for unusually controversial business. In 1857 Carnarvon moved the adjournment of a debate on Derby's resolutions censuring the government's China policy because it was midnight, but Granville objected:[33]

> Considering the length of time usually occupied by their debates did not exceed two hours and a half each evening, and that the other night a noble and learned Lord had postponed a most valuable motion on an important subject because he declined to address benches that were nearly empty, it was to be hoped, now there was such a full attendance of their Lordships, the House would not shrink from devoting more of its time to the discussion of a great question like the present.

VOTING AND PROTESTING

Also different from the procedure in the Commons was the method of taking votes in a division. Instead of swarming into the lobbies to be counted, the Lords remained in their places and when the question was put answered individually and orally, in order of rank and precedence, beginning with the lowest baron. The prescribed form was to declare 'content' or 'not content'. If numbers were equal, there being no casting vote in any Speaker, the measure was deemed to be lost. When the votes were taken, the 'contents' went below the bar and the 'not contents' remained in the House. Proxies, if called for, were read over and declared after all those present had voted. As in the Commons, strangers were required to leave the gallery during a division. This ancient method of taking divisions was, however, changed by a standing order of 16 June 1865, the new procedure being similar to that of the Commons.[34]

One major difference between the two Houses until 1868 was the peers' right to vote by proxy. It was still the case in the nineteenth century that personal attendance in the House was formally required by law and that any peer could move to enforce a 'call of the House' on any occasion. The duke of Newcastle, for example, gave notice on 2 March 1829 of his intention to do so to ensure a full attendance at the forthcoming debate on the Catholic Emancipation Bill.[35] Absence from such a 'call' could be punished by fine or even imprisonment, unless the peer could provide evidence of incapacity to attend. Mrs Arbuthnot wrote that on the occasion of the 'Queen's Trial' in 1820 'all the Peers were ordered to attend on pain of paying 500 £ and being imprisoned in the Tower.[36] It was, however, possible for a peer to appoint one of his colleagues to vote as his proxy, either for a whole session or for particular occasions. A form had to be filled in and signed by the absentee and submitted to the Clerk of the House by the peer appointed as the proxy. No peer could hold more than two proxies at a time. The details were entered in the proxy book for reference. Proxies were not used in a division unless called for by a member of the House, and they were counted separately and added to the votes of those present.[37]

Peers might lay down strict conditions as to the use of their proxies. After Grey had retired from the premiership in 1834 he chose to attend Parliament less frequently and in 1835 and 1836 he deposited his proxy with his successor, Lord Melbourne, professing 'both from my personal friendship for you and from the general conformity of our opinions, . . . my sincere disposition to give to your Administration all the support in my power'. He did not entirely trust Melbourne, however, to stand up to O'Connell and the Radicals as firmly as he himself wished, and so he made two reservations. The first was that if they should differ on any government measure, 'it will always be in my power to write to you in time to prevent its being used'. Second, he laid it down explicitly that it was not to be used in support of either of two measures to which he was implacably opposed, namely, any further reform, either of the House of Lords or the House of Commons, in particular the ballot, the extension of the right of voting, or shorter Parliaments, and second the appropriation of the surplus revenues of the Irish Church to secular purposes, should that question be brought forward again, without his further instructions. Grey's warning was in fact intended to influence Melbourne and the government to resist these measures: he found it convenient to use the device of placing conditions on the use of his proxy to indicate the strength of his views and the extent to which he expected his successor to respect them.[38]

It was not uncommon, however, for peers to lay down conditions for the use of their proxies. Lord Spencer in 1834 instructed his son Lord Althorp to enter his proxy with any peer of his choice, subject to the limitation that it was not to be used for 'every kind of appropriation [of Irish Church revenues] which may hereafter be proposed'.[39] Proxies could be and sometimes were revoked during the course of a session and transferred to another holder, especially if the first recipient ceased to attend, and they were automatically revoked if the giver attended the House himself on any occasion. Otherwise they remained valid until the end of the session.

The use of proxies was normally confined to major divisions. They could not be used in any judicial business, nor in committees. Between 1815 and 1868, they were called for on 104 occasions, and on twelve they determined the outcome against the majority actually present. In 1823 the Roman Catholic Election Franchise Bill was defeated by 43+30 proxies to 41+39, and Lord John Russell's government was saved from defeat three times in 1849 by proxies, though the opposition carried a vote of censure on Palmerston's Danish policy in 1864 by 119+58 against 123+45. Proxies were often numerous. In 1834, 175 were counted in a division on the Irish Tithe Bill, and in the exceptionally large division of 9 June 1837 on the Irish Municipal Corporations Bill the Tory majority of 205 included 76 proxies, while the Whigs counted 45 out of 119. The proxies then accounted for 37.3 per cent of the total vote of 364 peers.[40]

In general, the use of proxies in this period became more an instrument to maintain party strengths, irrespective of actual attendance, than a means by which individual peers sought to compensate for unavoidable absence or to salve their consciences for non-performance of their duties. As the Upper House came more to mirror the parties in the House of Commons, and as the diminished 'influence of the Crown' no longer gave the government of the day a powerful lever to keep the Upper House in line, the party whips and managers gave more attention to the organisation of the proxy system and tried to induce their supporters to nominate proxies before the start of each session as a safeguard against non-attendance. In 1838 the House debated proxies on the initiative of the marquess of Westminster, who remarked that it was 'manifestly improper' that questions should be decided by the votes of individuals who had not been present to hear the discussion. He even alleged that 'questions had actually been carried by the proxies of noble Lords who were dead at the time their authority was made use of', though he gave no evidence, and it was contested by Earl Fitzwilliam as being impossible. Fitzwilliam defended the practice as being a remedy for lords who were unable to attend because of illness or necessary duty, and pointed out that lords gave their proxies to people with whose views they tended to agree and that if the proxy-holder was influenced by the debate he would use his judgement whether to use the proxy. Brougham scoffed at proxies as 'most absurd and preposterous', but remarked sardonically that since the arguments in debate never made any difference to the way anyone voted they might as well decide everything by proxy. There was no wish, however, to pursue the matter and the reporter ended with the terse remark 'subject dropped'.[41]

The proxy system came under increasing attack from the press and public during the middle years of the nineteenth century and their use diminished sharply after 1850. Lords Derby and Redesdale defended them in the debate on the business of the House in June 1867, on the grounds that there were many aged or infirm peers who could not easily attend in person, as well as those holding diplomatic, military, or naval posts abroad who would be disfranchised by abolition.[42] Derby admitted that proxies had been called for only twice since 1849. In July Disraeli put forward the defence that peers who were unable to attend in person were in the position of constituents of the House of Commons who had the right to choose a representative to vote on their behalf.[43] A select committee recommended the termination of the system and it was discontinued by a standing order 32A of 31 March 1868.

Finally, members of the Lords had the unique right to record their dissent from any vote which was passed by the House. This took the form of a 'protest', when one or any number of peers present could record their reasons for voting in opposition to the majority and have them printed in the *Journals* of the House.[44] In the eighteenth century protests were frequently used by oppositions as propaganda, since they could be published in the newspapers even during the period when the reporting of debates was prohibited.[45] After the 1770s, however, their use declined as the newspapers gave more space to the reports of the debates themselves and they became superfluous as political propaganda. Thorold Rogers noted that down to the period of the American War of Independence protests 'were generally . . . instruments by which that portion of the opposition which acted together, and was most energetic in resisting the administration of the day, expressed its united opinion', but afterwards 'they became the record of the reasons which a small minority or even an individual had for dissenting from the policy which Parliament or the Upper House adopted'.[46] Protests were still occasionally used by members of the opposition to record the grounds of their political dissent against a major bill: the Whigs thought the 'Six Acts' so repressive that they entered 9 protests against them in December 1819. Catholic Emancipation attracted 9 protests in March and April 1829 and sixty-one members of the Tory opposition entered no less than 12 protests against the third reading of the Reform Bill on 4 June 1832, the number of signatures on each ranging from two to thirty-two. There were 4 protests against the Irish Church Temporalities Bill on 30 July 1833. Protests with the largest number of signatures were those against the repeal of the Corn Laws in 1846 (89), the Reform Bill on 13 April 1832 (77), the disestablishment of the Irish Church in 1869 (60), the Bill of Pains and Penalties against Queen Caroline on 20 October 1820 (55) and the repeal of the Navigation Laws in 1849 (43). Only 10 protests, 9 before 1850, were signed by more than twenty peers; the great majority (279 out of 373) were signed by five peers or less, including 148 signed by only one individual.

After 1850 the protests became less frequent, averaging just over 3 per session between 1850 and 1875, against 8.2 per session between 1815 and 1849. Only 14 out of 84 protests after 1850 were signed by more than five peers, and 44 were single protests. Whether this represents an increasing feeling of powerlessness among the peers, or simply a falling out of use of an outmoded procedure, it is difficult to determine. Thorold Rogers suggested that after 1832 protests became an absurdity and that they had ceased to perform any useful purpose. Some individuals and groups, particularly legal peers, continued to enter them, either to ride hobby horses or to try to set the record straight on matters of procedure or legal technicality. Eight peers during this period signed 8 or more single protests. In the earlier years, Lauderdale (11), Stanhope (10) and Holland (9) led for the Whig opposition, and Radnor signed 8 single protests between 1824 and 1847. After 1832 the leading single protesters were lawyers: Denman, 13 (all after 1856), and Brougham, 10 (after he ceased to be Lord Chancellor in 1835), while Lord Monteagle, a politician, also scored 10. As an instrument of party, however, protests really died out in the middle years of the nineteenth century. Thus, by the end of this period the procedures of the House of Lords had in several respects been assimilated more closely to those of the Commons, and in most cases they have subsequently remained unchanged.

Other proposals made from time to time to modify the procedures in the chamber were unsuccessful. In 1868 Lord Denman moved a bill to limit the length of speeches in the House, which failed to pass its second reading after Cranbrook argued that it was unnecessary. In 1888 Lord Stratheden proposed that the Lords should appoint a Speaker who would call on peers to speak, as in the Commons, but he withdrew his motion for similar lack of support. In the following year the select committee on standing orders suggested the creation of four standing committees to examine all bills before they came to a committee of the whole House, to expedite the process of revising legislation. Two committees were appointed, one for 'legal' and one for 'general' bills, and the House also agreed to a proposal that there should be a quorum of thirty members for any division in the House, but backbenchers disliked the idea of the removal of business from the whole House to select committees and the scheme collapsed after two years. In 1890 Lord Ribblesdale unsuccessfully suggested that a peer's right to vote on any question should be dependent on his having attended the House during the preceding session.[47] Such proposals with the purpose of making the procedures of the House more effective or improving attendance did not find favour and were abandoned. From the 1880s attention was directed towards reforming the composition of the House rather than changing its procedures for dealing with business.

REFERENCES

1. Lord Eldon in the House of Lords, 12 May 1829; Hansard, NS XXI, 1286, 1291.
2. *Ibid.*, IX, 1246–51.
3. *Ibid.*, 1246–53. A penalty of £50 was prescribed for non-attendance: *Diary and Correspondence of Charles Abbot, Lord Colchester* ed. Lord Colchester (1861), III, p. 299. Liverpool rejected Colchester's proposal that a temporary tribunal, of a Deputy Speaker (being a peer) and two assessors be appointed to clear off the arrears. He consulted Colchester as to whether the Deputy Speaker, if not a peer, could give his opinion to the House: *ibid.*, pp. 284–5, 289.
4. Hansard, NS X, 640 (2 March 1824), 830–6 (9 March).
5. *Ibid.*
6. Gifford (1779–1826), Chief Justice of Common Pleas, was raised to the peerage as Baron Gifford and became Deputy Speaker and Master of the Rolls (1824): *DNB*; G.E.C., *The Complete Peerage* (1910–59); Colchester, *Diary*, III, p. 309. Colchester said his judgements were given 'in a clear

and masterly style' but that his achievements in clearing off the Scottish arrears had led the senior lawyers to neglect their business in Chancery to give time to the appeals: *ibid.*, pp. 462, 495.

7. Hansard, NS XVII, 573–6 (7 May 1827): see T. Beven, 'The appellate jurisdiction of the House of Lords', *Law Quarterly Review*, XVII (1901) pt II, 357–71.

8. *Ibid.*

9. L.G. Pine, *Constitutional History of the House of Lords* (1894), pp. 376–82. On the Wensleydale peerage affair, see Olive Anderson, 'The Wensleydale peerage case and the position of the House of Lords in the mid-nineteenth century', *English Historical Review*, LXXXII (1967), 486–502.

10. Hansard, NS CXCV, 452–73, 1648–77; CXCVI, 1172, 1204, 1370–91; CXCVII 1387–1401. Lord Malmesbury, *Memoirs of an Ex-Minister* (1854), II, pp. 393–8.

11. R. Stevens, 'The final appeal: reform of the House of Lords and the Privy Council, 1862–76', *Law Quarterly Review* LXXX (1964), 343–69; V.M.R. Goodman, 'Appellate jurisdiction', *Parliamentary Affairs* VII, no. 1 (1953), 77–87; Beven, *'Appellate jurisdiction'*. The defeat of the attempt in 1873 to remove the final jurisdiction of the Lords was attributed to Redesdale's 'determined action': *Memories by Lord Redesdale (1867–76)*, ed. Lord Redesdale (1915), I, p. 23.

12. Pine, *Constitutional History*, pp. 247–85, 294–5.

13. In 1827 a person who had served a messenger of the House with a process from the Court of Requests for taking away his umbrella while he was below the bar was summoned to the bar and reprimanded: Colchester, *Diary*, III, p. 471.

14. *Journals of the House of Commons* IX, 509: 3 July 1678.

15. Emily Allyn, *Lords versus Commons: a Century of Conflict and Compromise, 1830–1930* (New York, 1931), pp. 4–5. For the 1860 and 1909 episodes see below, pp. 123–4 and 174–6.

16. Pine, *Constitutional History*, pp. 335–6.

17. J.Grant, *Random Recollections of the House of Lords* (1836), p. 27.

18. Diary of Lord Hatherton, Hatherton MSS, Staffordshire Record Office, 22 August 1835.

19. Lord Forbes, *The House of Lords, 1874–1891: A Sketch* (Edinburgh, 1891), pp. 13–16, 24–31.

20. Diary of Lord Hatherton, 18 July 1835 and 9 July 1836. For details of the various classes of private bills, and the procedures on each, see House of Lords Record Office Memorandum 16, *Private Bill Records of the House of Lords*.

21. Diary of Lord Hatherton, 2 July 1845.

22. *Life of John, Lord Campbell*, ed. Mrs M.S. Hardcastle (1881), II, p. 163.

23. Diary of Lord Hatherton, 5, 19 and 21 July 1836.

24. Hansard, CLIX, 2129–50; CLX 179–92.

25. *Ibid.*, 3rd ser., CLXXXVIII, 129–44.

26. Jan. 1808: Grey MSS, Durham; E.A. Smith, *Lord Grey, 1764–1845* (Oxford, 1990), p. 155.

27. Lord Edmond Fitzmaurice, *Life of . . . second Earl Granville*, I, (1905), p. 239.

28. *Letters, Remains, and Memoirs of Edward . . . 12th Duke of Somerset*, ed. W.H. Mallock and Lady Gwendolen Ramsden (1893), pp. 394–5. The

dullness of debate might also be punctuated by long silences: since the chancellor had no role in conducting the debate or calling on speakers it was often uncertain towards the end of debates whether any further lords wished to rise or whether it was opportune to put the question.

29. Fitzmaurice, *Life of . . . second Earl Granville*, 1905, I, pp. 233–9.

30. *Ibid.*, I, pp. 512–14; II, p. 379; Hansard, CCXC, 796.

31. Malmesbury; *Memoirs of an Ex-Minister*, I, pp. 262–3.

32. *Ibid.*, II, pp. 23, 119, 227–8.

33. Hansard, CXLIV, 1243–4, 24 Feb. 1857.

34. *Ibid.*, CLXXX, 347–8, 16 June 1865.

35. *Ibid.*, XX, 646–7, 2 March 1829.

36. *The Journal of Mrs Arbuthnot 1820–1832*, ed. F. Bamford and the Duke of Wellington (10 July 1820),I, p. 28.

37. The House of Lords Record Office, proxy books (150 vols) 1626–1864. See J. Enoch Powell, 'Proxy voting in the House of Lords', *Parliamentary Affairs* IX, 2 (1955–6), 203–12. Proxies could be inspected by peers on the day before a division after notice had been given of the intention to call for them.

38. Grey to Melbourne, 29 Jan. 1836; Grey MSS, Durham, G41/3. After 1837 Grey fell out with Melbourne. He gave his proxy to the more conservative duke of Richmond in 1840.

39. D. Le Marchant, *Memoir of John Charles Viscount Althorp, Third Earl Spencer* (1876), pp. 492–3. See also Wellington, *Despatches, Correspondence and Memoranda*, V, p. 502 and VIII, p. 356 for examples of the withdrawal or non-use of proxies.

40. Colchester, *Diary*, III, pp. 292, 326; Hansard, CVI, 547–8; CVII, 724, 1139–40; XXV, 1204; XXXVIII, 1329.

41. *Ibid.*, XLIII, 1087–9.

42. *Ibid.*, CLXXXVIII, 129–44.

43. Disraeli had used this defence before, in his *Vindication of the English Constitution* (1835) reprinted in W. Hutcheon (ed.), *Whigs and Whiggism: Political Writings by Benjamin Disraeli* (New York, 1914), p. 193.

44. In 1823 Colchester noted that the duke of Somerset entered a protest on the address though he had not voted in the division, but the House decided that 'he having been present at the debate, though he had not voted', his protest should stand on the *Journal*: Colchester, *Diary*, III, p. 273. For the Lords' protests see J.E. Thorold Rogers, *A Complete Collection of the Protests of the Lords . . .* (1875), II and III.

45. Though there were sometimes prosecutions of printers who did so, even as late as 1801, *ibid.*, I, p. xxxvii.

46. *Ibid.*, p. xxxviii.

47. *Diary of Gathorne Hardy* ed. N. Johnson (Oxford, 1981), pp. 703, 695, 729, 771.

PART TWO

Evolution and Adaptation, 1815–80

CHAPTER THREE
The Members of the House of Lords: The Hereditary Peerage

The House of Lords in this period comprised all those holders of hereditary peerages of England, Great Britain and the United Kingdom who were of age, not incapacitated by reason of insanity or conviction of a felony, and male, provided they had sworn the necessary oaths of allegiance and supremacy, abjured Popery and been formally introduced and taken their seats. It also included a number of elected representatives of the separate Scottish and Irish peerages (dating from the Acts of Union of 1707 and 1800 respectively), the two archbishops and twenty-four bishops of the Anglican Church, and four bishops of the Church of Ireland.

The hereditary peers fell into two categories: those whose ancestors had attended by writ of summons from the Crown at any time during the Middle Ages, and whose descendants could claim the right of attendance, and those (the great majority) whose peerages had been conferred by royal letters patent at a particular date.[1] The second type of peerage normally descended only by primogeniture in the male line, unless provision had been made by 'special remainder' for inheritance by another close relative. Peeresses might fall into either category, but in neither case could they sit in the House. Peerages by writ, as they were loosely known, were heritable by women and heirs general, and passed through women to their eldest sons or, in default of male heirs, to their daughters as coheirs and *their* male descendants by primogeniture. Peerages passing to female coheirs fell into abeyance until only one coheir was left alive or until a coheir was succeeded by a son. The barony of North, for example, dated from 1534 and was considered to be a barony by writ though the editor of the *Complete Peerage* suggested that it might have originated in an earlier patent, since lost. The earldom of Guilford was conferred on the family in

1752, but on the death of the 3rd earl without male issue in 1802, the earldom passed to his brother, but the barony of North fell into abeyance among his three daughters and coheirs and was revived in the person of the surviving daughter when the second daughter died in 1841. She became Baroness North in her own right and when she died in 1884 the barony passed to her son.

CREATIONS AND PROMOTIONS

Apart from the bishops, all members of the House of Lords during this period held hereditary titles, whether the first of their creation or not and whether elected to the House or sitting by right.[2] England in 1815 was a country still dominated by the wealth and influence of the landed aristocracy, of which order the peerage formed the pinnacle in rank and social primacy, and men wishing to rise to that eminence had to prove their worth and respectability. Few imagined, as Thomas Hope of Deepdene, Dorking, that they could reach the House of Lords by bribery: Mrs Arbuthnot noted in 1823 that the Duke of Wellington had been approached on his behalf with a gift of £10,000 if he would make him a peer, to which the duke replied that the intermediary 'had made an egregious mistake in coming upon such an errand and sent him out of the house'.[3] During the Napoleonic Wars, additions to the peerage had been made chiefly from men who had given outstanding service to the state in the armed forces, the diplomatic service and in public office at home, but these men were in any case mainly drawn from the old governing families or shared their educational experience and social environment. Where, as in the case of Wellington, they lacked substantial landed property of their own, they were provided with the means to obtain it, so as not to dilute the peerage with families who could not keep up the lifestyle of the aristocracy. The Lords thus contained not only 'country' peers, political backwoodsmen who had little time or inclination for politics unless they perceived a threat to their order or interests, but also a number, large among the politically active minority of the House, of ex-ministers and public servants whose experience of political affairs was in total extensive.

The close links between the monarch and the peerage sprang not from political manipulation but from a natural feeling of identity of interest. In return, the monarch exercised a jealous control over new creations and promotions in the peerage, ensuring that it was not cheapened by being too extensive or bestowed on men whose family, property, or social acceptability would diminish its respectability. When, after 1784, the younger Pitt became more generous in proposing candidates for the peerage, he did so for two reasons: to reward those who had used their political, and particularly electoral, influence on his behalf to help establish him in power, but also to yield to some extent to the growing demand from men whose increasing wealth and respectability seemed to qualify them for the advance in rank. George III expressed his doubts, particularly about the second category. The removal of men of weight and property from the House of Commons might reduce that House's social prestige and its reliability as a support of the old order. Liverpool wrote in 1814 that a large creation of peers was objectionable because it would withdraw 'the natural aristocracy of the country' from the Commons.[4] This consideration was much in the minds of William IV and his Prime Minister Earl Grey in 1831–2 when the obstruction to the Reform Bill in the House of Lords led Grey, with much reluctance, to demand that the king should, if necessary, create sufficient new peers of liberal views to overcome the opposition. Gladstone too tried later in the century to avoid taking too many useful and active men out of the Commons, though he was anxious to make the Upper House more representative of the various classes and interests in society. He gave Rothschild a peerage though, Granville wrote, 'the notion of a Jew peer is startling', so as to attach an increasingly powerful class to the aristocracy.[5]

After 1815, therefore, the pace of new creations did not keep step with the mounting demand for the distinction, and queues of applicants built up in the files of every Prime Minister's secretary – providing, incidentally, an excuse for the rejection or turning aside of requests on the grounds that the minister was already committed to more creations than could be expected to materialize in the near future. As it was, criticism of the suitability of new peers was frequent. In 1821 Lady Cowper described the coronation peers as 'a sad rum set' and five years later Mrs Arbuthnot, a fervid Tory partisan, scoffed at Liverpool's batch of new peers as 'the most absurd that ever were but all more or less *Canning-ites*, and every body of his own party are very much displeased', though Liverpool denied to Wellington that they were 'chosen by Mr Canning'. Grey's coronation peerages in 1831 were described by Greville as 'a set of horrid trash most of them' and Mrs Arbuthnot remarked in 1831 that the Whig ministers had made twenty-five peers in the ten months they had been in office 'and some of them such as Lds Cloncurry, *Segrave*! & Panmure, are such blackguards that one would think they must have gone into the high ways and hedges to seek for them'.[6] When the Whigs were contemplating a large creation of peers in 1831–2 to swamp the Tory opposition to the Reform Bill, they found it difficult to drum up enough names of sufficient respectability from outside the existing ranks of the peerage. The king tried to insist that the list should be restricted to eldest sons or collateral heirs to existing titles, who would not add permanently to the size of the House, and Grey's recommendations in May 1832 included thirty-eight in that category out of the first forty.[7]

Like Grey, Melbourne after 1834 was reluctant to swamp the Lords with new creations in order to redress the adverse political balance resulting from generations of Whig exclusion from office. In any case, peers often grew conservative in time. By 1841 the Whigs had created 86 peerages, a number roughly equivalent to that which Grey had envisaged as necessary in 1831, but Melbourne found that he could not rely on them or their successors to give steady support in return for their elevation. Of the 175 temporal peers who cast votes for the Reform Bills in 1831 and 1832, 54 were classed as 'Tory' after 1837, including six out of sixteen heirs who had succeeded their fathers.[8]

Though most new peerages and promotions were conferred in this period in return for political services, therefore, ministers were reluctant to respond too freely to pressure. When Russell suggested in 1836 that the government should strengthen itself in the Lords by a 'steady and gradual creation of peers', Melbourne refused to agree. He feared that the measure would not in fact serve the purpose, and that by taking respectable men out of the House of Commons he would lose support there to both Conservatives and Radicals in by-elections. He was content, and perhaps glad of the excuse, to modify or abandon contentious legislation to avoid conflict with the Upper House.[9]

Melbourne's new peers were for the most part relatively undistinguished men, raised for past political services rather than in the expectation of future benefit to the Whig Party. His coronation list in 1838 was drawn up mainly with an eye on not vacating seats in the Commons and it included such men as Lord Kintore who, Melbourne wrote, was 'though a little mad & very drunk is the richest and most Whiggish Scotch peer out of Parliament' and who attended the Lords only ten times during the remainder of the administration and never spoke. His retirement honours list in 1841 was similarly undistinguished. The other major batch, in 1839, included some elderly Whig politicians who had a record of service in diplomacy, such as Auckland, Ponsonby and Lamb, but two of them, Seaton and Keane, had to be granted pensions of £2,000 *p.a.* to enable them to support the dignity. Though Melbourne tried to maintain a standard of ownership of 3,000 acres and an income of £3,000 for new recruits, it was not always possible to reconcile that with other considerations. Eleven of the peers created by liberal governments between 1833 and 1874 were 'consolation peerages' given to men who had suffered defeat at the most recent general election, and a further seven were given to ex-ministers, four Liberal and three Conservatives, who were 'shelved' when their party subsequently returned to office.[10]

The net increase in the number of peerages (taking into account reductions by extinction or abeyance of titles) between 1810 and 1880 was therefore moderate, and the pace of increase slowed down after the 1830s. Between 1810 and 1840 the number of the English, British and UK peerages rose from 292 to 393, an increase of 34.5 per cent, but between 1840 and 1880 the net total increased only by a further 41, to 434. The number of new creations was greater than the increase in the total size of the peerage. Between 1837 and 1866, 118 new peerages were created, 50 from families already in the peerage, 52 from the landed gentry and only 16 from 'other backgrounds'. The number of Scottish and Irish peers given UK titles rose from 67 in 1810 to 124 in 1880.[11]

THE PEERAGE AND PROPERTY

Only one in five of those ennobled between 1833 and 1885 had less than 3,000 acres in the 1890s: three of Gladstone's nominations in 1869 possessed land of an aggregate value of nearly £200,000 *p.a.* In 1883, 400 peers and peeresses owned a total of 5.7 million acres in England and Wales, amounting to 17.4 per cent of the cultivated land in the kingdom. The 'New Domesday' enquiry in 1876 credited the peerage with even greater property: 28 dukes owned 158 separate estates, amounting to 4 million acres, 33 marquesses 121 estates and 1.5 million acres, 194 earls 634 estates and 5.9 million acres, 270 viscounts and barons 680 estates and 3.78 million acres. Not all the increase in acreage owned by peers was attributable to new men coming into the Lords: the 3rd and 4th dukes of Northumberland, for example, spent £469,000 between 1817 and 1865 on buying land to add to their already vast estates, and in 1883 possessed 186,000 acres, the largest of any family. It has been calculated that in the 1880s there were twenty-nine landowners whose gross incomes exceeded £75,000 *p.a.*, all of whom were peers. The Lords still held primacy of place in the landowning class, and ownership of land still conferred social leadership and prestige.[12]

Not all peers, of course, were great landowners, nor was landownership the only or even major source of wealth even for those who were. When men with little or no property were ennobled, usually from the law or armed services, adverse comment was sometimes heard: Greville noted in 1826 that 'everybody cries out against Charles Ellis's peerage; he has no property, and is of no family . . .' and in 1829 that Lord Wynford, a new legal peer, 'is poor and has a family, by which another poor peerage will be added to the list', in addition to the allegation that he was 'unfit for the situation he is to fill – that of Deputy Speaker of the House of Lords, and to assist the Chancellor in deciding Scotch causes, of which he knows nothing whatever'. In 1834 the peerage for another eminent lawyer Thomas Denman was criticized, though he was a Lord Chief Justice, because 'he has no fortune and a feeble son to succeed him'. Men of distinction in the legal profession were in fact unlikely to acquire adequate status to receive a peerage without having made a great deal of money. Distinguished senior officers in the armed services and other public offices were more likely to lack large fortunes and estates, though they were often well connected. Wellington was granted £400,000 in 1814 for the purchase of a fitting property to support his rank as a duke. Thomas Graham, one of Wellington's most distinguished generals, was created Baron Lynedoch in 1814, but he had no heirs and he refused to accept a pension.[13]

Though ownership of land conferred status and influence and provided an important source of wealth from rents, agriculture was not regarded in the nineteenth century as the most profitable investment for capital. Urban development, for those fortunate enough to possess land in and around growing towns and cities, was a much greater advantage. The growth of London, particularly of the fashionable west end, greatly increased the incomes of ground landlords such as the dukes of Bedford, Norfolk, Portland and especially Westminster. The 1st duke of Westminster succeeded his father as marquess in 1869 to find his estates valued at £4 million, with an income from London property amounting to £115,000 *p.a.* as against £37,000 from the Cheshire estates.[14] The growth of provincial towns and cities also enriched the nobility. Lords Salisbury, Sefton and Derby had productive estate in Liverpool, the dukes of Cleveland, Westminster and Devonshire in Bath, Chester and Eastbourne. Between 1800 and 1837 Lord Derby's income quadrupled, largely from urban rents.[15]

Mineral resources, especially coal and iron, also provided sources of increasing incomes from property. Lord Durham's collieries provided most of his income, with a profit of nearly £50,000 in 1835 alone, and the Fitzwilliams increased their incomes from coal and industrial enterprises substantially during this period. In Staffordshire the Leveson-Gower mining and industrial empire was one of the greatest in the country. In addition to their personal stake in industrial enterprise, such peers acted as patrons to local trades and industries which were interconnected with their own interests, such as canal and railway companies, and served on parliamentary committees on economic matters.[16] From the early stages of the Industrial Revolution, peers had helped to finance enterprises on or near to their estates, and to assist with their influence and parliamentary position schemes for the improvement of inland communications. The duke of Bridgewater and the earl of Ellesmere were only two outstanding examples of peers who provided capital for the promotion of trade and industry in this way. As Parliament took a closer interest in the promotion and regulation of economic activity during the nineteenth century, peers were much in demand as chairmen and directors of private companies or of public bodies such as the Railways Commission of 1865 of which the duke of Devonshire was chairman. Investments in government funds and on the stock exchange became increasingly important elements in peerage incomes during the nineteenth century. The 1st duke of Cleveland (1766–1842) left £1.25 million in consols and £1 million in plate and jewellery among his personal estate.[17] In many ways the peerage participated in the economic growth and diversity of the Victorian period, so that the House of Lords did not lose touch with the changes in social and economic life which were transforming Britain in this period.

MARRIAGE AND EDUCATION

The peerage also maintained its connections with a wide range of society through marriage. The peerage was closely interrelated, so that a new peer on introduction to the House would recognize and be known to a considerable number of those sitting. The 2nd marquess and 1st duke of Abercorn (1811–85) had seven daughters who all married peers, so that for sons-in-law he had two dukes, one marquess and four earls.[18] However, not all peers married within the closed circle of their own order. It has been calculated that just over 55 per cent of peers in the period 1830–41 married daughters, granddaughters, nieces, or sisters of British, Scottish, or Irish peers, the remainder being unmarried or finding brides elsewhere.[19] The landed gentry supplied many, but a number came from commercial, professional, or financial families, though their fathers had usually acquired landed estates and country houses. Younger sons and daughters of peers tended to be less restricted in their choices, and as the society in which they moved admitted more of the wealthier middle classes, alliances were formed with their sons and daughters. Only a quarter of all children of peers married within the peerage. Arranged marriages were still common, especially where the succession to the title and property was involved, but marriages for love were becoming more general in the upper ranks of society as young people were allowed more freedom of choice. Six peers during this period married brides who had been actresses, including the 9th duke of St Albans and the 2nd duke of Cambridge; none had issue who succeeded to the titles.

Education too was shared increasingly with the middle classes, as they penetrated the aristocratic preserves of the greater public schools. Eton was the alma mater of over a third of the peerage in the first half of the nineteenth century, followed in 75 per cent of cases by Christ Church, Oxford, and they remained predominantly aristocratic in their entry. Other old established public schools such as Westminster, Winchester and Harrow provided education for most eldest and younger sons, but at the newer foundations like Marlborough the sons of both peers and middle class mixed on terms of social equality.[20] The world of the 'upper ten thousand' in nineteenth-century England was a small and exclusive one, but the peerage did not form a caste within it. Whether the education it received was adequate has been questioned, and there are many examples of peers whose intellectual accomplishments were decidedly limited. Wellington once remarked that he did not see the necessity of learning to read and write, since the Pagets seemed to get on very well without it, and Hatherton remarked of the head of that family that 'Lord Anglesey once told me . . . that he never read a paper – or (I believe he might have added) anything else'. The 8th duke of Devonshire was strongly inclined towards idleness, and wrote to his father after visiting the Louvre in 1854 that 'perhaps a slight taste for pictures may be beginning to show itself', but, his biographer remarked, 'these early blossoms never came to fruit'.[21]

Peers with notable literary, artistic and scholarly interests included the 3rd Baron Braybrooke (1783–1858) who edited Pepys's *Diary* (1825), and his son the 4th baron (1820–61) who was the author of a number of antiquarian works. The 9th earl of Bridgewater (1756–1829) was a distinguished scholar, collector and patron of literature, who bequeathed his collection of the Egerton MSS to the British Museum. Other literary patrons and collectors included the 2nd duke of Buckingham (1797–1861) who went spectacularly bankrupt and was sold up in 1849, and the 4th Earl Ashburnham (1797–1878), who bought Buckingham's collection of MSS and added it to his own 'vast assemblage of MSS', part of which was bought for the British Museum in 1883. The 1st Baron Carysfort (UK, 2nd earl in the Irish peerage, 1751–1828) was author of *Dramatic and Narrative Poems* (1810) and 'a good and elegant scholar', and the 14th earl of Derby (1799–1869), besides being a notable politician and three times Prime Minister, found time to translate the *Iliad*. The 1st earl of Ellesmere (1800–57) was a book collector and author of forty-six works mentioned in the *Dictionary of National Biography*, though now largely forgotten. More distinguished author–peers included Byron, Lytton the novelist (1803–73), Tennyson, Macaulay and the 1st Baron Broughton (1786–1869) to whom his friend Byron dedicated the fourth canto of *Childe Harold*. The 1st Baron Acton (1834–1902) who was described as 'perhaps the most learned and widely-read man of his day' became Regius Professor of Modern History at Cambridge (1895) and was ennobled on Gladstone's recommendation as an eminent scholar. The 2nd Baron Londesborough (1834–1900) was a writer, collector of antiquities and silver, and an archaeologist. Peers distinguished in other branches of the arts included the 3rd Baron Crofton (1834–1912), an accomplished musician and composer, and the 1st Baron Chichester (1813–83) who was also a notable musician. In the visual arts, the 1st Baron Farnborough (1760–1838) was a successful painter and the 2nd Baron Northwick (1770–1859) had a magnificent collection of pictures which was sold after his death, many of them to the National Gallery. The 1st Baron Houghton (1809–85) had a range of artistic, literary and other intellectual interests and pursuits and was depicted by Disraeli as Mr Vavasour in *Tancred*.[22] Other distinguished scholars among the peerage included the 1st Baron Grenville and the 3rd Baron Holland.

CHARACTERS AND CHARACTERISTICS

If cultural pursuits provided a hobby and occupation for these and many other lesser known peers during this period, love of sport and country life was even more common, naturally enough in a class brought up on country estates and introduced from their earliest years to outdoor sports. Fox-hunting was the winter recreation of the landed classes in general, and provided one of the bonds which held together rural society at all levels from landowners to farmers. Several peers were inevitably Masters of Foxhounds, including the 1st duke of Cleveland (1766–1842) and the 8th duke of Beaufort (1824–99). The turf was a natural outlet for both the upper class's love of horses and sport and its addiction to gambling. Lord George Bentinck, a younger son of the 4th duke of Portland (1802–48), though not a peer, was a major figure in the reform of the turf before his death in 1848, and a fearsome figure to the crooks and sharpers who infested the sport. Aristocratic owners who devoted themselves to racing and whose horses won the Derby included the 3rd Viscount Clifden (1825–66), the 7th Viscount Falmouth (1819–89) (twice), and the 5th earl of Jersey (1773–1867) (three times). The 10th duke of Richmond (1791–1860) was a notable owner and patron at Goodwood. Not all owners were as sensible as the 7th Viscount Falmouth, who never betted though he won the Derby twice and built up the Mereworth stud, which was sold for 75,440 guineas eight years after his death. It was more common for aristocratic fortunes to suffer depletion or destruction from betting on horses: the 6th Viscount Anson (1795–1854) inherited an estate worth £70,000 *p.a.* but was forced to sell up in 1842. The 3rd earl of Ellesmere (1847–1914), though a member of the Jockey Club, was not successful as an owner, and the 3rd marquess of Exeter (1795–1867) encumbered his estates with heavy expenditure on racing. The 4th marquess of Hastings (1842–68) was known as the 'King of the Plungers'. The 3rd Baron Ribblesdale (1828–76) shot himself after suffering heavy losses in betting. Other sporting peers included the 3rd Baron Henley (1825–98), who (appropriately) was an Oxford rowing blue in 1843, and the 7th earl of Jersey, who ran for Oxford against Cambridge. The 1st Baron Gwydir (1754–1820) was a well-known cricketer.

As men of wealth and leisure, peers were able to defy Victorian conventions of behaviour with impunity. Eccentrics abounded. The 5th duke of Marlborough (1766–1840) not only led a disreputable private life, but ruined himself by his activities as a book-collector and arboriculturalist at Whiteknights, Reading, and lived the last years of his life as a recluse at Blenheim after selling up his Whiteknights estate. The 5th duke of Portland (1800–79) was 'a lonely, self-isolated man' who spent years digging under his house at Welbeck Abbey and making tunnels and underground rooms, it was thought because he disliked being seen by other people. He erected frosted-glass screens round his London house and when he travelled by train he never left his own carriage, which was loaded on to a truck with its blinds closely drawn. He lived in four or five rooms in the west wing, all the rest of the house being bare of furniture except for a working water-closet with water laid on in the corner of almost every room.[23] The 8th duke of Bedford (1809–72) also lived as a recluse in his London house, which he never left except to drive out in a carriage fitted with wooden shutters. More spectacularly eccentric were the 13th earl of Eglinton (1812–61), whose attempt to revive the medieval tournament in 1839 cost him £40,000, and the 4th earl of Harrington (1780–1867) who was a Lord of the Bedchamber to both George III and George IV. Known until 1829 as Lord Petersham, he was a dandy, a crony of the Prince Regent and a connoisseur of tea and snuff who gave his name both to a snuff mixture and to his own design of an overcoat. He collected 2,000 lb. of various snuffs which were sold for £1,000 in 1851. He married in 1831 Maria Foote, daughter of the manager of the Plymouth theatre, who had played Juliet at the age of 12. 'Tall, handsome, and faultlessly clad', he never went out before 6 p.m. and provided the model for Disraeli's Lord Fitzbooby.[24]

Eccentricity sometimes showed itself in pride of rank: the Smithsons, for whom the dukedom of Northumberland was revived in 1766, outdid even their predecessors the proud Percies. The 2nd Baron Alvanley (1789–1849), a crony of George IV, was a reckless spendthrift and fought a duel with the son of Daniel O'Connell who had called him 'a bloated buffoon'. The 7th Earl Waldegrave (1814–46), who married his illegitimate half-brother's widow Fanny (Braham), an ex-actress, was noted, according to his obituary, for 'wild excesses [which] were wont to adorn the records of the public courts, and made his name unfortunately notorious'.[25] The 7th earl of Cardigan (1787–1868), famous for his gallantry at the head of the Light Brigade at Balaclava, was 'quarrelsome, arbitrary, unpopular, and a loose liver'. He fought a duel in 1840 on Wimbledon Common with a Captain Harvey Tuckett, and was tried by his peers in Westminster Hall in 1841 on a charge of intent to murder and acquitted on a technicality. This was the first trial of a peer before the Lords since the duchess of Kingston in 1776, and the only one in this period.[26] Cardigan's affair with the lady who became his second wife during his first wife's lifetime also led to scandal, and her social ostracism. The 6th duke of Marlborough (1793–1857) seduced a young woman by a mock marriage, performed by one of his brothers dressed up as a clergyman. The 3rd earl of Egremont (1751–1837) fathered six illegitimate children by the mistress who later became his wife, and was also the putative father of the 2nd Viscount Melbourne, the Prime Minister, who was himself cited twice as a co-respondent in divorce proceedings and had a private taste for flagellation.[27] Egremont was nevertheless a worthy and hospitable man, patron at Petworth of the painter J.M.W. Turner and liberal in his charity: he gave away £1.2 million in the last sixty years of his life.

Nineteenth-century peers were not all idle drones given to dissipation and excess. Several of the most distinguished senior officers in the armed services were peers, or were ennobled for their achievements. Besides Cardigan, already mentioned, the 3rd earl of Lucan showed his bravery at Balaclava, and four of Wellington's senior generals in the Peninsular campaign were ennobled in 1814. Among them was Thomas Graham (1748–1843), created Baron Lynedoch, who was also a keen sportsman: he played in the first recorded cricket match in Scotland in 1785, and was a lover of horses and hunting. He started a racing stable when he was turned 90 years of age. The 1st Baron Napier (1810–90) was another distinguished officer who was promoted to the Lords in 1868 after service in command at Lucknow during the siege and in China and Abyssinia.

The navy too acquired its share of heroes ennobled for their services. The 1st Baron Lyons (1790–1858) served in the navy from the age of 11, and rose to be a Vice-Admiral and Commander in Chief of the Mediterranean fleet in 1855–8. He received his peerage for his service in the Crimean campaign, and also distinguished himself in civil life by being Minister successively at Athens, Berne and Stockholm between 1835 and 1853. He had the rare distinction of being invested with both the civil and military branches of the GCB.[28]

By the end of the period, men of distinction in learning, scholarship and public life were being considered suitable for the peerage. Besides Macaulay, Lytton, and Tennyson, already mentioned, Baron Blachford (Frederick Rogers) who received his peerage in 1871, had been a public servant: he was the first peer to come from the Civil Service, and the only one before 1875.

Peers suffered like lesser mortals from mental illnesses: the 3rd Earl Cadogan (1749–1832) was insane for over twenty-five years before his death, the 4th Baron Lyttelton (1763–1828) was also insane at his death, while the 6th baron (1817–76) committed suicide by throwing himself downstairs. The 1st earl of Munster (1794–1842), one of the ten illegitimate children of the duke of Clarence, later William IV, and 'Mrs Jordan' the actress, shot himself in 1842, 'tainted with the hereditary malady' and provoked by 'a dawdling, ill-conditioned, vexatious wife' who was herself an illegitimate daughter of the 3rd earl of Egremont. Other suicides included the 3rd Baron Rivers (1777–1831), a reformed Regency rake and gambler who drowned himself in the Serpentine out of shame and remorse when he failed to keep his promise to a friend never to touch cards or dice again.

The Victorian age was one of religious revival and religious controversy. Leading evangelicals among the peerage included the famous 7th earl of Shaftesbury (1801–85) who devoted his life to the cause of children exploited in factories and as chimney-sweeps, the 3rd marquess of Cholmondeley (1800–84) who was a generous subscriber to evangelical societies and good works, and the 1st Baron Ebury (1801–93) who tried to get the prayer book altered in accordance with his evangelical views. The 4th earl of Mount Edgcumbe (1832–1917) was a staunch churchman who promoted the restitution of the bishopric of Truro and the building of the cathedral. After Catholic Emancipation in 1829, peers of the Catholic faith were admitted to the House: the 7th duke of Norfolk (1765–1842) took his seat on 28 April 1829; unlike some of his forbears who had converted to Anglicanism to enable them to sit and to hold the hereditary office of Earl Marshal, he had been permitted by special act of Parliament in 1824 to exercise that office as a Roman Catholic. His son and heir, however, who was elected for Horsham in 1829 and was the first Roman Catholic to sit in the Commons since the reign of James II, seceded from Rome to the Anglican Church in 1851, twelve years after inheriting the dukedom. The 20th duke (1847–1917) who succeeded in 1860, remained a Catholic and was leader of the Catholic communion in England. His influence helped to gain John Henry Newman the cardinal's hat. A number of Catholic peers were, of course, Irishmen: the 1st Baron O'Hagan (1870) (1812–85) was the first Catholic to be Lord Chancellor of Ireland (1868–74) since the Glorious Revolution.

POLITICIANS

The House of Lords also contained a share of 'men of business' and of practical experience in politics. Many heirs to peerages entered the House of Commons, sometimes as soon as they were of age, in order to gain experience and establish contacts. Lord Harrowby opposed the Reform Bill in 1831 on the grounds that nomination boroughs provided opportunities for future peers to become acquainted with the representatives of the people, and Grey himself agreed that peers' sons who sat in the Lords were the best links between the peerage and the people.[29] On average, each House of Commons elected between 1790 and 1820 contained nearly 170 sons of peers, peeresses and Irish peers. In 1832 it was alleged that 98 sons and 155 other relatives of peers sat in the Lower House, and in 1835 an observer calculated that there were still 61 eldest sons, 132 other close relatives and 42 MPs related by marriage to the peerage, as well as three Irish peers, present in the Commons. It has been estimated that the aristocracy as a whole – peerage, baronetcy and landed gentry – still occupied 74 per cent of the seats in the House of Commons in 1865.[30]

Peers who had been MPs provided a valuable source of party strength in the Lords. During the 1830s, 48.74 per cent of peers had such experience, with a further thirty-two who had sat in the Irish House of Commons before the union. Melbourne admitted in conversation with Hatherton in 1840 that he and Grey had erred 'in making so many peers who had not the claim of Parliamentary service'; their fear of losing by-elections had deprived them of useful friends in the Upper House. Melbourne also, however, complained that some MPs who were promoted to the Lords tended to lose their political vigour: 'we peers who had been educated in the House of Commons became enervated by the climate of the House of Lords, and unfit for toil, which is quite true', Hatherton commented: 'no stimulant of constituency behind us – our objects in many instances gained . . .'.[31] Among the minority of politically active peers, the proportion who had served an apprenticeship in the Commons was large. The benefits to the country as well as to individual peers of such close connections between the two Houses were stressed by the 8th duke of Argyll, who wrote in his autobiography that he felt a great disadvantage, on entering the Lords in 1847, in not having previously served as an MP, though as a young man he had attended the Commons debates assiduously as a spectator. As a member, however, he would have made many personal friends in the House, and 'acquired a knowledge of men which nothing else can supply. It is not generally observed', he added, 'how very large a number of the peers have been members of the House of Commons for a longer or a shorter time, and what an effect this has on the silent and automatic causes which smooth the working of our old and hereditary constitution.' The House of Commons, he concluded, was 'an assembly of men which it is of importance for every politician to belong to, even for a time, however short, that he may know its members as widely as he can'.[32] Men who had been drawn to a political career were likely to sustain their interest and commitment after elevation despite the less stimulating atmosphere of the Lords. J.W. Croker, paying a visit to see the new House of Lords in 1857, remarked to Hatherton that only about thirty peers were present, all of whom he had sat with during his time in the Commons: 'It shows how completely the House of Commons has been the nursery of the House of Lords,' he remarked.[33]

OFFICE AND PATRONAGE

By no means all ex-MPs who arrived in the Lords, by inheritance or by creation, were silent backbenchers. Most of the Prime Ministers of the period sat in the Lords while holding the office. Only Canning, Peel, Lord John Russell (before he became an earl), Palmerston (an Irish peer in the Commons) and Gladstone and Disraeli were Prime Ministers in the Commons during this period, and their total length of time in office amounted only to some twenty-eight years out of the sixty-five.

Peers also occupied a large number of Cabinet offices in the governments of the period: besides 13 Lord Chancellors, 26 Lord Keepers of the Privy Seal and 15 Lords President of the Council, offices almost always held by peers, 5 peers held the Home Secretaryship (approximately 15 years in total), 9 the Foreign Secretaryship (30 years), 9 the Admiralty (42 years), 12 the Chancellorship of the Duchy of Lancaster (34 years), 12 the combined or separated offices of Secretary for War and the Colonies (50 years) and 8 were Presidents of the Board of Trade (19 years). Seventeen peers served continuously as Lords Lieutenant of Ireland, with a break only in Peel's ministries of 1834–5 and between 1841 and 1844.[34] During the first half of the nineteenth century, peers comprised the majority of members in every Cabinet down to 1834, and formed the minority only by one in Melbourne's Cabinet of July to November 1834. They were again in the majority in Peel's Cabinet of 1841–5. Writing in September 1841, Hatherton remarked that Peel's Cabinet, in which nine of the fourteen offices were held by peers, was 'too Lordly and Aristocratic for these days – being more so, than any former one within our memory – no commoner, really connected with the commonalty in it – for neither Peel nor Graham, nor Goulburn can be said to be so. Where are the Tom Macaulays, Barings, Hobhouses?' After 1846, the numbers of peers and commoners in Cabinets tended to be evenly balanced, as in the Cabinets of Russell (1846 and 1865), Palmerston (1855) and Disraeli (1874), or there was a slight majority of commoners (Aberdeen, Palmerston (1859), Derby (1866), Disraeli (1868) and Gladstone (1868)). Derby's Cabinets of 1852 and 1858 had a majority of one for the peers. Between 1806 and 1855 peers and their heirs comprised 56.7 per cent of Cabinet membership.[35]

As men of rank and influence, peers also took a major share of honours and patronage. *The Extraordinary Black Book*, published in 1832, listed 122 peers holding pensions (67), sinecures (25), or offices (57). The editor's assertion that this proved the power of the aristocracy to be more absolute than ever, and that it constituted an 'uncontrolled and irresponsible ascendancy', was certainly radical propaganda, but it was only an exaggeration of fact. Carpenter listed 64 pensioners in the Lords in 1837. Not all pensioners, however, were idle drones or parasites on the body politic. Wade admitted that most of the larger pensions in his list were granted after retirement from public service. The fact that large numbers of members of the House of Lords were in receipt of favours and patronage reflects not the necessity of bribing an otherwise independent and unruly body, but the natural outcome of a coincidence of attitude and interest between the state and its governing elite. Peers received patronage because they were the natural beneficiaries of royal favour and because they were often too powerful to offend: they did not acquire social or political importance by receiving it, but received it because they were important and it would have been disruptive of the social order to prefer others. This was openly acknowledged in the case of the most prestigious honour, the Garter. Melbourne's famous remark that he liked the Garter because there was 'no damned nonsense about merit' in it was illustrated in August 1835 when the recently ennobled Lord Hatherton suggested to him that it ought sometimes to be given to men of distinguished talent, such as Peel, rather than reserved for noblemen of high rank. 'He replied "I could never give it except to the highest rank"', and instanced the recent case in which even the duke of Somerset, whose peerage was one of the most ancient in the House, had sulked by refusing to attend because a vacant Garter had been given to the fellow, but greatly junior, duke of Grafton.[36]

Locally, too, peers filled the greater offices. Almost all Lords Lieutenant in the counties were peers: of the 120 English, Welsh, Scottish and Irish counties in 1830, 100 were governed by noble Lords Lieutenant. This was an office which was now more important for its dignity and its symbolic nature than for its administrative responsibilities, but it still had considerable patronage attached to it and remained a channel for the recommendation and conferment of honours and local offices, as well as bearing ultimate responsibility for the maintenance of law and order before the spread of the new police forces in the middle of the period. The expense of supporting the office, however, far outweighed any financial benefit to be gained from it, and increasingly only the wealthier families were willing to undertake it. Nevertheless, together with their patronage of local societies, charities and church livings, it embodied and symbolized the dominant social position of the leading families in the counties. It was still considered a political office, conferment and acceptance usually being taken to indicate support of a particular administration, but rank and position in the county sometimes overrode political considerations. When in 1856 Palmerston offered the Lord Lieutenancy of Nottinghamshire to the Tory duke of Newcastle, he made it clear that it carried no hint of political commitment:

> I consider these offices to be in the present state of things, posts of great importance in many essential respects, and I hold that the Government of the Day is under obligation to men of Rank, Influence, and large Property, and ability who will undertake to give their time and attention to the performance of the duties of their situation.
> I therefore accept your acceptance on the clear understanding that any obligation involved in the transaction is an obligation conferred on me, and not by me.

The duke accepted on these terms, writing that 'I frankly confess that I should not be willing to sacrifice my political independence'. Whatever their political allegiances, peers remained men of proud independence and gave the House of Lords a character and a status which prevented its ever being taken for granted.[37]

The House of Lords therefore represented many facets of national life in the nineteenth century. As Lord Lyveden said in his speech on 20 June 1867 on the business of the House,[38]

> In it were to be found the descendants of the ancient nobility, lawyers who had raised themselves by their learning and talents to the highest rank in their profession, eminent diplomatists, distinguished military men, and a bench of bishops no less remarkable as scholars than as divines – some men eminent in commerce, others beloved for their philanthropy – so that among them were many of the most highly educated men in the kingdom: with experience gained by many in the more active arena of the House of Commons, and by nearly all in the local tribunals of their country, their Lordships' House was formed of those whose education peculiarly fitted them to fill the office of legislator.

This reflected the fact that in the nineteenth century, particularly in and immediately after the Napoleonic Wars, peerages were conferred on men who had given distinguished service to the country, rather than on those with the largest property. By the later part of this period, the possession of large landed estates was less important as a qualification for the peerage: whereas in the eighteenth century few aristocrats possessed less than 10,000 acres, in the 1860s it was claimed that an independent annual income of only £2,000 was sufficient.[39] Malmesbury, speaking in the debate on Russell's bill to introduce life peerages in 1869, said that it was no longer necessary for peers to be rich:[40]

> It might have been very well to use such an argument as that 70 or 80 years ago, when public opinion obliged every peer to live ostentatiously: when he could not drive out without having four horses to his carriage, and being attended by outriders, and when he wore his stars and ribands morning and night. . . . [Now, however,] A peer . . . comes up to Town by railway, in the company of every person who chooses to travel in that way; he moves about as unostentatiously as any other class of persons . . . and there is therefore, I contend, no necessity whatever why they should require to have large fortunes to maintain what is called their dignity. . . . They are respected, not according to their riches, but their usefulness as members of the legislature and in their several localities.

Nobility became a reward for public service rather than a mere badge of extensive property and great wealth, and so the House of Lords was able to justify its survival as a part of the legislature and an institution of continuing utility. Granville, speaking on Disraeli's death in 1881, remarked:

> It has been said of the British aristocracy, sometimes as a matter of praise, sometimes of blame, that they are proud, wealthy, and powerful; there is an element of a democratic character mixed with the constitution of the House of Lords, which has certainly added to its wealth and strength: possibly to its pride. It is the unexclusiveness which is peculiar to the institution. Of the smoothness with which the portals of this country roll back before distinguished men without reference to caste or to blood, of the welcome which is given to such, of the distinguished place which is assigned to him, I know of no brighter or more brilliant example than that of Lord Beaconsfield.[41]

Disraeli was not the only Prime Minister from the professional classes to rise to the peerage: Addington had done so in 1805. Granville said in 1884 that when he entered the House thirty-five years ago, 'there were in it remarkable men, eminent statesmen, eloquent Prelates, great lawyers. I must say that I do not see the slightest degeneration in this respect at the present time.'[42] Throughout the century the House of Lords was an assembly containing not only the leisured rich, but men of the highest ability and distinction in public life. No further reason need be sought for its survival as a part of the British political system.

REFERENCES

1. For baronies by writ see L.G. Pine, *Constitutional History of the House of Lords* (1894), pp. 108–39. The first barony by patent was conferred on Lord de Beauchamp in 1387. He never took his seat, and was beheaded in the Tower in 1388: G.E.C[ockayne], *Complete Peerage*, 13 vols (1910–59) for details of subsequent references to individual peerages.
2. For Scottish and Irish peerages see Chapter 2; for attempts to create life peerages in this period see below, pp. 110 and 138–9.
3. *The Journal of Mrs Arbuthnot*, ed. F. Bamford and the Duke of Wellington (1950), I, p. 222.
4. Liverpool to E. Wilbraham Bootle, 5 Nov. 1814: BL Add. MS 38260, ff. 95–8, quoted in *English Historical Documents, 1783–1832*, IX, ed. A. Aspinall and E.A. Smith (1959), pp. 205–6.
5. Lord Edmond Fitzmaurice, *Life of . . . second Earl Granville*, 1905, II, pp. 16–18.
6. *Lady Palmerston and her Times*, ed. Mabell, Countess Airlie (1922), I, p. 93; *Journal of Mrs Arbuthnot*, II, pp. 27, 429; *The Greville Diary*, ed. P.W. Wilson (1927) I, p. 380.
7. E.A. Smith, *Lord Grey, 1764–1845* (1990), pp. 271–4.
8. R.S. Fraser, 'The House of Lords in the first Parliament of Queen Victoria, 1837–41', unpublished Ph.D. thesis (Cornell University Ithaca, NJ, 1967), 780–2, 806–20.
9. Spencer Walpole, *Life of Lord John Russell* (1889), I, pp. 266–7.
10. Fraser, 'The House of Lords', pp. 775–95, 840–905, for a full account of creations and promotions in the 1830s. Even the standard of £3,000 *p.a.* seemed low to some: see Sir Frederick Lamb's letter to Lady Cowper, 1829, in *Lady Palmerston and her Times*, I, pp. 146–7: 'You people who have had profusion all yr lives are apt to imagine that it can be done very well upon, but I can tell you it is a privation of anything.'
11. Figures from J.V. Beckett, *The Aristocracy in England, 1660–1914* (Oxford, 1986), pp. 121, 487–8. Beckett's figures include peeresses and minors. For the difficulty of arriving at precise figures see *ibid.*, pp. 482–3. Representative peers who did not also hold UK peerages are not included.
12. *Ibid.*, pp. 46, 50, 292; A.S. Turberville, 'The House of Lords and the advent of democracy, 1837–67', *History* XXIX, 152–83; W.D. Rubinstein, *Men of Property* (1981), pp. 194–5.
13. C.C.F. Greville, *Journal of the Reigns of George IV and William IV*, ed. H. Reeve (1874), I, pp. 83, 210; III, p. 74; for Wellington and Lynedoch, G.E.C[ockayne], *Complete Peerage*.
14. G. Huxley, *Victorian Duke: the Life of Hugh Lupus Grosvenor, 1st Duke of Westminster* (Oxford, 1967), p. 91.

15. J.M. Sweeney, 'The House of Lords in British Politics, 1830–41', unpublished D. Phil. thesis (Oxford, 1973), pp. 65–72.

16. M.W. McCahill, 'Peers, patronage and the Industrial Revolution, 1760–1800' in C. Jones and D.L. Jones (eds), *Peers, Politics and Power, 1603–1911* (1986), pp. 433–56.

17. He had his wine-glasses made without feet, so that they would not stand upright and had to be emptied at a single draught. For this and the following references to individual peers, see the entries (and especially the footnotes) in G.E.C., *Complete Peerage*.

18. His widow was photographed with her 101 descendants in 1894.

19. T.H. Hollingsworth, 'The demography of the British Peerage', *Population Studies*, suppt. XVIII (1964), 9; Sweeney, 'The House of Lords', 19–25.

20. T.W. Bamford, 'Public schools and social class, 1801–50', *British Journal of Sociology* XII (1961), 225.

21. Hatherton Diary, 23 March 1841; B. Holland, *The Life of Spencer Compton, 8th Duke of Devonshire*, 2nd edn. (1911), p. 17.

22. See the sketch of Houghton in G.W.E. Russell, *Collections and Recollections* (1903), pp. 51–9.

23. Mary Soames, *The Profligate Duke* (1987); R. Gathorne Hardy, *Ottoline* (1963), pp. 171–4, quoted in M. Girouard, *A Country House Companion* (1987), p. 16.

24. *Letterbag of Elizabeth Spencer Stanhope, 1806–73*, ed. A.M.W. Stirling (1913) I, p. 15.

25. *Gentleman's Magazine*, quoted in *Notes and Queries* CLXIX, 10 Aug. 1935, 94.

26. The 3rd Baron Northwick (1791–1887) fought Peter Borthwick, father of Lord Glenesk, at Wormwood Scrubs in 1838 over the Evesham election of 1837.

27. P. Ziegler, *Melbourne* (1978 edn.), p. 229.

28. It was calculated in 1837 that there were 91 army officers, 9 naval officers and 84 civil officials in the House of Lords: W. Carpenter, *A Peerage for the People* (1837).

29. Hansard, 3rd Ser. VII (1831), 1169; Grey to Sir Herbert Taylor, 10 April 1832; *Corresp. of Earl Grey with H.M. King William IV and with Sir Herbert Taylor . . .*, ed. Henry Earl Grey (1867), II, p. 348.

30. R. Thorne (ed.), *The House of Commons, 1790–1820* (1986), I, p. 282; *The Assembled Commons: or Parliamentary Biographer*, by a member of the Middle Temple (1838), quoted in Sweeney, 'The House of Lords', 42; M.L. Bush, *The English Aristocracy. A Comparative Synthesis* (Manchester, 1984), p. 150.

31. Hatherton Diary, March 1840 and 5 July 1836.

32. Argyll, *Autobiography and Memoirs of George Douglas, 8th Duke of Argyll*, ed. Dowager Duchess of Argyll (1906), I, pp. 268–9.

33. *The Croker Papers* ed. L.J. Jennings (1884), I, p. 85.

34. Calculated from *Handbook of British Chronology* ed. E.B. Fryde, D.E. Greenway, S. Porter and I. Roy (1986). The figures quoted exclude Palmerston (who sat in the Commons as an Irish peer) who was Foreign Secretary for a total of 10 years and 4 months as well as Prime Minister for a total of 9 years and 4 months. Of other senior

office holders Castlereagh (marquess of Londonderry), Lord John Russell (Earl Russell) and Disraeli (earl of Beaconsfield) are counted only for the time they sat in the Lords.

35. A. Aspinall, 'The Cabinet Council, 1783–1835', *Proceedings of the British Academy* XXXVIII (1953), appendix; E.L. Woodward, *The Age of Reform 1815–70*, 2nd edn. (Oxford, 1939); and R.C.K. Ensor, *England, 1870–1914* (Oxford, 1936); Hatherton Diary, 4 Sept. 1841; W.L. Arnstein, 'The survival of the Victorian aristocracy', in F.C. Jaher (ed.), *The Rich, the Well-Born and the Powerful* (Urbana, Ill., 1973), p. 210, gives the percentage of peers in each Cabinet, 1830–95. There was some variation in the relative numbers of peers and commoners during the lifetime of cabinets: the figures are those relating to the original formation of each cabinet.

36. Hatherton Diary, 22 Aug. 1835.

37. Palmerston to Newcastle, 19 Nov. Newcastle to Palmerston, 18 Nov. 1856: Newcastle MSS, Nottingham University Library NeC 12603, 12602.

38. Hansard, 3rd Ser. CLXXXVIII, 129–33.

39. Beckett, *Aristocracy in England*, p. 46.

40. Lord Malmesbury, *Memoirs of an Ex-Minister* (1854), II, pp. 396–7.

41. Hansard, CCLXI, 4–6.

42. *Ibid.*, CCLXXXIX, 961 (20 June 1884).

CHAPTER FOUR

The Non-Hereditary Members of the House of Lords

The House of Lords did not contain all the members of the hereditary peerages of the three kingdoms of England, Scotland and Ireland, nor of the peerage of the United Kingdom which came into being in 1801. The Scots peerage at the time of the Act of Union of 1707 contained 134 members, almost as large a number as the 157 English peers, and in 1800 on the eve of the Irish Act of Union the Irish peerage numbered 169 against 267 in the English and British, and 72 in the Scots peerages. Both in 1707 and in 1800, however, the English, who largely dictated the terms of both unions, were determined that England should remain the dominant partner and that the interests of the newcomers should be subordinated to their own. On both occasions the representation of the new adherents in both Houses of the united Parliament was reduced in order to bring this about, in the Commons by reducing the number of electoral constituencies and in the Lords by the introduction of a representative system to limit the number of peers from Scotland and from Ireland. The unions were designed to promote English security and English economic as well as political domination, and until the twentieth century the composition of the House of Lords reflected this aim.

A third non-hereditary element (in the sense that these members did not pass on their membership of the House by descent to their next of kin) consisted of the higher clergy of the Church of England and, between 1801 and 1869, of the Church of Ireland (though in the latter case, as with the lay Irish peerage, by a system of minority representation). Archbishops and bishops had by long usage and precedent been important figures in the governance of the realm, and although by the eighteenth century it was no longer customary to appoint them to political offices they remained titular lords and had precedence as such. Their presence in the House also confirmed and symbolized the union of Church and state, and the position of the Anglican Church as the Established Church of the nation, with the monarch as its temporal head. The archbishops and bishops were the monarch's spiritual advisers, as his secular peers and ministers were his advisers in material affairs. Though the archbishop of Canterbury no longer sat in the 'efficient' Cabinet of Ministers which since the later eighteenth century formed the select group of 'His Majesty's Confidential Servants', he retained a seat in the 'Grand' or 'Formal' Cabinet which met on regular occasions solely to advise the king on the use of the royal prerogative of mercy on condemned criminals facing the death sentence.[1] George III also consulted the archbishop of Canterbury, without the knowledge of his Prime Minister or Cabinet, in 1795 and again in 1801 when he got wind of possible proposals to free Roman Catholics from religious discrimination, the king acting on the grounds that it was a matter which affected his conscience, and involved the interpretation of his coronation oath.[2] As the Church continued to play an important role in national life, even after the repeal of laws discriminating against Protestant Dissenters and Roman Catholics in 1828–9, the archbishops and bishops continued to sit in the Lords; but their political conduct, and even their presence, was challenged over the Reform Bill in 1831–2, and thereafter they tended to confine themselves to matters with some spiritual or ecclesiastical dimension.

THE SCOTTISH REPRESENTATIVE PEERS

Under the provisions of the Act of Union of 1707 the peers of Scotland received all the privileges of Parliament enjoyed by peers of England or, after the union, of the new peerage of Great Britain, except the right to sit in the House of Lords in person. Sixteen of their number were to sit as representatives of the whole. They were elected afresh at each general election and so held tenure for a maximum of seven years at a time, after 1716.[3] During the eighteenth century, governments and oppositions had put forward rival lists of approved candidates and had used all the arts of political management and persuasion to achieve a majority. The advantages clearly lay with the ministry of the day, the Scots being notoriously eager for the benefits of place and patronage, and most of the Scots peers therefore made up a part of the government's majority in the House. During the younger Pitt's long administration Henry Dundas, later 1st Viscount Melville, took on the job of managing Scottish affairs and he built up a commanding position: in 1796 no less than thirteen of the sixteen were returned through his endeavours.[4] It became a moot question whether they were the governments' followers, or Dundas's personal supporters; the question was avoided by Pitt's successors employing his son Robert, the 2nd viscount, to continue his father's role down to 1830, save for a brief interval in 1827–8. He continued the practice of drawing up and circulating a list of the candidates endorsed by the government, and in general the Scottish peers continued to provide steady support: fourteen out of sixteen on Melville's list were elected in 1820, for example.

In 1827, the issue of whether they followed the administration or Melville personally came into the open. Melville adhered to Wellington's group which refused to serve under Canning, and ten of the sixteen voted against the ministry, three abstaining and only three giving it support. 'Almost all the great leading interests [in Scotland] are on our side', Melville told Arbuthnot, and D.C. Large concludes that 'the Scottish representative peers were becoming members of a party in the Lords – that section of the Tories led by Wellington'. So entrenched were they that Grey's ministry failed in 1831, when elections to the Commons were sweeping the board for reform, to win more than four of the sixteen places. It was a hard blow to the government, which needed to muster all the support it could in the Lords to avoid having to make new peers to overcome the opposition to the Reform Bill. Some of the result was attributable to the convention that existing representative peers would not normally be disturbed, though this also worked in favour of two of the four Whig candidates who had served since 1820, but in general it reflected the political opinions of the great majority of the Scottish peers. In 1832 Melville secured fifteen of the sixteen for Wellington's conservative opposition, and by 1838 all sixteen were included in his following. Thus, 'in the 1830s the sixteen representative peers became part of the Conservative party in the Upper House . . . and the conservative leaders made arrangements for the management of the elections and of Scottish business in the House as part of their party organization.'[5]

Between 1815 and 1880, sixty-six individuals sat in the House as Scottish representative peers, serving on average 20.7 years.[6] The longest terms of service were those of the 8th Marquess of Tweeddale with 58 years (1818–76) and the 6th earl of Selkirk with 54 (1831–85), each without a break and ending only with their deaths, and the 4th Lord Sinclair with 50 years in two spells, 1807–31 and 1833–59. A further thirteen served for 30 years or longer. Altogether, thirty-seven of the sixty-six died while still serving, and a further seventeen were given peerages of the United Kingdom during their period of office and so vacated their representative seats at the end of the Parliament in which they were so created. Thus only twelve of the sixty-six Scottish representative peers either did not stand for re-election or were not re-elected at the end of their service, though a further twelve had broken periods of service. One of the first twelve (the 10th earl of Home) died shortly after the dissolution of 1841 and one (the 11th earl of Home) was made a UK peer in the year following the end of the Parliament of 1874, so presumably neither stood for re-election. The tenure of Scottish representative peers was therefore remarkably continuous, and once elected the majority remained in the House until death.

In 1869, Lord Grey introduced a bill to make the Scots representative peers elected for life, with power to resign their seats, and with a penalty of expulsion for persistent non-attendance: the duke of Buccleuch objected to the proposal on the grounds that while the number of representatives was so small, thirty-five of the present eighty-six Scots peers who were neither representatives nor holders of British or UK peerages would have little chance of entering the House. The bill was eventually lost.[7]

The process of election was laid down in Articles xxii and xxiii of the Treaty of Union and the act of 1707, with a few small subsequent modifications.[8] Those entitled to vote were men holding titles which appeared on the 'Union Roll' of peerages valid in 1707, minus those disqualified by attainder after the Jacobite rebellions of 1715 and 1745 (though the majority of these were later restored) and also any Scots peerages called out of abeyance after 1707. The roll was headed after 1716 by the duke of Rothesay, a peerage held by the sovereign's eldest son, but between 1812 and 1865 there was no holder of the title (except for the Prince Regent between 1812 and 1820) and after 1812 its holder has not voted. The original Union Roll numbered 154,[9] but the number actually in existence and entitled to vote at an election was always less, and the number who actually attended to vote between 1815 and 1875 never exceeded 31 (1835), and on eight occasions fell below 9.[10] Peers could vote at the election by proxy through a colleague, or *in absentia* by sending in a signed and certificated list to the returning officers, the Lord Clerk Register, the Principal Clerk of Session and the Deputy Principal Clerk. Peers holding more than one title could vote only in respect of one, usually the oldest.[11] Minors and females holding peerages in their own right could neither vote nor stand as candidates. The number of votes actually registered in 1835 was 70–31 present, 18 proxies and 21 signed lists. In 1847 an act[12] modernized the roll and the procedure for claims to dormant peerages, requiring that no claim could be added to the roll unless the House of Lords had admitted its validity, and adding that titles which had not voted since 1800 should be removed from the list. Previously, the clerks made it a practice to allow the votes of claimants in cases of dispute and to leave it to the House of Lords to determine, to avoid delays and wrangles at the election meeting. Between 1825 and 1837 Alexander Humphreys, the son of a Birmingham merchant, was allowed to vote in respect of his claim to the earldom of Stirling, but in 1839 the documents on which he based his claim were found to be forgeries and he was not permitted to vote again. In addition to the exclusion of minors, females and holders of attainted peerages, the election was barred to Roman Catholics until 1829 and thereafter until 1868 by the necessity to swear the oaths of allegiance, supremacy and abjuration and to make a declaration against Popery. The Promissory Oaths Act of 1868[13] abolished the last two and revised the former, so that Roman Catholic peers of Scotland at last became eligible to vote and to be elected to serve in the House.

Scots peers after 1782 were able to receive grants of British or UK peerages and, as increasing numbers did so, the sixteen were no longer the only representatives of their order. The House resolved in 1787 that representative peers who received grants of British and UK peerages should be replaced by others, but in 1793 that all Scots peers, whether or not also holding British or UK titles, should continue to be eligible to vote in the election of the representatives. Unlike the Irish peers, however, Scots peers who could not sit in the House of Lords were not eligible to be members of the Commons.[14] There were between eighty-five and eighty-eight Scottish peers throughout this period, and during the nineteenth century increasing numbers of them received grants of UK titles. In 1880 forty-seven Scots peers were eligible to sit in the House under a British or UK title. Subtracting the sixteen representative peers and three peeresses in their own right, only twenty-three Scots peers did not have seats in the Lords in 1880.[15]

Like their English counterparts, the Scots peerage, whether representative or not, contained a variety of types. Prominent among those with scientific interests was the 8th duke of Argyll (1823–1900), who sat in the Lords as Baron Sundridge. He had interests in geology, chemistry and ornithology among other intellectual and literary pursuits and, said the *DNB*, 'exerted a useful influence on scientific progress'.[16] The 25th earl of Crawford and Balcarres (1812–80) wrote

a *History of Christian Art* among other works, the 8th marquess of
Lothian (1832–70) was a distinguished author and book collector,
and the 7th earl of Elgin became famous for his purchase and
donation to the country of the 'Elgin Marbles'. The 9th Baron
Kinnaird (1807–78) was not only an antiquarian and archaeologist
who conducted excavations at Rome, but was also interested in
steam ploughs, railways, popular education, free trade and social
reform. The 34th earl of Caithness (1821–81) invented a steam
engine and a form of compass. Sporting peers included the 9th
and 12th dukes of Hamilton who were addicted to the turf. The
9th marquess of Queensberry (1844–1900), famous for his insult to
Oscar Wilde and successful defendant in Wilde's action for libel, was
'notorious as a supporter of Bradlaugh and secularism' and in 1880
failed to be elected a representative peer 'on account of his agnostic
opinions'. He was even more famous as the finest amateur boxer of
his day and the framer, with J.G. Chambers, of the Queensberry
Rules which still govern professional boxing.

Scotsmen since the eighteenth century had followed careers in the
armed forces of the Crown. Among their number in this period were
the 7th earl of Northesk (1758–1831, representative peer 1790–1807
and 1830–3) who was Nelson's third in command at Trafalgar and
Commander-in-Chief Plymouth 1827–30. Thomas Cochrane, 10th
earl of Dundonald (1775–1860) had an unusually adventurous career;
after distinguished service in the Royal Navy he was struck off the
navy list and the Order of the Bath (and expelled from the House
of Commons where he was radical MP for Westminster) for alleged
frauds on the stock exchange and imprisoned for a year, but then
entered the naval service of Chile and Brazil, played a leading part
in securing their independence, and also commanded the Greek navy
from 1827 to 1828. He was pardoned and restored to the British
rank of Rear Admiral in 1832, and was Commander-in-Chief the
West Indies and North America, 1848–51. Another adventurer abroad
was the 9th earl of Lindsay (1787–1851) who entered the East India
Company's service, became Agent at the Court of the Shah of Persia,
and was instrumental in defeating the Russian attacks on Persia and in
quelling a rebellion there in 1834. He stood 6 feet 8 inches in his socks
and was regarded by the Persians as 'a veritable Rustam'.

More unusual careers were those of the 26th earl of Buchan
(1815–98) who before his succession to the title in 1857 earned his
living as a jockey, the 9th earl of Dundonald (1748–1831), who gave
up a naval career to pursue scientific experiments 'of great ingenuity,
but (in his lifetime) of little practical result', and died in poverty in

Paris. The 2nd Earl Cathcart (1783–1859) was a distinguished general who served in the Peninsular War and at Waterloo, and also wrote papers on geology and discovered a new mineral which he named Greenockite, after the family's second peerage.

Politically too the Scots provided distinguished public servants, including one Prime Minister (Lord Aberdeen) and several diplomats and governors of imperial dominions. Relatively few as were its numbers by the mid-nineteenth century, the Scots peerage contributed many men of energy, talent and public service to Victorian Britain. As Lord Cockburn wrote in 1848:[17]

> As an aristocracy of rank our Scotch Peerage is also sunk by the penury with which so much of it is sprinkled. It is adorned by some great fortunes and splendid estates, but too many of its members are sadly poor. . . . Though containing only about eighty-one individuals, one of whom is a lady, there are at present at least twelve who hold, or have recently held, places of such high public importance . . . and at least twenty more who, exclusive of honorary offices and naval and military rank, are respected and looked up to on account of the lead which they take in general or local public affairs. The twelve include one Foreign Secretary, one Governor-General of India, one Governor of Jamaica and Canada, two of Madras, and one Lord-Lieutenant of Ireland. The twenty include several great estates, all *resided on*, considerable political influence, and respectable pursuits and character. On the whole it is at present a very respectable body.

THE IRISH REPRESENTATIVE PEERS

By the terms of the Irish Act of Union which came into force on 1 January 1801, twenty-eight of the peers of Ireland were to be elected by their fellows to represent them in the UK Parliament. The Irish peerage, numbering 220 in all in 1815, had long been used, and regarded, as a second-rate consolation prize for men, in England as well as Ireland, who sought a title but were not regarded as worthy of the British peerage, either because of their lack of wealth or of the requisite social background, or of both, or because they were regarded as, and expected to be, lackeys of the ministry. The Act of Union was forced through the Irish Parliament by extensive promises of future patronage, including peerages, and these 'Union engagements' hung round the necks of British governments for decades afterwards. No less than 37 peerages and promotions (4 marquesses, 6 earls, 4 viscounts and 23 barons) were granted in 1800 alone. Mainly for this reason, and unlike the regulations in the Scottish Act of Union of

1707, the act made provision for future creations of Irish peerages after 1801, subject to the limitation that no new Irish peerage could be granted until three existing ones had become extinct, until their total number was reduced to 100. Thereafter, new peerages might replace extinct ones on a one-for-one basis. Until 1831 there were also no restrictions on the grant of promotions to a higher grade in the Irish peerage, but in that year the Law Officers ruled that it was illegal to make such promotions except under the same limitations as applied to creations. In the thirty years after the Union 29 promotions were made, but none thereafter.[18]

Attempts were made to establish higher standards for Irish peerages after the union. Liverpool and Peel, as Prime Minister and Chief Secretary in Ireland respectively, made it their rule to grant Irish peerages only to men resident in Ireland and for 'services and *personal consequence*' in that country.[19] The rate of new creations slowed appreciably after 1801 as a result. No less than 141 additions and promotions had been made in the last forty years of the eighteenth century, but between 1801 and 1880 there were only 14, of which 3 became extinct during the same period. The total size of the Irish peerage thus declined from 220 at the union to 179 in 1880.[20]

In addition to the reduction in the total number of the Irish peerage, there was a steady process of granting UK titles to Irish peers, as in the case of Scotland. Between 1801 and 1880, 67 such promotions were made, to which should be added 31 dating from before the union. Taking extinctions into account, a total of 78 Irish peers also held British or UK titles in 1880 and so were entitled to sit in the UK House of Lords by right. In total, 118 separate Irish titles, belonging to 76 individuals, were extinguished by 1887.[21]

Unlike their Scottish counterparts who were re-elected at each general election, Irish representative peers sat for life in the UK House of Lords, so that by-elections took place only on the death of a representative. Any representative peer who received a UK title continued to sit in both capacities and did not vacate his representative place. Between 1815 and 1880, eleven representative peers were given UK titles,[22] but in 1880 all the representatives but one were holders of Irish peerages only.

A total of 100 individuals served as Irish representative peers during the period 1815–80. Their average period of service, at 25.6 years, was only slightly longer than that of their Scottish counterparts, emphasizing that, in practice, Scots representative peers also tended to serve for life. Those with the longest periods of service were the 2nd earl of Charlemont (1806–63) and the 4th Earl Mountcashell (1826–83), each with 57 years. The 4th Earl Belmore served 56 years (1857–1913) and the 3rd Lord Clonbrock 55 (1838–93). The 3rd Viscount Gort, however, died four months after election in 1865. As in the case of Scotland, elections of Irish representative peers were dominated by government influence, usually exercised indirectly through friendly intermediaries to avoid too blatant an exercise of patronage. The elections, after the first in 1800 which took place in the Irish House of Lords, were conducted by post. In return, the Irish in the Upper House could normally be relied on to give steady support to government or, after 1830, to the party which had secured their election – naturally, therefore, to the Conservatives. However, the life-tenure of their seats enabled them to act independently if they wished, and they were not such a solid phalanx as the Scots in the divisions, nor was any member of the government appointed to manage them.[23] In 1827 when the Scots followed Wellington on Canning's appointment as Prime Minister, five of the fourteen Irish who voted on the corn question supported the opposition. On the Reform Bill, however, nineteen voted with Wellington and only four with the government, and thereafter the majority continued to support the Conservatives. From 1832, as Large writes, 'the choice . . . was virtually made by the leader of the Conservatives in the Upper House, or as one disgruntled Irish liberal peer put it a generation later, they were made in Lord Derby's drawing room'. In the Lords' debate on the Reform Bill in July 1867 the Liberal leader Lord Granville declared that Derby 'has a power almost superior to the Queen's prerogative of making Peers, by practically having the selection of the Scotch and Irish representative peers . . . . No individual, whatever his position, his ability, or his character, has the slightest chance of representing either of those Peerages in the House unless his political opinions perfectly coincide with those of the noble Earl.'[24]

English prejudice against all things and men Irish did not disappear after the union, and the Irishmen in the Lords rarely acquired the respect and acceptance given to others. In part this also reflected the relative poverty of many families in that troubled island. Poor Irish peers were unlikely after 1801 to be elected to the UK House of Lords, and so their existence did not in fact detract from the status of the House. Poverty was, however, sometimes noted in the Irish peerage. Matthew Barnewall successfully claimed the descent of the Irish viscountcy of Barnewall in 1814, but had to be given a small pension to relieve his poverty. Others became poor through extravagance or misfortune: the first marquess of Drogheda (1730–1822) was addicted to gambling, and had to give up his property to his creditors and live on an allowance from them. Joshua, 6th Viscount Allen, was described by Creevey in 1834 as 'A penniless Lord and Irish pensioner, well-behaved, and not encumbered with too much principle'. The 3rd Baron Montfort (1773–1851), whose estates had been alienated, received a pension of £300 *p.a.* after 1800 as 'a decayed member of the peerage': in 1793 he married Betty Watts, daughter of the owner of a 'sponging house' where he was confined for debt. When the 6th Viscount Strangford succeeded to his title in 1801 he had only a salary as a clerk in the Foreign Office plus what he earned by writing articles for magazines. He subsequently became a diplomat and held two ambassadorships, and was awarded a UK peerage in 1825 for his public services, but he pleaded exemption from the fees of £600 required to obtain his letters patent on the grounds of poverty. A pension of £2,300 on his retirement was said to more than double his income. Lord Westmeath, who was promoted to marquess in 1822, according to Lady Cowper 'is said not to have money enough to pay the Fees'. On the other hand, the 2nd marquess of Clanricarde (1832–1916) left a fortune of £2,500,000 – though his estates in County Galway were worth less than one tenth of that sum. He attended the House so rarely that he was once unrecognized and was refused admission.[25]

Other eccentrics were more disreputable. The 2nd Viscount Frankfort de Montmorency (1806–89) tried to make money by inserting advertisements in the press offering assignations, quoting the names of respectable people who were alleged to have taken advantage of the service. He was sentenced to twelve months in a house of correction. The 4th earl of Kingston (1796–1867) was charged with sodomy in 1848 but forfeited his bail of £10,000 when he did not appear to stand trial. In 1860 he appeared several times in the police courts, accused of drunkenness, refusing to pay cabmen and assaulting the police. Lord Glentworth (1789–1834), heir to the 3rd earl of Limerick, 'fell a victim to a career of reckless indulgence' and spent 'the greatest part of his time, after he came of age, in prison'. The 4th earl of Mornington (1788–1857) led a notoriously profligate life. His obituary notice remarked that 'Redeemed by no single virtue, adorned by no single grace, his life has gone out without even a flicker of repentance . . . [he was] deservedly avoided by all men.' The 5th earl of Aldborough (1784–1849) divorced his first wife in 1826 and went through a form of marriage with Mary Arundell at the British Embassy in Paris, but later denied its validity, and she lived in Florence as 'Mrs Gerard'. Her son unsuccessfully disputed the succession of the 6th earl, a son of the first marriage, in 1849, the 5th earl having left all his property to Mary's children and declared that his first marriage was invalid and his children illegitimate, since he had previously married a Miss Devonport, who was still alive at the time of that marriage. 'By his own showing', remarked the editor of *The Complete Peerage*, 'the Earl must have been an exceptional scoundrel and bigamous betrayer of women under cover of pretended marriage'.

Not all Irish peers were unworthy of the peerage as a whole. The 6th Viscount Haberton (1836–1912) published the first English translation of *The Lately Discovered Fragments* of the Greek poet Menander. The 9th Viscount Galway (1782–1834) was a topographer and antiquary and the 3rd earl of Dunraven (1812–71, given a UK peerage as Baron Kenry in 1866) was an archaeologist and antiquarian, renowned for his knowledge of Celtic and mediaeval remains. He was a believer in spiritualism and assisted at seances. The 5th earl of Rosse (1800–67) was an expert in astronomy, chemistry and civil engineering: he built a great telescope costing £20,000 at his country estate. Some Irish peers were also affected by religious zeal. The 3rd earl of Roden (1788–1870) was 'one of the most determined Orangemen of the North of Ireland', and a strict sabbatarian, who taught all his life in his Sunday school. 'The Orange scarves hung in the chapel of the house. The great iron shutters put up to protect the household from the Fenians could still shut with a clang against nocturnal bandits. An atmosphere of stern and uncompromising piety brooded over the house.' Lady Roden 'gathered the young maidservants round her to read the Scriptures on Sunday afternoons.'[26] Their eldest son unfortunately, and perhaps predictably, rebelled against his upbringing and became a libertine.

Irish peers were by no means immune from pride in rank. The 1st marquess of Abercorn (1756–1818) always wore his Garter riband when out shooting, and required his housemaids to wear white kid gloves when they made his bed. When his second wife left him in 1798 he sent her a message begging her to go in the family coach, 'as it ought never to be said that Lady Abercorn left her husband's roof in a hack chaise'.[27] The 1st Marquess Wellesley, Wellington's elder brother, wore his Garter star and ribbon on his dressing gown and when Lawrence painted his portrait he wore lipstick and rouged his cheeks.

Irish peers to suffer violent death were the 2nd Baron Mount Sandford (1805–28) who died of his injuries after being assaulted by a drunken labourer at Windsor, and the 2nd earl of Norbury (1781–1839) who was assassinated on his Irish estate by a 'Ribbonman' who was also his servant: on this occasion, the butler did it.

THE BISHOPS

At the beginning of this period the two archbishops and twenty-four bishops of the Church of England, and four bishops of the Church of Ireland, one archbishop and three bishops serving in rotation of sees as prescribed, sat in the House of Lords. During the first fifteen years of this period, they tended to form a section of the 'party of the Crown' in the House, though there were always a few who were independent, or even supporters of the Whig opposition. As appointees of the Crown, and even after first appointment dependent on royal or ministerial favour for translation to a higher rank and income,[28] they were regarded in the eighteenth century as little better than placemen, to be herded into the lobbies in support of any measure proposed by the government or to defeat any opposition measure which could not be decently disposed of by other means. There were certainly time-servers on the eighteenth-century bench, but the picture was over-coloured by later radicals and evangelicals. It was natural that men, often in the later eighteenth century sons of wealthy, propertied and even aristocratic families,[29] should support the existing order, and that bishops should see it as their spiritual as well as political duty to uphold lawfully constituted authority and the social hierarchy which underpinned it. After the American and French Revolutions the upper and middle classes became more concerned at what they believed was the national degeneracy and decline of moral standards, and religious revival, within as well as outside the Church of England, affected the attitudes of politicians and laymen towards ecclesiastical patronage, and of their nominees towards their pastoral duties. Wilberforce exhorted his friend the younger Pitt to pay more attention to learning and piety in appointments to the episcopate, and though Pitt was not averse to pressing the claims of his old Cambridge tutor and private secretary George Tomline to the archbishopric of Canterbury in 1805 – which George III refused on the grounds that it was a party political nomination – Pitt's successors paid more heed to the principle. Perceval and Liverpool in particular both resisted the wish of George III and his eldest son to control ecclesiastical patronage (even though George III took a responsible attitude towards it) and also tried to appoint men worthy of the spiritual and pastoral duties of the Church. Spencer Perceval told the marquess of Ely in 1810 that the practice of appointing Irish bishops on grounds of parliamentary interest had been abandoned, and in 1819 Liverpool wrote to Lord Talbot that in England also 'no Minister has ever paid more attention to merit or so little to political objects as myself'. Nevertheless, he added, 'the aristocracy of the country will naturally expect to have some share in the patronage of the Church, and it is desirable even for the sake of the Church itself that this should be the case . . . . It is of great consequence, however, that the proportion of men of rank raised to the bench should not be too large'.[30] The Duke of Wellington, faced with a vacancy for the see of Oxford in 1829, was, as Mrs Arbuthnot wrote,

> a great deal puzzled, for the B. of Oxford, unless he is a very celebrated divine, shd be a man of family and a gentleman. We have no particularly learned man to put on, and the Duke burst forth into one of his tirades at the laziness and inefficiency of our aristocracy. He said he wd give anything to know a man of rank or family, well-informed and respectable, to put into this Bishoprick, and there is not one. It is, however, [she added] very true that those men of family who go into the church think of getting livings and preferments but never of studying & making themselves fit for the dignities of the church.[31]

In 1826 Liverpool refused the solicitations of Wellington and Wellesley to make their brother Gerald an Irish bishop, on the grounds that he was separated from his wife – hardly a reason, one would think, that would much concern George IV – and in 1820 the king himself was unable to persuade Liverpool to translate Bishop Pelham from Exeter to Winchester.[32]

Some early nineteenth-century bishops nevertheless climbed to the bench up the ladder of royal favour, including royal tutors like John Fisher (Exeter, 1803–25), George Davys (Peterborough, 1839–64), H. W. Majendie (Bangor, 1809–30), or personal friends of the Prince Regent (Law of Chester 1812–24, Bath and Wells 1824–45, and William Jackson, Oxford 1812–15). Great aristocratic families also continued to obtain episcopal preferment for younger sons, tutors and chaplains, and prominent party men in both Houses secured it for their followers. As time went on, however, the 'saints, theologians, pastors, preachers, philosophers' listed by Gladstone as the men best fitted for the episcopate began to predominate over those who were purely 'gentlemen & men of business'.[33]

The bench of bishops in the early and mid-nineteenth century thus consisted of a variety of types, reflecting the broad views comprised within the Church itself, but naturally tending to conservative principles and generally voting on the side of government, whether from self-interest or not. Since the French Revolution many churchmen had become more conservative, fearing that the welcome which liberal and radical circles seemed to have given to revolutionary ideas threatened both political and religious establishments, and even Christianity itself. This reinforced their willingness to resist reforms which did not come before the House with the imprimatur of government, to the despair of liberal reformers in the years following Waterloo. Yet their attitude was not wholly reactionary, as their conduct in the later 1820s showed over the issue of religious toleration. It was perhaps unexpected that thirteen out of twenty-one voted in favour of the repeal of the Test and Corporation Acts in 1828, although in the majority of cases it was not out of liberal views but because they believed that the security of the Church would be better protected by the new declaration to be taken by office holders not to do anything to injure the Church of England. 'The question', wrote Van Mildert of Durham, 'is not whether the fortress shall be surrendered, but whether the outworks shall remain as they are or be reconstructed on a somewhat different plan.'[34] On Catholic Emancipation they were also divided, some influenced by the pressure which Wellington's reluctant advocacy of the measure placed on them as supporters of government. Both evangelicals and high churchmen had doctrinal reasons for opposing emancipation, and even some of its supporters did so with 'fear and agony and sorrow', as Peel's protégé Lloyd of Oxford wrote. On this occasion, the archbishop of Canterbury summoned them to a meeting at Lambeth to discuss what they should do, but they could not agree on any common action, only that 'each should take his own line'. Eventually, ten voted for it and seventeen against it.[35]

The Irish bishops were more united in their hostility, believing that the Irish Church had far more to lose. Greville reported that fourteen of them were 'coming over in a body to petition the King . . . and most foolish they. The English bishops may by possibility be sincere and disinterested in their opposition (not that I believe they are), but nobody will ever believe that the Irish think of anything but their scandalous revenues.'[36]

On the Reform Bills in 1831–2 the bishops were more determined. Only two voted with the government on the second reading in October 1831 and twenty-one were found in the majority of forty-one.[37] It was possible to argue arithmetically that they were responsible for the defeat, and they were attacked by radicals and in popular demonstrations. 'The Ministers are furious with them', wrote Mrs Arbuthnot, 'and all the venom of the Radical press is let loose against them & *disfranchising* the Bishops is now openly preached by "The Times" & petitioned for by all the blackguards all over the country.' *The Times* wrote on 12 October 1831 that 'The people everywhere regard the Bench of Bishops as enemies to the civil rights of Englishmen, and no man opens his mouth upon the fate of the Reform Bill without asking the question, "Why are the Bishops suffered to meddle in any manner with legislation?"' Nevertheless, it would be an oversimplification to say that they voted on purely self-interested grounds: many of them were naturally of a conservative disposition, and there is no reason to suggest that they were any more, or less, responsible in the use of their votes than their lay colleagues. On the second reading of the third bill in 1832, after strong pressure from Grey, with the king's approval, twelve of the thirty English and Irish bishops supported it with fifteen against – enough to give a majority of nine in the division, but hardly evidence that the bishops as a whole were more susceptible to political manipulation than true to their political beliefs. Seven bishops were among the seventy-four who signed the protest against the second reading. Radical opinion seized on the bishops' opposition in order to attack the Church: the bishop of Worcester who deserted to the opposition in May 1832 was compared to Judas Iscariot by a graffiti artist on the walls of his cathedral. Phillpott's palace at Exeter had to be protected by a garrison of coastguards, and his effigy was burnt on 5 November 1831.[38]

It was not only their opposition to the Reform Bill that made the bishops disliked: rather it focused popular complaints against the Church in general and its financial exactions in particular. *The Poor Man's Guardian*, a radical 'unstamped' newspaper, described a bishop-burning ceremony at Huddersfield in November 1831 which was allegedly attended by between 15,000 and 20,000 spectators, to watch 'a great, fat, bloated, blundering bishop, whom we have bartered for the poor, deluded, murdered Guy Faux' being paraded to a bonfire. It proclaimed:

> This is the last fifth of November which shall constitute the anniversary of a bloody church and state conspiracy, in support of tithes, Easter offerings, oblations, obventions, and all the horrid and dreadful train of business . . . for the purpose of rioting in holy luxury out of the *grindings* of our bones, to our utter ruin and past and present degradation.[39]

It concluded with a verse which encapsulated the radical objection to the supposed alliance of Church and state in support of corruption:

> Good Lord! put down aristocrats,
> Let Boroughmongers be abhorred;
> And from all tithes and shovel hats
> Forthwith deliver us good Lord!

The opposition of the majority of the episcopal bench to the Whig governments of the 1830s is in truth not surprising. The Whigs of the

1830s were the successors of, or in the person of Grey, the very people who had welcomed the French Revolution and opposed the war to destroy it. Also, the Whig defence of 'civil and religious liberty all over the world' from the days of Fox, and their championship of Catholic Emancipation and the repeal of the Test and Corporation Acts in the 1820s, branded them in the eyes of some churchmen as enemies of the establishment. In the 1830s their attempts to reform the Irish Church also aroused the fears of the High Church that an age of secularization was dawning. Many faced the dilemma that, with the Whigs in charge of government, their secular and spiritual duty to uphold lawfully constituted authority seemed to conflict with their equally binding responsibility to their Church. The crucial question became, how far should they go in supporting general opposition to the government by enlisting under Wellington's banner? The king himself addressed a reproof to them for voting for Wellington's motion of censure on the government's policy towards Portugal in 1833, on the grounds that this was a 'purely political' question 'in which the interests of the Church were in no way concerned', and he warned Archbishop Howley that the bishops ought not to 'put themselves forward in party questions'. As Greville pointed out, it was a strange proceeding, 'So unconstitutional, so foolish; but his Ministers do not seem to mind it, and are rather elated at such a signal proof of his disposition to support them.'[40] The bishops, like the House of Lords as a whole, had to be aware that unwavering opposition towards a government backed by the House of Commons and supported by the majority of the public might threaten their own survival. Duncannon said in 1833 that if the Lords threw out the Irish Church Bill, the House of Commons would vote to expel the bishops by a great majority. In fact 11 voted for the second reading, 15 against it. In 1834, 3 voted for the Irish Tithe Bill, 21 against it, and in 1836 the opposition to the Irish Municipal Corporations Bill included 19 bishops out of 23 who voted. In 1839, 21 out of 24 supported the archbishop of Canterbury's resolutions against secular interference with education.[41]

Nevertheless, the cooling of the people's enthusiasm for reform after the achievement of the Reform Act, the setting up of the Ecclesiastical Commission in 1836, which remedied some of the more glaring abuses in the Church, and the general wish for stability and order after the disturbances of 1831–2, resulted in the dying down of agitation against the bishops in the House of Lords. Lord Henley, Peel's brother-in-law, proposed in 1832, as part of an extensive 'Plan of Church Reform', which anticipated much of the later work of the Ecclesiastical Commission, that the bishops should be excluded from Parliament to avoid their becoming 'gladiators in the [political] strife of bitterness and personality'. But even Radical attacks on the political role of the bishops failed to make headway. Proposals in 1834, 1836 and 1837 to exclude them were heavily defeated in the Commons. The Church was still a powerful institution and the Whigs had no desire to encourage the Radicals by an outright attack upon it.[42]

Nevertheless, there was opposition to any increase in the number of bishops sitting in the Lords when new sees were created to deal with the changing size and distribution of the population in the mid-nineteenth century. In 1847 two new dioceses, Ripon and Manchester, were created by act of Parliament, but the new bishops were to sit in the Lords only when vacancies arose among the existing members. In 1867 a further bill proposed to create additional sees, with the proviso, added by the House of Commons, that these bishops should not sit in the Lords. The House of Lords, led by the archbishop of Canterbury, rejected this amendment and the bill was dropped. It was reintroduced in 1869 and again rejected. Eventually, in 1875, a compromise was reached. The two archbishops and the bishops of London, Durham and Winchester would always sit in the Lords, followed by the first twenty-one in order of seniority of appointment. The Irish bishops disappeared from the House after the disestablishment of the Church of Ireland in 1869.

Bishops therefore continued to take part in the proceedings of the House of Lords, and as in the case of lay peers tended to a large extent to divide on party lines. A few such as Phillpotts of Exeter were notorious 'Ultra' Tories and took Wellington's party whip, though he was described by the duke as 'one of the most unmanageable gentlemen in the House of Lords, and the person who requires the most attendance and attention'. The Irish bishop of Elphin who became a representative by rotation in 1835 wrote to the duke to offer to come for the beginning of the new session, even at the cost of personal inconvenience, 'if it would assist the Conservative party'. Wellington's intended reply was somewhat curt, sensing the arrival of another reinforcement for Cumberland's band: 'You must judge for yourself whether you will or will not attend your duty in Parliament', he wrote, though his secretary toned down the phrasing. Phillpotts in particular was a combative and pugnacious speaker against the Whig governments. He had participated in a notorious scene with Lord Grey in the House on the Reform Bill, in which he 'got a most tremendous dressing', Greville wrote. 'It would be an injury to compare this man with Laud', continued Greville: 'he more resembles Gardiner; had he lived in those days he would have been just such another, boiling with ambition, an ardent temperament, and great talents. He has a desperate and a dreadful countenance, and looks like the man he is.'[43] As time went on, however, for the most part, the greater 'seriousness' of the Victorian Church and its episcopate and the greater awareness of the social and pastoral problems which it had to face moderated the political role of the bishops, the majority of whom became independents rather than merely party men in the mid- and later nineteenth-century House of Lords.

Ministers did not, however, refrain from using their power to designate bishops in accordance with their own views and interests. The difference was that, whereas in the eighteenth and early nineteenth centuries the candidates' political views were the major criterion, in the mid-nineteenth century it was the views of the politicians on church questions which carried weight. Lord John Russell, for example, as Prime Minister from 1846 to 1852 appointed two archbishops and eight bishops, all representative of the 'Broad' church party rather than of the High Church or Tractarian persuasion, including R.D. Hampden, appointed to Hereford in 1848 'in order to spite the Tractarians' and to become the centre of the most famous of the religious controversies of the age.[44] Later ministers tended to be more impartial, although Shaftesbury appears to have been given control of church patronage by Palmerston, and between 1856 and 1865 was responsible for the nominations to three archbishoprics and sixteen bishoprics, all men representing the evangelical rather than the High Church party, and some men of narrow views and little distinction. Even the queen, with Gerald Wellesley, now dean of Windsor, as her ecclesiastical adviser, was unable to contest at least two of Shaftesbury's nominations. Samuel Wilberforce, 'the spiritual ancestor of the modern busy bishop', left the strongest mark on the bench, setting by example and precept the model of both spiritual zeal and administrative efficiency, and others like Blomfield (Chester 1824, London 1828–57) were distinguished for their contributions to the reform of the Church and its clergy.

By the 1870s, the Anglican episcopate had 'gained the general respect of the nation' and the cry for its reform or removal from the House of Lords had died a natural death.[45] The issues which were now being discussed were not those concerning the Church's interference in politics, but the politicians' interference with the Church. The reversal by the Privy Council in 1850 of the judgement of the Ecclesiastical Court in the Gorham case, arising out of the bishop of Exeter's refusal to institute Mr Gorham to a living on the ground of his views on baptismal regeneration, aroused the fury of high churchmen that such a decision should be taken by a purely secular court. Lord John Russell's declaration that the case involved 'the Queen's supremacy over all matters in the Church, spiritual as well as temporal' and that the alternative would be the erection of 'a priestly supremacy over the Crown and people'[46] was hardly conciliatory, though the furore over the 'Papal aggression' which followed shortly afterwards reunited the Church and the politicians in defence of the Protestant establishment. In general, relations between Church and state were not seriously disturbed, and the position of the bishops in the House of Lords attracted little adverse comment for the rest of the century. In contrast to the outcry over the Reform Bills in 1831–2, only two bishops voted in the division in committee on Disraeli's Reform Bill in 1867, one for and one against, and even on the disestablishment of the Irish Church two years later only nine voted on the third reading, seven of those in favour.[47]

REFERENCES

1. A. Aspinall, 'The Grand Cabinet, 1800–1837', *Politica* (Dec. 1938). This Cabinet ceased to meet after the accession of Queen Victoria and its function was transferred to the Home Secretary.
2. D.G. Barnes, *George III and William Pitt* (New York, 1965), pp. 348–9, 391–2.
3. Sir James Fergusson, *The Sixteen Peers of Scotland* (Oxford, 1960).
4. H. Furber, *Henry Dundas* (Oxford, 1931), pp. 175–6, 279–82.
5. D. Large, 'The decline of the "party of the Crown" and the rise of parties in the House of Lords, 1783–1837', *English Historical Review*, LXXVIII, 672–80; A.S. Turberville, *The House of Lords in the Age of Reform 1784–1837* (1958), pp. 109–10. Of the sixteen elected in 1831, twelve had been in the 1826–30 Parliament.
6. Listed in J.C. Sainty, *Representative Peers for Scotland, 1707–1963, and for Ireland, 1800–1961*, House of Lords Record Office Memorandum no. 39 (1968).
7. Hansard, CXCV, 473–6, 1677–94.
8. Full details in Fergusson, *The Sixteen Peers*, cha. 1.
9. *Ibid.*, pp. 23–33 and Appendix A, pp. 156–8.
10. There were 8 in 1825, 1842, 1843 and 1872; 7 in 1867 and 1870; 6 in 1824, and 2 at a by-election in 1869: *ibid.*, pp. 133–5.
11. In 1872 the marquess of Lothian answered to two other titles in addition: *ibid.*, p. 7.
12. 11 and 12 Vic. c. 52.
13. 31 and 32 Vic. c. 62.
14. Turberville, *The House of Lords in the Age of Reform 1784–1837*, pp. 103–7. Scots peers holding English peerages before 1707 were allowed to vote

from 1708.

15. *New Edinburgh Almanac* (1880), 524; *General Almanac of Scotland, and British Register* (1813), 57. A further two listed, the earl of Fife and Earl Macdonald, actually held Irish peerages. The total of 88 included 3 peeresses in their own right.

16. Argyll, *Autobiography and Memoirs of George Douglas, 8th duke of Argyll*, ed. Dowager Duchess of Argyll (1906), pp. 70–122, *passim*. For other examples see entries in G.E.C., *The Complete Peerage*, and Sir James Balfour Paul, *The Scots Peerage*, 9 vols (Edinburgh, 1904–14).

17. *Journal of Henry Cockburn, 1831–54* (1874), II, pp. 225–6.

18. *Gentleman's and Citizens' Almanac* (Dublin, 1815), 91–108. For the Irish peerage in the nineteenth century see G.E.C., 'The peerage of Ireland', *Genealogist* V (1889), 1–16, 82–9, 145–52, 180–205. The representative peers for each Parliament are listed in *38th Annual Report of the Deputy Keeper of the Public Records* (1877), 783–7 and in Sainty, *Representative Peers*. The last Irish peerage to be created was Rathdonnel (1868), until Curzon was given an Irish title in 1898 in order to keep him in the Commons. A subsequent attempt to prevent further creations was lost in the Commons, but none was ever given afterwards: G.E.C., *Complete Peerage*, III, p. 581.

19. Liverpool to George IV, 22 Jan. 1822: *Letters of King George IV*, ed. A. Aspinall (Cambridge, 1938), II, p. 498.

20. *Gentleman's and Citizens' Almanac; New Edinburgh Almanac* (1875), 507.

21. G.E.C., 'Peerage of Ireland', 9–16, 82–5.

22. 1815: the earl of Enniskillen (Baron Grinstead) d. 1840, earl of Limerick (Baron Foxford) d. 1844 and earl of Clancarty (Baron Trench) d. 1837; 1821: earl of Kingston (Baron Kingston) d. 1839, earl of Longford (Baron Silchester) d. 1835, earl of Conyngham (Baron Minster) d. 1832, earl of Donoughmore (Viscount Hutchinson) d. 1825; 1826: earl of Thomond (Lord Tadcaster) d. 1846; 1835: earl of Gosford (Lord Worlingham) d. 1849; 1837: earl of Charlemont (Baron Charlemont) d. 1863; 1876: earl of Erne (Lord Fermanagh) d. 1885: Sainty, *Representative Peers*.

23. *Memoirs and Correspondence of Viscount Castlereagh*, ed. marquess of Londonderry III (1849), pp. 368–70; D. Large, 'The House of Lords and Ireland in the age of Peel, 1832–50', in Jones and Jones, *Peers, Politics and Power, 1603–1911*, pp. 373–405.

24. Large, 'The decline of the "party of the Crown"', 682; Hansard, NS CLXXXVIII, 1861–2.

25. W.D. Rubinstein, *Men of Property* (1981), p. 201; *Lady Palmerston and her Times* (1922), I, p. 93.

26. *Ibid.*, II, p. 48.

27. G.W.E. Russell, *Collections and Recollections* (1903), pp. 73–4.

28. D.H. Akenson, *The Church of Ireland, 1800–85* (New Haven, Conn., 1971), p. 72. The value of sees ranged from £19,182 *p.a.* (Canterbury), with five others over £11,000, to £924 (Llandaff): N. Ravitch, *Sword and Mitre* (The Hague, 1966), p. 96. Akenson gives a figure of £23,518 for York in 1830 down to £962 (Rochester), and for the Irish, £17,669 for Armagh down to £4,081 for Killala and Achonry (p. 84). For the incomes of the altered and amalgamated Irish sees in 1867 (Armagh and Clogher £8,882 to Cloyne, Cork and Ross (£2,106)), *ibid.*, p. 223. G.W.E. Russell,

Collections and Recollections, p. 69, remarked of the bishops before the time of the Ecclesiastical Commission that they were the heirs of a 'grand tradition of mingled splendour and profit', and that even the poor bishoprics were usually held with a rich deanery, prebend, or living, 'so that the most impecunious successor of the Apostles could manage to have four horses to his carriage and his daily bottle of Madeira'.

29. Ravitch calculates that for the period 1791–1836, of 51 bishops appointed, 12 were sons or near relatives of peers, and 16 from gentry families. Two were sons of bishops, and altogether 10 sons of clergymen. He estimates that the proportion of bishops appointed from aristocratic families during the period was 24 per cent and from the gentry 31 per cent. For the Irish the figure was 32 per cent in each case. Of the 26 Irish bishops appointed in that period, 12 were sons or close kin of peers and 12 sons of gentry, about half of them being English or Scots: N. Ravitch, *Sword and Mitre*, pp. 120–2, 145–6.

30. *English Historical Documents, 1783–1832*, ed. A. Aspinall and E.A. Smith (1959), XI, pp. 649–50; Large, 'The decline of the "party of the Crown"', 684.

31. *The Journal of Mrs Arbuthnot*, II, p. 282. Dr Bagot, dean of Canterbury 1827–45, was appointed to Oxford in 1829.

32. The appointment of Dr Gray as bishop of Bristol in 1827 allowed Liverpool to give Wellesley Gray's living at Bishop Wearmouth, worth £3,000 *p.a.*: 'The duke is quite delighted and perfectly satisfied', wrote Mrs Arbuthnot, and Liverpool 'does it with a good conscience, for tho', from the circumstances of Dr Wellesley's situation with his wife, Ld. Liverpool never wd make him a Bishop, yet knowing him to be an excellent private character & a most exemplary clergyman, he feels that he is perfectly competent to the situation'. *Ibid.*, II, pp. 80–1; Large, 'The decline of the "party of the Crown"', 684.

33. C.K. Francis Brown, *A History of the English Clergy 1800–1900* (1953), p. 123. For a discussion of categories and types see *ibid.*, pp. 86–125.

34. W.L. Mathieson, *English Church Reform 1815–1840* (1923), pp. 36–7; Hansard, NS XIX, 236–7.

35. Mathieson, *English Church Reform*, p. 39; C.C.F. Greville, *Journal of the Reigns of George IV and William IV*, ed. H. Reeve (1874), 21 March 1829, I, p. 194.

36. *Ibid.*, I, p. 187 (11 March).

37. Of the 21, 14 were appointed by Liverpool. Only one (Maltby of Chichester) was a Whig appointee (1831).

38. *Journal of Mrs Arbuthnot*, II, p. 430; Turberville, *House of Lords in the age of Reform*, pp. 297–318, for the politics of the bishops in the 1830s; Mathieson, *English Church Reform* pp. 287–318, for the attitudes of the bishops towards the Reform Bills.

39. *Poor Man's Guardian*, no. 22, 19 Nov. 1831.

40. *The Life and Times of Henry, Lord Brougham*, written by himself (1871), III, pp. 275–8; Greville, *Journal*, II, p. 393.

41. *Ibid.*, 15 July 1833; III, p. 9. For Alvanley's *bon mot*, *ibid.*, III, p. 197; Hansard, 3rd Ser. XIX, 1017–18; XXV, 1204–7; XXXIII, 306–9; XLVIII, 1332–5.

42. Mathieson, *English Church Reform*, p. 69; Hansard, XXXIII, 311–22, for Rippon's motion 26 April 1836. The division was 53 to 180.

43. *Correspondence of Lady Burghersh with the Duke of Wellington*, ed. Lady Rose Weigall (1903), pp. 89–90; *The Prime Minister's Papers: Wellington, Political Correspondence*, ed. J. Brooke and J. Gandy II (1975), pp. 358–9; Greville, *Journal*, II, pp. 205, 287.

44. Spencer Walpole, *Life of Lord John Russell* (1889), II, pp. 116–17; Brown, *English Clergy*, p. 119.

45. *Ibid.*, pp. 112, 115–17, 122; *Memoir of Charles James Blomfield, D.D. Bishop of London*, ed. A. Blomfield (1863), I, pp. 107–12 *et passim*.

46. Brown, *English Clergy*, p. 118.

47. Only one bishop (St David's) voted for the second reading, with 16 against; the 2 English archbishops and 10 English bishops abstained. The archbishop of Canterbury feared that the defeat of the second reading, especially if obtained by the votes of the bishops, would be dangerous to the Irish Church, and advocated amendment in committee. Gerald Wellesley, the queen's ecclesiastical advisor, mediated between the government and the bishops and a compromise was reached: Akenson, *Church of Ireland*, pp. 268–73. Henceforward Irish bishops ceased to sit in the Lords.

CHAPTER FIVE

Parties and Party Management in the House of Lords

THE NOVELTY OF PARTY

Party became the dominant political division in the House of Lords after 1830. The accession to power of the Whigs, who had been in almost perpetual opposition since the mid-eighteenth century, highlighted the division of political principles, and their Reform Bills, by presenting a stark choice between change and preservation of the old order, provided the stage for the process. Before 1830 there had been a small, ineffective, but generally coherent Whig opposition to a succession of governments which could only loosely be described as Tory. They had been composed of alliances of groups and individuals, formed in accordance with the royal preferences and supported by the 'influence of the Crown' and the general tendency of the peerage to support the monarch's views. The history of Catholic Emancipation in the 1820s demonstrates the importance of this attitude. As long as George IV's hostility to the question prevented the government from giving it ministerial support, the majority of the Lords continued to block attempts to pass it. When in 1829 Wellington accepted the necessity of emancipation and compelled the king to withdraw his resistance to it, the measure passed the Upper House, the earlier majorities of between 39 and 181 against it being transformed into a majority of 107 for the bill. The true nature of party was shown, not by the numbers in the division, but by the effect of emancipation on the government's previous supporters. The defection of the 'Ultras' from Wellington signified the beginning of a realignment on the principle of reform or conservation, while the Canningite group, led in the Lords by Melbourne, drifted towards the Whigs whom they joined formally in 1830. The Reform Bills completed the tendency to divide into two major parties, some of the 'Ultras' reuniting with the main body of Wellington's supporters but others adhering to the Whigs, whose desire was in any case not to destroy but to preserve and strengthen the aristocratic constitution by removing those abuses which made it unpopular.[1]

At the same time, the dismantling of the place and pensions system was virtually completed, with the abolition of the remaining sinecure offices in 1834. This did not put an end to patronage, but since patronage was falling almost wholly into the hands of ministers as party leaders it no longer cemented a party looking exclusively to the king. Ministers like Grey and Melbourne, unlike their predecessors, faced a hostile majority in the Lords because there was no 'party of the Crown' for them to call upon to supplement their own followings.[2]

Elements in the House of Lords who had hitherto been mainly supporters of the Crown thus tended to become party men after 1830, when the onset of a long period of mainly Whig and Liberal governments meant that they had to choose between support of government and resistance to reform, two principles previously not incompatible. The swing of the majority in the Lords towards opposition was the consequence, not so much of any change in the perceived role of the Upper House, as of the change in the nature and programmes of governments. The natural conservatism of the Lords had now to find expression through party, and in opposition.

To Greville, writing in 1838, this nevertheless intimated 'a great practical change in the constitutional functions of the House of Lords'. Before 1830, the House had supported the Crown and the ministers chosen by the monarch. During the reign of William IV, at any rate after 1835, when Peel's ministry fell because of the hostility of the House of Commons, the Tories might have justified their opposition on the grounds 'that they were only supporting the Crown when they opposed the Ministers whom the House of Commons had forced upon him' – a sound eighteenth-century principle. That excuse, however, was patently untrue while Victoria gave her open support to Melbourne's Whigs. Greville wrote:

> It is a departure from the character and proper province of that
> House to array itself in permanent and often bitter hostility to
> the Government, and to persist in continually rejecting measures
> recommended by the Crown and passed by the Commons . . . it is,
> I believe, the first time that there is no party in the House of Lords
> supporting the Crown, nor any individual acting upon that principle,
> but all are either Whigs or Tories arrayed against each other and
> battling for power.

Even before 1830, Mrs Arbuthnot had commented in May 1827 that 'party spirit seems as if it wd now run most furiously high in both Houses. In the Lords they are becoming like the H. of Commons in violence.' In 1833 Greville described the Tory lords as 'perfectly rabid. . . . They care for nothing but the silly vain pleasure of beating the Government.'[3]

As feelings ran high on a number of Whig reforms after 1832, particularly on the English and Irish Municipal Corporations Bills, observers noted the tendency towards polarization. Greville remarked in August 1835 that 'the majority in each House grows daily more rabid and more desperate' and accordingly on both sides, the management of party became crucial to success.[4] The Whigs had regarded themselves as a party since long before 1830, bonded together by common if rather general principles. They had opposed the repressive policies of governments since 1790 and advocated economy in government expenditure, reduction of establishments and of the 'influence of the Crown', and civil equality for members of all Christian Churches. Their number was relatively small but they were a close-knit social group, interrelated by marriage and family connections, and they included several of the 'great Whig families' who traced their political descent from the revolution of 1688–9. Russells, Cavendishes, Wentworths, Ponsonbys, Spencers, Howards and their various branches formed the 'sacred circle of the great-grandmotherhood'[5] and provided both a nucleus of party in the Lords and before 1832 a good deal of the territorial and electoral influence that helped to fill the ranks in the Commons. Their titles were generally of older descent than many of the 'Tories', since the great majority of those originating after the 1760s had been created by the ministers of George III and IV, who did not belong to the mainstream Whig connection. They were indeed in many ways even more jealous of the status of aristocracy than those of recent ennoblement, so that the party conflict did not seriously threaten the continuance of the House of Lords. Grey and Melbourne set their faces against reform of the Upper House in the 1830s, preferring after 1832 to accept limitations on their political measures rather than destroy the power of the Lords to obstruct them. They relied rather on popular pressure, exerted either through a House of Commons claiming to be more representative of the people, or directly by public opinion expressed in newspapers or public meetings and by petitions, to make the Lords cooperate with liberal policies. There was indeed little else they could do. They could not hope for a numerical majority in the Lords. Grey had shrunk from carrying out the threat to swamp the House with new peers in 1832, and the great Whig families were reluctant to dilute the peerage with newcomers. Even after the creation of 86 new Whig peers between 1830 and 1841, the Whigs could muster only a maximum of 129 in the lobbies during the decade, while in the same division the opposition reached 240.[6] Lord Hatherton pointed out in 1835 that the Whigs could count on only 87 of the 430 members of the House of Lords, and that many of those were absentees or irregular attenders.[7] Government peers were more likely to be absent through employment on diplomatic missions abroad, though this could to some extent be countered by pairing and proxies, but not all the peers created by Grey and Melbourne were indefatigable in attending and voting. There was a steady diminution of support even among this group, until in 1841 less than half of them voted against the motion of no confidence in Melbourne's government.

PARTY MANAGEMENT: WHIGS AND LIBERALS

The division of the House of Lords into two political parties, save for a relatively few individuals, was reflected and assisted by the greater intensity of attempts at party management and the more overt recognition of party as a respectable form of organization. Whig management in the Lords was less effective under Melbourne than it had been during Grey's premiership. Grey had been a regular attender at the House, was a practised speaker in debate and master of the government's business in the House. Party management under his leadership was efficient. He continued the practice of previous Prime Ministers of giving a dinner to his leading friends in the House on the eve of the session, to hear the King's Speech and discuss the government's plans. Attendance implied a commitment to support, so that invitations were restricted to those who were considered reliable, though the Whigs were less selective than their opponents who had larger numbers to choose from. Grey's chief whip in the Lords, the duke of Richmond, was efficient and thorough. Circular letters were sent out to request the attendance of supporters before the opening of the session, and again before important debates, and proxies were solicited from peers who were unable or unlikely to attend. Grey wrote to Lord Stafford on 9 July 1833 asking him to send his proxy for a debate in which the issue was doubtful, and enclosed a form for signature. He also asked if the duke of Sutherland had left a blank proxy, which he would like to have.[8] Pairs were also arranged between the respective party whips to minimize the effects of absence.

Whig management in the House after 1834, however, was clearly not very effective. Melbourne had been an efficient Home Secretary under Grey, but as Prime Minister his freedom from specific departmental responsibilities brought out his natural indolence. Campbell remarked that the Whigs in the later 1830s lacked an efficient leader to take care of government bills:

> Lord Melbourne would give himself no trouble about them. They were
> left to Duncannon [the chief whip] who, though a man of excellent
> good sense, was wholly incompetent to enter the lists with Lyndhurst,
> and contented himself generally with reading the title of the Bill,
> moving that it be read a second time, and when it was opposed saying:
> 'Well, my Lords, if your Lordships object to the Bill, it would be vain
> for me to press it, and therefore I withdraw it.' In this way several
> other unexceptional Bills . . . met their fate.[9]

In 1842, when the Whigs were back in opposition, Campbell noted that

> Lord Melbourne lounged down to the House generally about five
> o'clock, and remained till it rose, or it was time to go to dress for
> dinner; but he seemed to feel as if he had been sitting at Brooks's,
> and that he had nothing to talk or think of beyond the gossip of the
> day. He would not have taken the trouble to repress activity in any of
> his party, but he had no desire to see activity in any of them, and he
> would have made little objection to a general resolution that all Bills
> proposed during the session should pass – the House to adjourn till the
> day of prorogation.

The consequence was 'the extreme listlessness of our friends'.[10]

The same problem was noted by Hatherton, a newcomer, in 1835. He found not only that over half the 'available numbers' in the House were out of town, but there was a 'squeamishness that exists about asking peers to stay in town, and attend the committees. Who shall make such a request to such august persons as the Dukes of Devonshire and Sutherland?' Lord Stafford, who had taken the job of whipping in the peers, was 'a perfect old woman, totally devoid of the address and tact requisite for the task'. The Postmaster-General was normally expected to act as government chief whip in the Lords but, Hatherton reported, 'neither he nor anyone else would now undertake it. Accordingly, the state in which things are even in our own party in the House of Lords is enough to break one's heart.'[11] Stafford was succeeded by Duncannon, who had been chief whip in the Commons before he was called up to the Lords in 1834,[12] and later Falkland. Both were less effective than their rivals on the other side. Nor did

Melbourne give the attention to his followers that Wellington did or Grey had done. Falkland's task was eased by the cooperative attitude of the chief Tory whip Lord Redesdale, who, Falkland told Hobhouse, 'had agreed with him to act upon honour, as it was called – that is, not to attempt any surprises or tricks . . . This, Lord Falkland told me, made his work somewhat less troublesome than it would otherwise have been; but it was still disagreeable enough.'[13]

Nevertheless, the general impression is one of laxity, not only due to Melbourne's natural disinclination to be otherwise, but also because the great Whig peers did not take naturally to party discipline and often preferred the rival attractions of their country houses and the exercise of their local leadership in the counties. Trollope's Duke of Omnium was a typical portrait:[14]

> He was a whig – a huge mountain of a colossal whig – all the world knew that. No opponent would have dreamed of tampering with his whiggery, nor would any brother whig have dreamed of doubting it. But he was a whig who gave very little practical support to any set of men, and very little practical opposition to any other set. He was above troubling himself with such sublunar matters. At election time he supported, and always carried, whig candidates; and in return he had been appointed Lord Lieutenant of the county by one whig minister, and had received the Garter from another. But these things were matters of course to a Duke of Omnium. He was born to be a Lord Lieutenant and a Knight of the Garter.

Duncannon, who succeeded to the earldom of Bessborough in 1844, resumed the office of chief whip on the Liberal side, serving until 1846. His son, the 5th earl, took up his father's duties as well as his title, and from at least 1848 managed the party in the Lords. He held the office of Master of the Buckhounds while his party was in office until 1866, and was subsequently Lord Steward of the Household in 1866 and between 1868 and 1874. After 1848 the government chief whip normally held an office in the Royal Household, as the earlier practice of combining the post with that of Postmaster-General was abandoned. Bessborough's counterpart on the Conservative side after 1852, Lord Colville, held the offices of Chief Equerry and Clerk Marshal in 1852 and 1858–9, and Master of the Buckhounds in 1866–8. His successor Lord Skelmersdale was Captain of the Yeomen of the Guard 1874–80. The tendency noted by D.C. Large for Household appointments to become political posts at the disposition of party leaders in the late eighteenth and early nineteenth centuries had clearly become established practice by the middle of the nineteenth century, and it provided further confirmation of the extent to which the Prime Minister had replaced the monarch as the fount of patronage as well as of political power, reflecting and assisting the increasingly two-party complexion of both Houses.[15]

PARTY MANAGEMENT: THE CONSERVATIVES

If the Whig government of Melbourne after 1834 suffered frustration at the obstinacy of the Lords over such measures as the Irish Church Bill and the English and Irish Municipal Corporations Acts, their opponents in the Lords also faced a dilemma. The Tories now found themselves, for the first time in twenty-five years, an opposition party. Accustomed to habitual support of the king's government they were now opponents of an essentially party government, which they could obstruct only at the risk of bringing it down without having the power to replace it, and of creating a dangerous antagonism from the electors of the Lower House.

The Conservative leadership was more inclined to impose party discipline. If, on the one hand, the existence of a permanent Tory majority might seem to suggest less need for organization to bring its weight to bear, on the other Wellington's anxiety to keep his troops in order and their greater tendency to disagreement made him keep a tighter rein on them. The lack of access to government patronage also removed an incentive to support and a means of discipline that were available to the Whigs, and made tighter party organization necessary.

The Tories in the early 1830s were not a united party. Wellington was never wholly a party man and was not happy in opposition. He believed that it was the duty of all political men to serve the Crown and the national interest, irrespective of party struggles for power. He was more concerned to see that power was exercised responsibly than to hold it himself. Nevertheless, his prestige, experience and commanding temper made him the only real choice as leader of the Conservative peers, even though there were those who disagreed with his attitude and tactics. Their efforts were directed, however, not at replacing him but at trying to make him follow the more active opposition which they favoured, to try to bring down the Whig ministries.

The Conservative peers in this period fall into three main groups: those who followed Wellington either from respect for him or because they agreed with his pragmatic approach; the 'Ultras' who had broken away on the Catholic question in 1829 and who continued to resist all reform; and for a time in 1831–2 the 'Waverers', a small group headed by Harrowby and Wharncliffe who wished to try to reach an agreed compromise on the Reform Bill with the Whigs in order to limit the damage, rather than fly in the face of public opinion by rejecting it. The last group was in fact ineffective. Greville described them as 'a patched-up, miscellaneous concern at best, of men who were half-reasoned, half frightened over, who could not bear separating from the Duke, [and] long to return to him'.[16] In May 1832 they returned to the main body of opposition after the failure of negotiations with Grey.

The Ultras, however, remained a thorn in Wellington's side. They were led by the duke of Cumberland, whose unrelenting opposition to every kind of reform made him feared and hated by all liberals. Slightly less extreme in their Tory views were the duke of Buckingham and the marquess of Londonderry, who wanted Wellington to be more vigorous in his opposition to the government's measures after 1832. In January 1831 Londonderry had suggested to Buckingham that they set up a separate group, independent of Wellington and Peel, consisting of 'men of the description both of ultra and moderate Toryism', in the somewhat naive hope that Grey would react against Radical pressure for the Reform Act and negotiate for a moderate coalition of the centre.[17] After 1832 they cooperated with Cumberland in the attempt to promote more active opposition, trying to force Wellington's hand by demanding party meetings to determine policy and tactics in the Lords. Wellington disliked such meetings as much as he disliked 'formed opposition'. He wrote in January 1833:[18]

> I have never relished . . . the seeking opportunities to carp at and
> oppose the measures of Government; the whole course of my life
> has been different. I dislike such conduct at present more than I did
> heretofore . . . . [I] consider Lord Grey's Government as the last
> prop of the monarchy, however bad it is and however unworthy of
> confidence . . . . It will not be wise for us to endeavour to break down
> Lord Grey without knowing what is to follow him . . . . The course
> then which I would recommend on the whole is one of attentive
> observation rather than of action . . . that we should not oppose
> and bring an opposition to the test of division excepting in a case of
> paramount importance essential to the best interests of the country.

He wrote in the same sense in March 1833:

> I cannot wish to remove from office men who profess at least to have
> good intentions in order to place the power in the hands of those who
> have not the grace even to make such professions . . . . I wish therefore,
> as far at least as I am personally concerned, to afford no ground for the
> charge of faction.

Recognizing that the government was backed by a strong majority in the Commons and by the weight of public opinion in the constituencies, Wellington realized that if the Lords attempted to block their measures, it would be the Lords who would suffer in the end. The waiting game was the only one he was prepared to play. 'This quarrel [between the two Houses] will occur in its time', he wrote to Londonderry, 'and the House of Lords will probably be overwhelmed; but it shall not be attributed to me.'[19]

Wellington therefore tried to impose his strategy on the Conservatives in the Lords and to avoid party meetings which might force him to modify it. The duke of Cumberland wrote in December 1832 to complain of 'the want of concert and communication' in the party, and to urge that meetings were '*gratifying* to the less conspicuous members of a party' since 'The very idea, even, of being *supposed* to be consulted often seals and confirms the bond of union.' Wellington's view as expressed again in January 1834 was that he was ready to consult those who wished to discuss the parliamentary course of the party, but

> I must observe . . . that I never knew that any benefit resulted from such consultations excepting possibly the gratification of the persons called to participate in them. They occasion great loss of time, they seldom lead to any decision, never to a wise or discreet one, and they expose the party to ridicule on account of what passes in discussion.

To Lord Roden he complained that

> People are telling me every day that noblemen and gentlemen like to be consulted, and to know the opinion of each other. I thought that I could not adopt a better mode of consulting them than to invite to dine with me on the day preceeding the meeting of Parliament every nobleman in the habit of speaking in the House of Lords or whose opinion was likely to have weight with others. I have invited as many as fifty. From some I am sorry to say that I have not received very civil answers. Many have not answered at all, some have excused themselves for not attending, very few have said that they will attend. I confess that I should find it difficult to give a reason for having sent these invitations. If a meeting was desirable, those who wish it might have met at a club or at the house of any other noble lord.[20]

When a meeting was held at Apsley House in the summer of 1833, Londonderry, wrote Lady Salisbury, 'went so far as to say that it was useless to summon him and his friends when the line of conduct was already determined upon', whereupon Wellington 'turned red with indignation' and retorted that 'he made no decision for others and assumed no power to himself, that he was there, happy to give his opinion to those noble lords who did him the honor to ask it.'

Wellington particularly resented the practice, adopted by the

Ultras at this time, of holding their own separate meetings at Holdernesse House before the eve-of-session meeting of Conservative peers at Apsley House, so that they came as delegates rather than as individuals. Rosslyn, Wellington's chief whip in the Lords, reported to Mrs Arbuthnot that the duke was so incensed by the activities of the Ultras' 'mutinous little troop' that he had told Buckingham that he would no longer act as head of the party and, if sent for by the king, 'he must as an honest man tell H. Majy that he had not the confidence and support of those peers in the House of Lords, nor could he trust them'. 'The party appears for the present to be broken up', Rosslyn concluded. 'The Duke of Cumberland is at the bottom of all this', wrote Lady Salisbury, '. . . Lord Londonderry and the Duke of Buckingham are the most unreasonable.'[21] Wellington had told the bishop of Exeter, another member of the Ultra group, that he could no longer consider himself 'as the leader of a party who put no confidence in him and who held meetings independent of him to decide upon their own course.' In June 1834 Wellington lost his temper with Londonderry and Buckingham when Londonderry forwarded one of Buckingham's letters to him. If he was to carry on warfare with Buckingham, Wellington exploded, he should at least write legibly – he could hardly read a word. 'To talk of my being leader of a party or anything but the slave of a party, or in other words the person whom any other may *bore* with his letters or his visits upon publick subjects when he pleases is just what I call *stuff.* I beg therefore to have no more of the Duke's letters.'[22]

Despite his troubles with Cumberland and the Ultras, however, Wellington maintained his authority and influence over the Conservative peers in general and, together with Peel, succeeded in keeping the Lords within reasonable bounds. The interlude of Peel's 'Hundred Days' administration in 1834–5 helped to strengthen Wellington's grip on his fellow peers and after the relaxation of tensions between the two Houses following the sessions of 1835–6 the Conservative peers on the whole fell into line. Wellington was helped until 1837 by Rosslyn, whose death in January was, Wellington wrote, 'a terrible loss, particularly to me.' He feared that no one else would undertake the duty of whip and that 'I shall have to perform it myself, as well as everything else that nobody chooses to do.' Redesdale, however, stepped into the breach and quickly became an efficient and hardworking servant of the party. He mastered all the details of procedure of the House and attended debates and committees with remarkable assiduity. He never married and so had no family to distract him from his political activities. He resigned as whip in 1846 because of the repeal of the Corn Laws and succeeded Shaftesbury as Chairman of Committees in 1851, holding the post until 1886. 'No man was more looked up to', wrote the later Lord Redesdale in 1915, 'and I don't believe he had an enemy in the world.'[23]

Wellington and Redesdale formed an effective partnership in managing the Conservative peers through the remainder of Melbourne's, and then Peel's, administration, though in 1842 Campbell thought Wellington aged and ineffective and the government front bench 'exceedingly feeble'. The duke regularly sent out circulars to the most reliable and active of his followers, gave dinners before the start of each session, known as 'speech dinners', and, as the channel to office and patronage when his party came into office in 1834 and 1841, maintained a strong hold over the politically active. He also chose the peers to move and second the address at the start of the session and invited them to the 'speech dinner'. Redesdale looked after all the necessary business of whipping, collecting proxies, soliciting attendance at important debates and divisions and keeping a close eye on his troops. He also managed efficiently the organization for electing Scottish and Irish representative peers. The party whips had a small office and salaried staff set up in 1831 in Charles Street, but closed down in 1832 and later reopened in Duke Street and known as 'the Duke Street establishment'.[24]

Supporters were assessed according to the regularity of their attendance, the degree or quality of their support and the importance of the business. There were four types of letter: Wellington's own pre-session letters (most of which were in fact written by his private secretary Algernon Greville, who could imitate his handwriting exactly); anonymous circulars sent round on occasions during the session when attendance was needed; circulars or notes sent over the name of a whip; and letters to individual peers, often those who were not on the normal circulation list, by close friends or relatives at the request of Wellington or of a whip. Bishops were not normally sent the first class of letter, but might receive the anonymous circulars if they requested their names to be on the list. Scots peers were handled by their own separate manager, the duke of Buccleuch until 1838 and then Lord Aberdeen. Peers who were sent letters were selected on the basis of their regular active support, or because they asked to receive them, or sent proxies to one of the party leaders, were attached to a leading Conservative peer, or were members of the Carlton Club. To avoid giving offence, informal enquiries were made before any new or less well-known peer was put on the address list. The Duke Street office was supported by regular subscriptions of £20 from the more active peers; over £700 was collected for the purpose in 1836, for example. Wellington preferred to leave these financial details to others – he 'dislikes the duty of tax-gatherer most exceedingly', Rosslyn wrote in 1833 – but he recognized their essential role in providing the means for party management.[25]

Besides their system of party management in the House of Lords, the Conservatives also used the Carlton Club, set up in early 1832, as an important party centre. Three of the four trustees of the club and twelve of the first twenty-nine committee members were peers. The membership numbered 700, and was later increased to 950, of whom between 18 per cent and 14 per cent were peers in the period 1836–41. The club moved to new quarters in 1835 and provided regular weekly dinners for leading Tories in both Houses, and for a time informal suppers on four evenings a week after debates in the Commons. It also acted as a clearing house for electoral management in the constituencies, particularly in helping to find prospective candidates. Members paid an entrance fee of 10 guineas and an annual subscription of the same amount.[26]

The organization and management of parties in the Lords during the remainder of this period reflected the increasingly firm establishment of the nineteenth-century party system. 'Parties in Parliament in England', wrote Wellington in 1837, 'are now placed as two opposing armies . . . There is seldom any defection in each case.'[27] Analysis of voting in the Lords from 1860 to 1886, for example, has shown that on fifteen major issues, 737 peers voted, of whom 306 peers showed a strong Conservative preference, against 188 Whig/Liberal, and only 26 behaved completely independently of party.[28] Although the Whigs, or Liberals as they became in the 1840s and 1850s, continued to suffer from their numerical inferiority in the Lords, Whig or Whig-Peelite governments were able to survive and to pass most of their measures because of the corresponding weakness of the Tories in the Commons, following the split of 1846, and the continuing reluctance of the Lords to create a constitutional conflict between the two Houses. Peel's difficulties with the Tory peers in 1845–6 were mitigated by Whig support for the Maynooth grant and the repeal of the Corn Laws, and his Whig successors similarly benefited from the alliance of Whig and Peelite peers for the next few years. The greater attention paid to the organization of Whig proxies during Russell's administration of 1846–52 also helped on a number of occasions to stave off government defeats in the Lords. In 1849 the Navigation Bill was carried by 105+68 proxies against 119+44, and Brougham's two hostile motions, on foreign policy and on the

Canada Rebellion Losses Bill, were defeated by 45+63 to 51+45, and 46+53 against 54+42 respectively.[29] In general, however, the period from 1846 to 1868 was one of general consensus among the governing elite represented in the Upper House.

LEADERSHIP: THE LIBERALS

It was during this period that the office of Leader of the House developed. The recognized 'leader' on the government benches was the Prime Minister himself when he was a peer – as, indeed, was commonly the case between 1812 and 1846, with the sole exceptions of the ministries of Canning and Peel. Canning promoted Robinson to the peerage as Lord Goderich with the purpose of making him leader in the Lords in 1827. After 1846, when Lord John Russell was Prime Minister in the Commons, the Whigs in the Lords looked for leadership in the House to the 3rd marquess of Lansdowne, who held the post of Lord President of the Council and who had succeeded Melbourne as leader of the opposition Whigs in 1842, though Campbell noted that out of delicacy he then refused to be designated or to act as leader in the Lords and did not even give the usual eve-of-session dinner, which was usually held at Brooks's Club.[30] In 1848, however, Campbell gave his wholehearted approval to Lansdowne, who performed 'admirably' as leader and 'not only manages the government business with admirable propriety, but he occasionally makes the most excellent speeches'.[31] Lansdowne has been called 'the first recognizable modern leader for the government in the Lords . . . carrying the main burden of speaking there, over-shadowing both his other colleagues and Lord Chancellor Cottenham in a manner virtually unprecedented.'[32] He was a classic example of the Whig aristocrat; wealthy, well-endowed with territorial influence, hospitable, and moderate and conciliatory in his political views. He used his considerable influence to keep the Whigs together and to maintain the power of the aristocracy against the threat of radical democracy. As such his views reflected those of many leading peers in both parties and gained him the respect of both sides. His affable and rather lethargic air, recalling Melbourne, masked, however, 'greater energy and discretion in managing the peers', as Campbell noted, and his willingness to accept such necessary measures as the repeal of the Corn Laws in the interest of maintaining respect for the aristocracy commended him to moderates on both sides.[33]

He was succeeded in 1855 by Granville. When Palmerston formed his administration in February, he asked Granville to be Lord President of the Council and to assist Lansdowne who would continue to be 'the organ of the Government in the House of Lords'. This, however, was a misunderstanding on the premier's part. Granville wrote a tactful letter to Lansdowne (who had declined Cabinet office), assuring him that

> When you are in the Cabinet, it is of course impossible that you should not be the first person in the assembly in which you sit, but I never imagined that you would consider yourself bound to be in the House at five o'clock and sit on to the close of the debate excepting on very important occasions, nor that you should take any trouble in ascertaining from different departments what was to be said in answer to insignificant questions.

He offered to be Lansdowne's 'temporary *locum tenens*' and added:

> I apprehend it will not be necessary to make any distinct statement to the House as to whether you lead it or not. The House will look for your guidance on all important occasions, and will think it perfectly natural that you should throw upon your younger colleagues all the routine work.

Lansdowne, however, had told Palmerston that he did not wish to take his former office of Lord President and he said that he believed it necessary for the leader of the House to be in office. All that he had undertaken was that 'I should not object on some particular occasions to represent the Government . . . reserving it to myself to judge of the necessity or expediency when the case arose.'

In the event, Granville was designated as Leader of the House, and except for the period of Russell's premiership in the Lords, he led the Liberals both in government and opposition until his death in 1891.[34] He offered to give up the post in 1861 when Russell was made a peer, since the latter was senior to him, being an ex-Prime Minister, but Russell did not press his claim, having been told by Palmerston that 'he presumed he did not mean to interfere with my position in the Lords. . . . Pam considered that it was desirable for the Government that no change should be made, and advised me personally to continue.'[35] He gave up the leadership during Russell's premiership in 1865 but resumed the post in 1868 under Gladstone.

Granville led the Liberal peers with quiet effectiveness for many years. He was not a dashing orator, in contrast to his rival the earl of Derby, 'the Rupert of debate' even in the Lords, but he was calm, conciliatory, good humoured and witty. He was a master of the telling phrase at the end of a speech which made his longer speeches memorable, and he understood his fellow peers. He wrote that he believed that what the House most dreaded was boredom, and that

> in addressing that fastidious assembly it was necessary to understand their little idiosyncracies, and to remember that they preferred new illustrations of an old story to a constant repetition of the old story itself.

He was wary, however, of anecdotes, for it was difficult to foretell what effect 'any statement might have had upon twenty undemonstrative peers'. He enjoyed speaking in the House, and they responded to him. He occasionally found the role burdensome, writing to Lord Canning in 1856 that he had had to speak on 'a quantity of little questions' on which he was not always expert, and that 'both for myself and the House and my colleagues a greater division of labour would be better'.[36] He endeared himself to the House in 1855 in reply to an opposition attack on the government as made up of a 'family party' of close Whig relatives:

> I am obliged to admit that some of those who went before me had such quivers full of daughters who did not die old maids, that I have relatives upon this side of the House, relations upon the cross benches, relations upon the opposite side of the House, and actually had the unparalleled misfortune to have no fewer than three cousins in the Protectionist Administration of my noble friend opposite.

This sally, records the editor of his memoirs, 'took the fancy of the audience' and the motion of censure was defeated.[37] He was also a strict disciplinarian and did not hesitate to remind his friend the marquess of Ailesbury, one of the leading Household peers, 'that I had accepted the lead on the express condition that members of the Household should constantly attend the House of Lords, unless when in attendance on the Queen, in the same way as the members of the Government.'[38]

After 1868 many Liberal peers became alarmed by Gladstone's apparent radicalism and Granville's period of office became 'a long struggle to keep together on the red benches a party worthy of the name in . . . numbers and reputation'.[39] In the debates on the Irish Church Bill in 1869 'the dry bones of many ancient Whig peers, who in their day had been men of renown, again stirred on the battlefield and executed more than one disastrous attack on the flank of their own party'.[40] Granville's difficulties were not eased by the abolition of proxies in 1868, and in the Lords he was faced by 'a huge array of hostile lay peers' and conservative bishops in dealing with Gladstone's extensive legislative programme affecting elementary education, the universities, Ireland, army reform, the ballot and reform of the judicial system. In the summer of 1869 he urged Gladstone to ask for 'a considerable creation of Liberal peers' and when the queen showed unwillingness to agree he wrote to her to point out that the government's position in the Lords was 'intolerable'; the opposition had a majority which was 'absolute in all ordinary matters of legislation, on which the credit and utility of a Government so much depend. It does not scruple to exercise that power, a course ultimately sure to create great dissatisfaction.' He estimated a Conservative majority of between 60 and 70 besides bishops and several Liberal peers who voted oftener for the opposition than the government. The twelve peerages Gladstone had asked for would at least provide some moral support. The queen eventually gave way, but the Liberals' difficulties were not solved: in 1884 the Conservative majority refused to pass the third Reform Act until the Redistribution Bill was agreed, on the grounds that reform of the franchise alone would be to the electoral disadvantage of their party. In face of these difficulties Granville could only strive to conciliate the majority. Lord Selborne summed up his achievement in 1891:

> in the face of adverse majorities he invariably made it an object of the deepest personal concern to keep the House in harmony with the other House of Parliament, and to preserve for it the respect and esteem of the public.[41]

LEADERSHIP: THE CONSERVATIVES

The Conservatives were led after the split of 1846 by Derby, who was one of the most accomplished parliamentary orators of the century, and who, though a sufferer from gout and intermittent in his enthusiasm for politics, was also more insistent on a degree of party discipline among the Lords. Granville commented in 1867 that attendances had been noticeably more numerous during the current year, 'partly owing to the pressure which it was understood he [Derby] had put upon all those connected with his Government'. Derby's oratory was greatly admired. He was, as the editor of Granville's correspondence remarked, 'one of the acknowledged masters of English eloquence and the despot of the House of Lords, who held proxies just as he owned racehorses. . . . A witty antagonist once said that he had "Newmarketised" the House, and the phrase lived.'[42] He was also believed to have complete control of the election of Scottish and Irish representative peers.

Yet despite these advantages, Derby was less successful in commanding the majority in the Lords than Wellington had been in the days of Grey and Melbourne. Campbell paid tribute to Derby's 'admirable powers as a debater' and noted that 'the old Tory aristocracy are much inclined to gather round him', but he observed that 'he is not regarded as a safe man', and was 'neither a great statesman nor the discreet leader of a party. Although he inspirits his followers, he does not fill them with confidence.'[43] Derby (or Lord Stanley as he was until 1851) was the acknowledged leader of the Protectionist peers after 1846, but the defection of the large number of Peelites seriously weakened his forces, and the Conservative majority which had hampered the Grey and Melbourne governments before 1841 no longer existed. Granville remarked that in 1852 'a goodly retinue' followed Aberdeen in joining the Liberal peers, and in 1856 that this so 'materially weakened the Opposition' that the Liberal government generally possessed 'the command of the House'.[44]

Derby in fact had some successes. His motion of censure on the government's foreign and domestic policies in the debate on the address in 1849 failed by only two votes, and when he renewed the attack on the repeal of the Navigation Laws both sides exerted themselves in what Greville declared was 'the greatest whip-up . . . that ever was known'. Russell called on the queen, Prince Albert and even Wellington for support.[45] The House was fuller of peers, and of peeresses in the gallery, than for many years. The government was saved only by proxy votes: 106+68 against 119+44, a majority of eleven. Derby's major success was in 1850, when the Lords passed his motion of censure on Palmerston's policy in the Don Pacifico Affair by a majority of thirty-seven.[46] In general, however, the Conservative opposition failed to control the Lords between 1846 and 1867. Derby's biographer counted 180 divisions during those years in which Derby himself voted, in 24 of which he supported government measures, and lost sixty-four: the only other important divisions which the opposition won under his leadership occurred on the Paper Duties Bill in 1860 and the motion of censure in 1864. The Peelites and neutrals, and often even the archbishops and bishops, would not support him regularly in opposition: in the 180 divisions referred to, the majority of the latter supported Derby thirty-two times but voted on the other side in seventy-one.[47] On the Oxford University Bill in 1854 Derby was unable to win their unanimous support for the maintenance of the Thirty-nine Articles oath. Greville remarked that

Aberdeen's government, a coalition of Peelites and Liberals, seemed to be stronger in the Lords than in the Commons, though he added that this depended on circumstances.[48]

Derby's influence over the Lords was strongest when he stood forward as the champion of their privileges, traditions and constitutional rights. His speeches against the admission of life peers to the House in the Wensleydale case were attentively heard by full benches and by large numbers of spectators in the galleries. On this occasion his reference to 'having myself the honour of being the fourteenth representative in this House of an hereditary earldom, which now for 400 years has, in hereditary succession, sent representatives here' was particularly telling.[49] He not only expressed the fear that life peerages would threaten the independence of the Lords and increase the prerogative of the Crown, but also the concern for the status of the peerage if men otherwise not qualified for admission should be brought in for the specious purpose of making it more widely representative. He was particularly scathing about the rumoured wish of Prince Albert to honour men of literary, scientific and other intellectual eminence. Granville remarked in his journal that Derby 'does not appear to have suggested that hereditary peers should be prohibited from gaining distinction by translations from Greek and Latin poets' (he had himself published a translation of Homer): perhaps it was to be 'assumed that the difficulties which he anticipated were of the character attributed to the Prime Minister in a modern play, when he suggests that his private secretary should attempt to discover some person the appearance of whose name in a Birthday Honours List would at least not excite general disapprobation'.

Derby's prejudices were, however, those of many of his fellows. Granville noted that in 1869 Russell's Bill for Life Peerages 'was thrown out on the third reading by one of those ugly rushes of the rank and file of the Tory peers which in the Upper House occasionally prove stronger than even a combination of the experienced leaders on the two front benches'. Perhaps Derby's greatest success was in persuading the Lords to accept his own government's Reform Bill in 1867. He soon afterwards retired from the premiership and the leadership of the House owing to his increasing gout.[50] He died in 1869.

Disraeli succeeded to the premiership, and asked Lord Malmesbury, the Lord Privy Seal, to take over as leader of the House of Lords, but after the defeat of the government in the general election a few months later he gave up the post in favour of Lord Cairns, a recently ennobled legal peer. The appointment was approved by Derby and confirmed at a dinner given by Malmesbury to twenty-three leading Conservative peers on the eve of the session in February 1869.[51]

Cairns was an Ulsterman who had risen to prominence as a barrister of distinction, became MP for Belfast in 1852 and served in Derby's administrations as Solicitor-General in 1858–9 and Attorney General in 1866. He was then made a Lord Justice of Appeal in Chancery and given a peerage. He had refused a peerage in 1866 on the grounds that he lacked the income to support it, having given up an enormous and lucrative practice at the bar to become a judge, but in 1867 a relative 'came to his assistance'. His rapid rise to high office was, one authority remarked, such 'as . . . has never been before witnessed, such proof of confidence is almost unparalleled'.[52] He made a big impression as a speaker in both Houses. Disraeli described his speech on the Reform Bill in 1859 as one of the greatest ever delivered in Parliament. In supporting Disraeli's bill in 1867 he made twenty-four speeches. His speech on Gladstone's Irish Church Suspensory Bill in 1868 was printed and widely circulated. He was a redoubtable champion of the Protestant Church in Ireland, and his resistance to disestablishment was described as 'vigorous and tenacious'.[53] He was instrumental in persuading the Lords to insist on their amendments to Gladstone's Bill in 1869, but when a constitutional crisis with the Commons seemed imminent he took it on himself to arrange the compromise with Granville that enabled it to pass with some changes.

All these activities marked Cairns out as a natural leader for the Conservative peers, though he was reluctant at first to assume the post for more than one session and stood aside in 1870 for Salisbury, whose more provocative style of speaking made a stronger public impression. Salisbury, however, refused to serve under Disraeli, and the duke of Richmond was elected leader, proposed and seconded by Disraeli and Salisbury as a compromise candidate. Richmond, however, was overshadowed in the debates by Salisbury and though he remained nominal leader until 1876 Cairns in effect resumed the post later in 1870. In 1874 Disraeli appointed Cairns Lord Chancellor and he presided over the House until the end of the ministry in 1880, though Disraeli's arrival in the Lords in 1876 meant that he took over the Conservative leadership. After Disraeli's death in 1881 many Conservative peers expressed a preference for Cairns to resume the office, but ill health obliged him virtually to retire and Salisbury succeeded to the post.

Cairns's greatest achievements were his contribution to the passage of Disraeli's Reform Bill in 1867, the compromise over disestablishment in 1869 and the passage of the legal reforms of the period, including the Supreme Judicature Act and the Married Women's Property Act in 1882. He was respected for his professional brilliance and for his calm and moderate – some said 'cold and unimpassioned' – but effective speaking in the Lords and his ability as leader of the Conservative peers at a time when the mounting pace of reform was arousing strong feelings for the future of the House in an age of social and political change.

REFERENCES

1. E.A. Smith, *Lord Grey, 1764–1845*, (Oxford, 1990) *passim*.
2. D. Large, 'The decline of the "party of the Crown" and the rise of parties in the House of Lords, 1783–1837', *English Historical Review* (1963), LXXVIII, 669–95.
3. C.C.F. Greville, *Journal of the Reign of Queen Victoria, 1837–52* ed. H. Reeve (1885), I. p. 129. *The Journal of Mrs Arbuthnot 1820–1832* ed. F. Bamford and the Duke of Wellington (1950), 5 May 1827, II, 115; C.C.F. Greville, *Journal of the Reigns of George IV and William IV*, ed. H. Reeve (1874), III, p. 16.
4. *Ibid.*, p. 129.
5. D. Southgate, *The Passing of the Whigs, 1832–1886* (1962), Appendix, Table B.
6. Figures from R.S. Fraser, 'The House of Lords in the first Parliament of Queen Victoria, 1837–41', unpublished PhD. thesis (Cornell University, 1967) pp. 780–2, p. 10.
7. Diary, 20 July 1835.
8. Sutherland MSS, Staffordshire Record Office 593/P/22/1/4.
9. *Life of John, Lord Campbell*, ed. Mrs M.S. Hardcastle (1881), II, p. 86.
10. *Ibid.*, pp. 163–4.
11. Hatherton Diary, 15 and 20 July 1835.
12. 'He was a bustling, zealous partisan & a very good whipper-in' in the Commons, according to Greville, 17 July 1834: *Journal* III, p. 109.
13. J.C. Hobhouse, 1st Baron Broughton, *Recollections of a Long Life* ed. Lady Dorchester V. (1911), pp. 219–20.
14. A. Trollope, *Framley Parsonage*: *Cornhill Magazine* (1860), I, 307–8.
15. Large, 'The decline of the "party of the Crown"'; on whips in the House of Lords see House of Lords Record Office Memorandum 31, 'Leaders and Whips in the House of Lords, 1783–1964' (1964).
16. 15 April 1832: *Journal* II, pp. 289.
17. *Ibid*, 25 Jan 1831; I, pp. 196–8.
18. To Aberdeen: *The Prime Minister's Papers: Wellington, Political Correspondence*, ed. J. Brooke and J. Gundy (1975), I, pp. 82–3.
19. To Roden: *ibid.*, pp. 120–1; to Londonderry, 17 June 1834: *ibid.*, pp. 561–2.
20. Cumberland to Wellington 3 Dec. 1832, *Despatches, Correspondence and Memoranda of Field Marshall Arthur, Duke of Wellington, K.G. 1819–32*,

ed. by his son VIII (1850), p. 506, and Wellington to Cumberland, 1 Jan. 1834, *Prime Minister's Papers*, I, pp. 406–7; to Roden, 17 Jan. 1834, *ibid.*, pp. 422–3.

21. *Ibid.*, pp. 268–9 (26 July 1833): Rosslyn to Mrs Arbuthnot, 24, 27 July, 5 Aug. 1833, *Correspondence of Charles Arbuthnot*, ed. A. Aspinall, Camden 3rd ser. LXV (1941), pp. 172–4.

22. *Prime Minister's Papers*, I, p. 569, 19 June 1834.

23. Wellington to Lady Burghersh, 29 Jan. 1837: *Correspondence of Lady Burghersh with the Duke of Wellington*, ed. Lady Rose Weigall (1903), p. 88: *Memories by Lord Redesdale* (1915), I. p. 23. Redesdale attended 418 out of 438 sittings of the Lords in the period 1837–41 (Fraser, 'The House of Lords', p. 178).

24. Ellenborough Diary, 16 June 1831 in A. Aspinall (ed.), *Three Early-Nineteenth Century Diaries* (1952), p. 93.

25. The Duke Street office was staffed by two secretaries, each at £250 *p.a.*, and an assistant at £100 *p.a.* Incidental expenses in 1836 amounted to £130. Individuals subscribed £20 *p.a.*: *Correspondence of Charles Arbuthnot*, p. 175; Large, 'The decline of the "party of the Crown"', 693. For examples of circular letters see *Memoirs of the Courts and Cabinets of the Reigns of William IV and Victoria*, ed. Duke of Buckingham and Chandos (1861), I, p. 290, and *Prime Minister's Papers*, II, pp. 409, 434–5. Fraser, 'The House of Lords' pp. 108–205. For examples before 1830, *A Political Diary (1828–30), by Edward Law, Lord Ellenborough*, ed. Lord Silchester (1881), I, pp. 12, 347, 398–9.

26. Sir Charles Petrie, *The Carlton Club* (1955); Aspinall, *Three Diaries*, pp. xiv–vi, lii–lviii; N. Gash, *Politics in the Age of Peel* (1953), pp. 397–401.

27. To Newcastle, 30 Oct. 1837: Newcastle MSS, Nottingham University Library, NeC 5325.

28. P.B. Zaring, 'In Defense of the Past: The House of Lords, 1860–86', unpublished Ph.D. thesis (Yale University, 1966), pp. 265–70.

29. See Chapter 2, p. 43. Lansdowne's major defeat occurred in the 'Don Pacifico' debate, 17 June 1850 when the opposition won 169 to 132, despite the efforts of Lady Palmerston, who 'has been in the House all night and has been very active' (Hardcastle, *Life of . . . Campbell*, II, p. 280).

30. *Ibid.*, pp. 173–4.

31. *Ibid.*, pp. 241–2, 255.

32. Large, 'The decline of the "party of the Crown"', 694.

33. Southgate, *Passing of the Whigs*, pp. 214–5; Hardcastle, *Campbell*, II, p. 242.

34. Lord Edmond Fitzmaurice, *Life of . . . second Earl Granville,* (1905), I, pp. 95–6. He wrote in 1858 that he had 'assumed the post of leader of Opposition' when Derby replaced Palmerston 'after much consultation with Clarendon, Lord Landsdowne, and Pam'.

35. To Canning, 17 July 1861: *ibid.*, pp. 399–400.

36. *Ibid.*, p. 165.

37. *Ibid.*, pp. 110–12, Hansard, CXXXVIII, 506.

38. Fitzmaurice, *Granville*, I, pp. 233–41.

39. *Ibid.*, p. 495.

40. *Ibid.*, II, pp. 10–11.

41. *Ibid.*, 503. Hansard, CCCLII, 468.
42. Fitzmaurice, *Granville*, I, p. 233. One writer has remarked that in opposition he occasionally 'gave the Lords a gallop': J.J. Bagley, *The Earls of Derby, 1485–1985* (1985), pp. 174–90; Hansard, CLXXXVIII, 138.
43. Hardcastle, *Campbell*, II, pp. 246–55.
44. Fitzmaurice, *Granville*, I, pp. 290–3, 495.
45. Greville, *Journal . . . Victoria*, 11 May 1849, III, p. 286; W.D. Jones, *Lord Derby and Victorian Conservatism* (Oxford, 1956), p. 136; Hardcastle, *Campbell*, II, p. 252.
46. *Ibid.*, p. 142; Hansard, CXI, 1293–332. The government countered with a motion of confidence from the Commons, passed by a triumphant majority after Palmerston's 'Civis Romanus Sum' speech.
47. In 35 divisions the bishops voted with Derby on questions involving the Church, but their votes were not given in support of the Conservative party: Jones, *Derby*, pp. 206–7.
48. Greville, *Journal . . . Victoria*, I, p. 169.
49. Hansard, CXL, 364–74.
50. Fitzmaurice, *Granville*, I, pp. 157–61.
51. Lord Malmesbury, *Memoirs of an Ex-Minister*, I (1854), pp. 388–90.
52. G.E.C. *The Complete Peerage*; (1910–59) *DNB*.
53. *Ibid.*

CHAPTER SIX
The Lords and the Commons

INFLUENCE AND COOPERATION

The eighteenth-century constitution was often praised by contemporaries on the ground that it was a perfectly balanced system in which a royal executive and a parliamentary legislature checked each other's power. The Crown had the power of dissolution against a House of Commons which overstepped its bounds, and George III used that power in 1784 to prevent the Commons from supplanting his constitutional control of the executive. The Commons in turn had the right to control the policies of the executive by the refusal of supplies, though Fox's attempt to exert this power in 1784 in order to change the composition of the ministry was considered too extreme a step in those circumstances. The Crown also had a check on the power of the House of Lords through the prerogative of making peers, which could be used to block any excessive obstruction by the Lords of the policies of the government as embodied in legislation. It was therefore seen as necessary for the two branches of the legislature to act in harmony. It was also maintained that the political system should reflect the predominance of landed property in society. The mechanism for ensuring that both these requirements were met was the influence of the House of Lords over the Commons. The number of MPs who were closely related to and/or returned by the patronal influence of peers was substantial, and it increased as the century went on. In this way the possibility of conflict between the two Houses was minimized, and the potentially supreme authority of the Commons as the people's representatives was kept in check. It also meant that the supremacy of landed property was upheld against the growth of other interests in the Lower House.[1] As time went on, however, the progress of economic and social change created increasing resentment against this aristocratic control. The parliamentary reform movements of the late eighteenth and early nineteenth centuries were at least as much directed against the overpowerful influence of the House of Lords as against the 'influence of the Crown' which was attacked by Dunning's resolution in 1780. By 1830, in fact, the influence of the Crown in the form of patronage controlled by the monarch had almost disappeared as a political force. The radicals and reformers of the time were well aware that the real obstacle to their objectives lay in the Upper Chamber. In the 1780s, Christopher Wyvill's County Association movement was rooted in the commonalty, the 'gentry, clergy and freeholders' who formed the body of the citizenry, and Wyvill tried to exclude the Yorkshire aristocracy from the movement. Indeed, the Yorkshire Association itself collapsed as a result of the split between Wyvill's followers and those of Lord Fitzwilliam, who was not only head of the old Rockingham Whig group in the county but who, with his fellow Whigs, represented the dominance of the aristocracy. Wyvill's support of Pitt in the 1784 elections was a natural consequence of this fact.[2]

In the 1790s, the reformers again identified aristocratic influence as the chief enemy to reform of the Commons. The Friends of the People calculated in 1792 that no less than 164 English MPs were returned by the direct nomination or powerful influence of 72 peers, while the reform propagandist T.H.B. Oldfield added that 30 of the Scots members were elected through the influence of Scottish peers. In 1816 he asserted that the numbers had risen to 249 MPs, elected by 114 members of the two peerages. Of the 100 Irish members added to the Commons by the Act of Union, 51 were said to owe their election to peerage influence, and in total, one third were sons of Irish peers. Thus, some 45 per cent of the Commons at the beginning of this period owed their seats in some degree to the patronage of peers. Croker calculated in 1827 that a mere 22 peers returned 150 MPs by '*direct nomination*', with another dozen returned by others. Five years later the total was estimated at 354, or 54 per cent of the Lower House returned by peers. Nor did the Reform Act entirely put an end to the practice: 44 peers retained sufficient electoral influence to control 59 seats, with significant influence in another 20 county seats, and Dod calculated that no less than 250 peers retained a degree of parliamentary influence in the twenty years after 1832. After 1868 there were still 28 borough and 15 county seats where peerage influence was significant.

Relatives of peers occupied many seats in the Lower House, whether returned by their influence or not. In 1832, 257 MPs were Irish peers, or sons, fathers, brothers, cousins, grandsons, nephews and uncles of 169 peers. In the 1841–7 House of Commons there were 172 sons, 27 grand- and great-grandsons of peers and 8 Irish peers, and in 1865 there were still 101 sons and 15 grandsons sitting.[3]

Nevertheless, the influence of the Lords over the House of Commons was weakening, despite the appearance of the figures, even before the Reform Act became law. The increasing cost and trouble of maintaining an electoral interest had been pointed out as early as the 1780s, and with the revival of radical political consciousness among the middle classes after 1805 it became increasingly troublesome. For example, the previously powerful Leveson-Gower influence in Staffordshire, where once they had virtually controlled three boroughs and one of the county seats, was destroyed between 1812 and 1831 in a concerted campaign by a determined 'radical' movement. In other 'proprietary' boroughs under aristocratic control like Pontefract, Knaresborough and Malton (all in Yorkshire) attacks were made, if not always successfully, on the patronal influence of Lord Galway, the duke of Devonshire, and Earl Fitzwilliam respectively between 1780 and 1807.[4] The Reform Act opened the franchise to a slightly wider range of the middle classes, but its chief feature was the destruction of a large proportion of direct aristocratic patronal influence through the inclusion of many of their boroughs in Schedules A and B and the redistribution of some of those seats to large towns where that influence did not operate to any significant extent. Thus, the resistance of the House of Lords to the passage of the Reform Bills in 1831 and 1832 was entirely understandable. It reflected not the conservative prejudices of a reactionary assembly, but the defence of the natural interests of a governing class.

However, although the defence was unsuccessful in terms of resistance to the provisions of the bill, the influence of aristocracy was not destroyed by it. It was never Grey's intention to do so. He saw the bill as a means of strengthening the legitimate influence of the aristocracy and reconciling the middle classes to the system by including them in it, but not giving them superiority. The bill also defused the confrontation between aristocratic patrons and radicals by removing the grievances over pocket boroughs. The influence of peers in county constituencies remained, and was strengthened by the 'Chandos clause' – a Tory amendment accepted by the government – which enfranchised tenants-at-will and so benefited their landlords in the absence of a secret ballot.

The Reform Act was indeed as significant for what it did not do as for what it did. It did not remove or lower the property qualification for MPs; it did not institute payment of salaries to MPs; it retained the distinction between county and borough constituencies and, by increasing the number of the former, balanced the increase in representation of urban interests. As long as society remained hierarchical and deferential towards the upper classes, aristocratic influence remained. As Walter Bagehot and John Bright were to remark in 1867, it was the second, not the first Reform Act which effectively brought it to an end.

THE LIMITS OF POWER

The question which the Lords had to consider after 1832 was, therefore, how far they could go in defying the claim of the reformed House of Commons to 'speak for the nation' when they might consider its proposed measures too radical, or hostile to the interests of the aristocracy. As *The Times* wrote on 3 October 1831,

> It is undoubtedly true, that among the uses of an Upper Chamber ought to be accounted that of checking occasionally the too impetuous flight of popular impulse, and subjecting that which may be but a light or transient caprice, to the test of calm, laborious, and reiterated deliberation.

On the other hand, as the leader writer put it a fortnight earlier on 13 September,

> The House of Commons has in effect told the House of Lords, 'You shall be a House of Lords, and we hope you will remain so while England remains a limited monarchy; but, under the title of House of Lords, you must not be in reality both Lords and Commons too . . . [otherwise] the constitution of England is not . . . a mixed monarchy, but an unmixed oligarchy.

Although, therefore, the House of Lords quickly recovered its confidence after 1832 and proceeded to assert its right to independence in considering legislation, there were limits beyond which it proved inadvisable to go. Wellington was one of the first to appreciate the new situation. He wrote in 1834 that the destruction of the House of Lords was now 'out of the question', and assured Aberdeen that 'we have only now to follow a plain course with moderation and dignity in order to attain very great if not preponderating influence over the affairs of the country.'[5] The key word was 'moderation'; it would not have been difficult for the Tory Lords to use their strength to emasculate the government's legislation and make it impossible for it to carry on, but the days of 1783–4 were long gone and if the Lords brought down a government with a sound majority in the Commons the king could no longer use his influence to reverse that majority by a general election, as George III had done.

In general, therefore, the Lords limited themselves to obstructing Liberal legislation on the principle that they formed a necessary check on the actions of the Commons in order to give time for reconsideration, rather than insisting on their own authority to prevent it altogether. Wellington took the view that the Lords had a function as the ultimate guardians of the constitution, but that they should not use their powers in this respect unnecessarily. He preferred to allow a 'bad' measure to pass rather than risk a civil disturbance. He also believed that it was more important to preserve the Lords' powers intact so that they could be used in case of need on great questions. While keeping the ultimate power of rejection in reserve, the Lords should seek to restrain extreme measures, and by their very presence induce the Commons not to press too far. Lord Ashburton told Hatherton in May 1836 'that his party were very sensible of the necessity of confining their exertions only to very great occasions, and that they should avoid trifling opportunities of showing their strength'.[6]

The period from 1833 to 1837 was one in which this relationship was developed. On the other hand, it quickly became an established convention that a government would not resign simply because of a defeat in the Lords, if it retained the confidence of the king and the Commons. The very first session after the Reform Act illustrated both these points. In June, Wellington proposed a motion on the affairs of Spain, intended as a virtual motion of censure on foreign policy, which was carried against the government by 79 to 69. The ministry, however, did not resign, nor did anyone seriously expect it to do so. Greville declared that the result was that 'the House of Lords has had a rap over the knuckles from the King' and 'their legislative functions are practically in abeyance', because they could not throw out a government bill without the risk of being swamped by new creations. In the following month Wellington attacked the Irish Church Bill in the Lords, but summoned his followers to Apsley House and told them that they must allow it to pass. He said, however, as Greville reported, that defeats in the Lords would impose a salutary restraint on the House of Commons, and 'that the Tories were by no means frightened or disheartened and meant to take the first opportunity of showing fight again'.[7]

The Lords thus did not hesitate to oppose what they considered to be dangerous radical legislation. In the 1830s, they destroyed or mutilated Whig measures such as the Jewish Disabilities Bill, the Universities Tests Bill and the Irish Tithes, Irish Church and Irish Municipal Corporations Bills, seeing themselves as guardians of the Church in particular. Hatherton accused them of acting out of 'thirst for power, and the most factious and restless indulgence of it'. Holland was critical of what he considered to be Melbourne's weakness in dealing with the Lords, advocating a 'more pugnacious' attitude. Lord Holland remarked in March 1832 that

> the present House of Lords never could go in with a Reformed
> Parliament, it being opposed to all the wants and wishes of the people,
> hating the abolition of tithes, the press, and the French Revolution, and
> that in order to make it harmonize with the Reformed Parliament it
> must be amended by an infusion of a more liberal cast.

This, as Greville tartly commented, 'goes upon the assumption that his party is that which harmonizes with the popular feeling, and what he means by improving the character of the House is to add some 50 or 60 men who may be willing to accept peerages upon the condition of becoming a body-guard to this Government'.[8]

However, the Prime Minister, like Grey before him, had no wish to involve himself in a constitutional crisis in order to destroy the Upper House and play into the hands of the radicals. It was the restraint advocated by Peel and Wellington that preserved the political compromise. Peel's recognition of the superior constitutional status of the Commons was reflected in his cautious attitude while in opposition, believing that his moderation would prevent the Whig government from falling into radical hands, and he tried to restrain the Conservative peers from their opposition to the Irish Corporations and Tithe Bills, though his defective communications with Wellington sometimes prevented him from doing so. Greville too rebuked the Tory peers for their determined opposition to the Municipal Corporations Bill:

> It does certainly appear to me that [they] will never rest till they
> have accomplished the destruction of the House of Lords. They are
> resolved to bring about a collision with the House of Commons, and
> the majority in each House grows every day more rabid and more
> desperate.

He believed, however, that public opinion neither desired the abolition of the House of Lords nor cared much about its preservation; so long as it acted in harmony with, and therefore in subordination to, the Commons, it would be tolerated.

Peel also drew attention to the relationship between public opinion and what the Lords might do. At an election dinner in Tamworth in

1837 he pointed out the necessity of increasing the Conservative vote in general elections so that the Lords might be assured that they acted 'in accordance with the feelings of the intelligent and thinking class of the community'. He also warned the Lords that they should not resist all reform indiscriminately, but accept 'salutary improvements' while also defending the existing constitution in general. Wellington warned Newcastle in 1837 that the government's majority in the Commons of between twenty and forty was sufficient and that 'I don't see how they can be shaken'.[9]

This realism on the part of the two most influential leaders of the opposition was the decisive factor in resolving what had in any case, as Greville remarked, been a party and not a constitutional conflict, in which the party which was dominant in the Commons must prevail: 'It can scarcely cross the minds of either party, or of any individual of either, that the substantive power of Government can or ought to be transferred from the House of Commons to the House of Lords', he wrote. After the battle over the Municipal Corporations Bill in 1836, when the Lords tried to destroy the bill by amendments which the Commons then rejected, and Howick spoke of the Lords being 'swept away like chaff', the political temperature cooled. As Greville admitted, the Lords could not be expected

> to yield everything, and . . . pass every Bill which the House of Commons thinks fit to send them . . . but common prudence and a sense of their own condition and their own relative strength under the new dispensation demand that they should exercise their undoubted rights with circumspection and calmness, desisting from all opposition for opposition's sake, standing out firmly on questions involving great and important principles, and yielding with a good grace, without ill-humour, and without subserviency on minor points.[10]

The accession of Queen Victoria in 1837 coincided with the virtual resolution of the questions on which Lords and Commons had been in conflict since 1830, and the loyal spirit engendered by the young queen helped to moderate conflict. Relations between the two Houses quickly settled into a conventional understanding. On the questions of the grant to the Irish Catholic Maynooth College and on the repeal of the Corn Laws in the mid-1840s the Lords were inclined to be obstructive but, as in the case of Catholic Emancipation in 1829, the fact that these were proposed by a Conservative administration and supported by the opposition made it difficult for the Upper House to carry its resistance too far. The Lords could, indeed, be justly accused of insincerity when they professed to act on principle when opposing measures of Liberal governments but accepted similar ones from Conservatives in response to the directions of Tory party leaders. In both cases, as it happened, the Whig peers came to Peel's assistance: 73 Tories and bishops voted against the government on the Maynooth grant, but the majority of Whig peers reinforced the loyal Conservatives and placemen to secure its passage. Almost all the 73 deserters on Maynooth also opposed the repeal of the Corn Laws, but the Whigs again came to the rescue. Among the majority of 211, 115 Whig peers assured the passage of repeal against 15 out of 164 in the minority.[11]

The Corn Laws episode was significant for the future. The repeal of the Corn Laws was seen as a victory for the commercial and industrial middle classes over the landed aristocracy, and it marked an important moment in the changing balance between the two Houses of Parliament. As in 1831–2, the Lords' resistance to a measure demanded by a large and powerful interest in the country backed by intense popular agitation threatened a crisis in the constitution and a revived campaign against the powers of the Upper House. It was to avert this danger that the queen and Prince Albert intervened to persuade Wellington to get the peers to allow the repeal through, and in the end the duke's influence, together with the support of the Whig peers, ensured its passage.

The split in the Conservative ranks which followed the repeal of the Corn Laws had the effect of changing the political balance in the Upper House. For the next twenty years, the existence of a bloc of Peelite peers, who often voted with the Liberals, and of a number of independent or neutral peers who saw themselves as politically impartial, counteracted the old Tory majority and held the balance between the two sides. Unlike Wellington in the 1830s, Derby in the 1850s and 1860s found that he could not muster enough support to defeat government measures in the lobbies. The first occasion when the Lords did collide with the House of Commons occurred in 1850, when they passed Stanley's motion of censure on Palmerston's conduct of the Don Pacifico Affair. A crisis was avoided by the Commons passing Roebuck's motion of confidence in the government. Lord Ashley warned the Prime Minister, Lord John Russell, that he should speak with caution about the conduct of the Lords, and not encourage public criticism: his views echoed what many people were thinking, but 'the House [of Lords] forms a part of the constitutional arrangement of these kingdoms' and could not be abolished without a revolution. After the Commons debate Clarendon congratulated Russell on his speech, which he believed would calm the situation; the Lords, he wrote, were 'not deficient in worldly wisdom' and would refrain from appearing as 'a public nuisance'.[12]

THE LORDS INSIST ON THEIR RIGHTS

Nevertheless, the Upper House did not wish to become a mere cipher in the constitution and its members remained convinced of their right to express an opinion critical of the government in opposition to the Commons. Lansdowne spoke in the chamber to that effect in 1852, when the Liberals were in opposition, warning the peers 'that, besides being mild and courteous, they must be more energetic and enterprising, so as to fill a larger space in the public eye, or they will soon be superseded and forgotten'.[13] In 1860 the Lords again caused a sensation by rejecting Gladstone's bill to abolish the paper duties, 'taxes on knowledge' which restricted the circulation of newspapers and periodicals. This threatened a constitutional crisis over their interference with what could be regarded as a money bill. It also aroused strong feelings in the country, for the repeal of these duties was seen as a means to extend popular knowledge of and participation in national affairs, and also as part of a process of shifting taxation from the general community towards direct taxes on land and property, following Gladstone's introduction in 1853 of reforms in the inheritance taxes.

The Cabinet discussed whether to resign in protest, and Russell suggested that if the Lords rejected it a second time they might dissolve and appeal to the country. The duke of Argyll warned the Lords that although they had the right to reject any bill sent up from the Commons, to do so in this case was to go counter to constitutional practice: 'in truth and substance you are striking at the very root of the constitutional usage which has hitherto regulated the relations between the two Houses.' The opponents of repeal admitted that the Lords ought not to entrench upon the financial powers and rights of the Commons, but they contended that the repeal of an existing tax involved wider issues than the imposition of a new one, since it implied a choice as to which tax to remove or retain, and also whether the resulting loss of revenue was in the national interest. It was not a secret that the Prime Minister himself was lukewarm about his chancellor's proposal, since Palmerston wished to keep up the revenue in order to pay for increased armaments and fortifications against France. The Lords' opposition was no doubt encouraged by this fact as well as by the claim, made in the debate by Lord Chelmsford, that if they were barred from discussing such matters of national policy the House would become a cipher compared with the Commons.[14] A crisis was averted by the government's decision to pass a resolution in the Commons against the Lords' action. Even John Bright, the leading radical critic of the Lords and protagonist of democracy, thought it best not to risk the resignation of the government but to resolve the matter in the following session. In the next session the repeal was incorporated in Gladstone's budget and the Lords shrank from further interference. The duke of Rutland moved to reject the budget, but Derby persuaded him to withdraw the motion.[15]

Nevertheless, the Lords continued to resist Liberal measures. On three occasions in the 1850s, as six times before 1852, they rejected bills from the Commons to allow Jews to sit in Parliament, despite Lyndhurst's warning in 1858 that it was dangerous to refuse assent to measures repeatedly passed by the Lower House and supported by public opinion. The most that the Lords would do was to allow the principle that each House should determine for itself what oaths should be required from its members – Jews were excluded by the need to swear 'on the true faith of a Christian' – and this allowed Rothschild to sit in the Commons to which he had been elected, in vain, five times by the City of London. In 1866 an act intended to relieve Roman Catholics of objectionable oaths, by omitting the phrase referred to, incidentally allowed Jews to sit in the Lords.

The Lords were particularly active on questions affecting the religious establishment. They blocked attempts to abolish religious tests for admission to Oxford and Cambridge Universities, and rejected the abolition of church rates until 1868, when they accepted from Disraeli's government a compromise effectively ending compulsory payment. In 1871 they similarly accepted on Disraeli's advice the ending of religious tests for universities. In 1868–9 they opposed Gladstone's plan to disestablish the Irish Church, again threatening a constitutional crisis. After Disraeli's resignation in 1868 Gladstone assumed the premiership, and before the general election which was to be held shortly afterwards he proposed that, pending the introduction of a disestablishment bill in the next Parliament, all appointments in the church hierarchy should be suspended. The Lords threw out the Suspensory Bill, Salisbury declaring that since the question had not been put before the electorate the House of Commons had no more right to speak for the people than the Lords. His opposition was, in truth, engendered more by his concern for the status of the Lords as a second chamber than by the bill itself. The

House, he declared, should not be the 'mere echo' of the Commons but it was

> a free, independent House of the Legislature, and that you will consider any other more timid or subservient course as at once unworthy of your traditions, unworthy of your honour, and, most of all, unworthy of the nation you serve.

The duke of Marlborough elaborated the point, saying that

> the other House . . . may represent more nearly the external fervour, the declamatory power, and the first impulses of the people; but I believe that your Lordships do represent, in an eminent degree, the inner feeling of the English nation, and, perhaps, that 'still small voice' which counsels prudence, moderation, and delay.

The importance of the issue was shown by the fact that the debate went on for three nights, the first such long sittings since 1832, and that no less than 289 peers voted, defeating the bill by a majority of 95.[16]

Salisbury's argument was answered by the general election, in which the question was put explicitly to the electorate and the Liberals were returned with a large majority. Nevertheless, the role of the House of Lords was still in question, and the strong feelings of the Conservative and many Liberal peers on religious questions came into play to reinforce general concern about the extent to which the Lords should submit to external pressure. Clarendon wrote to Lady Salisbury that they 'were more afraid of the pressure now brought to bear upon them than of the irreparable mischief they will do to their House and their order by throwing out the Bill'. Clarendon's speech in the Lords stressed the dangerous consequences of rejection, and Salisbury, though insisting on the Lords' right to do as they thought best, accepted that the popular mandate required the concession of the second reading, though it did not extend to every detail of the bill, which the Lords were free and entitled to amend in committee:

> If we do merely echo the House of Commons, the sooner we disappear the better. The object of the existence of a second House of Parliament is to supply the omissions and correct the defects which occur in the proceedings of the first.

It was true that sometimes the Commons would justly reflect the views of the nation, but at other times it might be mistaken, and if it was thought to be the case the Lords had the duty to insist that the nation be consulted; it was important

> that one House without the support of the nation shall not be allowed to domineer over the other. In each case it is a matter of feeling and of

> judgment. We must decide by all we see around us and by events that
> are passing . . . upon our consciences and to the best of our judgment
> . . . whether the House of Commons does or does not represent the
> full, the deliberate, the sustained convictions of the body of the nation
> . . . . [If it does, the House of Lords] must devolve the responsibility
> upon the nation, and may fairly accept the conclusion at which the
> nation has arrived.

The debate continued for four nights, and the second reading passed,
179 to 146, by virtue of Salisbury's leading thirty-six Conservative
peers into the government lobby.[17]

The Lords then passed several amendments in committee, which
were rejected by the Commons. The Lords voted to insist on their
amendments and deadlock ensued, to be broken by the initiative
of Lord Cairns, the Conservative leader, who despite his strong
objections to the measure (he was a Protestant Ulsterman) took it upon
himself to negotiate a compromise with Granville, the Liberal leader.
Assisted by the influence of several English bishops, the compromise
was accepted by the House and the crisis passed.

Granville too had assured their lordships in the second reading
debate that by allowing the bill to pass they would not confess
themselves powerless:

> Will noble lords . . . tell me that this House is powerless? Why,
> looking around me, when I see your Lordships' House crowded with
> representatives of enormous wealth, of great social position, and of
> eminent services rendered in public and private life – when I see
> the precincts of this chamber crowded with Privy Councillors, with
> Members of the other House, with the representatives of Crowned
> Heads and great Republics, and our galleries adorned . . . with a
> portion of the human race not altogether without influence – I venture
> to say that in this world never was erected a more magnificent
> platform on which men, by their wisdom, their eloquence, and their
> knowledge, could influence the opinions of their fellow-men. . . . . My
> Lords, you have power – great power – immense power – for good;
> but there is one power you have not . . . you have not the power
> of thwarting the national will when properly and constitutionally
> expressed.

As Lord Cairns remarked four days later, this left open the question
of whether the verdict of a general election was to be taken as decisive
on every question included in the winning party's programme: the
Lords must be satisfied that the will of the country had indeed been
properly expressed, but Cairns's speech amounted to an admission
that the Lords must, in their legislative capacity, bow to the wishes
of the country at large, or even express the country's wishes more
precisely by amending unsatisfactory legislation.[18]

It was in that sense that the Lords behaved in the following decade. The 1870s began the opening of a new era, marked by an intensification of party conflict which reflected changes in the nature of parties after the second Reform Act. The electorate became more dominant, the press and the platform began to supplant the House of Commons as the voice of the people, and politicians found themselves obliged to look to the country for their power base. The House of Lords tried to use this development to strengthen its ability to maintain its authority and prestige. Under Salisbury's doctrine of 'the mandate', developed during the crisis over the Irish Church, the Lords sought to establish a claim to refer unsatisfactory legislation from the Commons back to some kind of popular referendum. If indeed this had been a genuine attempt to check the constitutional power of the Lower House, in which the majority, under tighter party discipline, might be seen merely as the legislative arm of the government, it might have had some justification. What negated it in practice was the way in which the increasingly conservative majority in the Lords used the doctrine for party rather than national ends. This was exemplified in the Lords' treatment of Gladstone's extensive reforming programme after 1868. Though the Lords were relatively cooperative on a wide range of social reforms, which hardly touched their own interests but might be considered to restrict the freedom of the industrial middle classes, they were less so on the political front or when their own social or economic interests were involved. In 1871, when the government proposed the abolition of the purchase system for commissions as part of a reform in the army, the Lords rose up in wrath to defend a vested interest. Aristocratic families had long regarded the army as a suitable career for their sons and had invested large amounts in the purchase of commissions and promotions. The substitution of a system of promotion by merit (though social cachet and patronage were not to disappear from the officer class for a considerable time to come) might threaten aristocratic leadership in a number of ways. The question was recognized as being one involving the class system, and it brought out the latent conflict between a House which still embodied the interests of an exclusive social elite and one which was becoming more socially as well as politically radical. The Lords threw out the bill by a majority of 155 to 130. The government avoided direct confrontation by the device of abolishing purchase by prerogative action, through royal warrant, and though the Lords passed a motion of censure by 162 to 82 there was nothing they could do to prevent it.[19]

Other acts in the government's programme, on the rights of trade unions and other social questions, passed with less difficulty and though in 1871 the Lords rejected the ballot, they allowed it to pass in the following session. Salisbury again asserted the rights of the Lords to reject a bill of which they disapproved. Writing to Lord Carnarvon, he declared:

> If we listen to the Liberals we should accept all important Bills which had passed the House of Commons by a large majority. But that in effect would be to efface the House of Lords. Another principle . . . is to watch newspapers, public meetings and so forth, and only to reject when 'public opinion', thus ascertained, growls very loud. This plan gives a premium to bluster and will bring the House into contempt. The plan which I prefer is frankly to acknowledge that the nation is our Master, though the House of Commons is not, and to yield our own opinion only when the judgment of the nation has been challenged at the polls and decidedly expressed. This doctrine, it seems to me, has the advantage of being: (1) Theoretically sound. (2) Popular. (3) Safe against agitation, and (4) so rarely applicable as practically to place little fetter upon our independence.

When, however, a series of by-elections in 1871–2 indicated a strong popular feeling in favour of the ballot, the Conservative front bench abstained and allowed the bill to pass, Salisbury firing a parting shot that

> If it be true that the House of Lords is a mere copying-machine for the decrees of the House of Commons, the sooner its duties are remitted to that useful instrument the better.

As Salisbury's descendant and biographer remarked, 'From his first entry into the House he had been painfully impressed by the apathetic indifference of its members and by the consciousness of weakness which he believed to be its cause.' His remedy, as the 'doctrine of the mandate', became the constitutional rule for the Lords in the immediate future and enabled the House to retain at least the appearance of a residual constitutional function both as a revising chamber and as a check on the excessive activity of the Lower House.[20]

For the immediate future, the diminishing popularity of Gladstone's government weakened its will to carry controversial legislation, and its defeat at the polls in 1874 brought in a Conservative government under Disraeli that was more congenial to the majority in the Upper House.

Disraeli's programme of 'Imperium et Sanitas' heralded in his Crystal Palace speech of 1872, did not disturb the smooth relations between his government and the House of Lords. Party discipline on the Conservative side and support on principle from the Liberals for a programme of social reforms kept the debates in the Upper House free from acrimony despite the growing signs that the government was adopting 'collectivist' policies. Increasing state intervention affecting rights of private property, for example in the Artisans Dwellings Bill and Public Health Bill in 1875, failed to arouse partisan or class conflict: the debates in the Lords were relatively short, and constructive, showing that the peers were amenable to party discipline when they had a government of which they approved. During the second half of Disraeli's administration the pace of social reform slowed, as foreign and imperial affairs took a greater share of the Prime Minister's attention. Here the Conservative peers were fully behind him. Domestic legislation during those years proved relatively uncontroversial.[21]

The Lords were, however, unlikely to remain passive indefinitely. Changes in the world outside Westminster were beginning to impinge on the status and role of the aristocracy. In particular the agricultural depression of the 1870s resulted in a sharp fall in land values and in rental incomes both in Britain and in Ireland. Peers who did not profit from the ownership of urban property or lacked substantial investments or resources in industry and business suffered a fall in their wealth relative to the rising middle classes and they began to see the House of Lords as a means to resist this advancing tide. The predominantly middle-class House of Commons reflected the growing radicalism of men like Joseph Chamberlain and of the larger towns they represented and whose populations were enfranchised in 1867. The Lords became uneasy, fearing that they would be threatened as in 1832, and the tone of the Upper House became increasingly aggressive. The 1880s were to begin a new, less cooperative era in the relations between the two Houses.[22]

REFERENCES

1. *Blackwood's Edinburgh Magazine* XXIX (1831), 147.
2. N.C. Phillips, *Yorkshire and English National Politics* (Christchurch, N.Z. 1961).
3. *English Historical Documents, 1783–1832*, ed. A. Aspinall and E.A. Smith (1959), XI, pp. 234–5, 229, 236; T.H.B. Oldfield, *Representative History of Great Britain and Ireland* (1816); *The House of Commons, 1790–1820*, ed. R. Thorne (1986), I, pp. 106, 282–4; *The Croker Papers*, ed L.J. Jennings (1884) I, pp. 368–9, 371–2; A.S. Turberville, *The House of Lords in the Age of Reform 1784–1837*, pp. 246–7 and Appendix VII; N. Gash, *Politics in the Age of Peel*, (1953), pp. 438–9; C.R.R. Dod, *Electoral Facts, 1832–52* ed. H.J. Hanham (1972), pp. xxxiv–xxxvi; W.L. Guttsman, *The English Ruling Class* (1969), pp. 149–58; J.V. Beckett, *The Aristocracy in England*

1660–1914 (Oxford, 1986), pp. 430–3; *A Key to Both Houses of Parliament* (1832), 440.

4. S.M. Hardy and R.C. Baily, 'The downfall of the Gower interest in the Staffordshire boroughs, 1800–30': *Historical Collections, Staffordshire* (1950–1), 267–301; E.A. Smith, 'Earl Fitzwilliam and Malton', *English Historical Review* LXXX, no. 314 (1965), 51–69; Chatsworth MSS, Knaresborough election papers.
5. 23 August 1834: B.L. Add. MS 43060, ff. 113–14.
6. Hatherton Diary, 20 May 1836.
7. C.C.F. Greville, *Journal of the reigns of George IV and William IV* ed. H. Reeve (1874), II, pp. 377, 379–80.
8. S. Walpole, *Life of Lord John Russell* (1889), I, pp. 244–7, 274–82, 293, 297–302; Hatherton Diary, 2 Sept. 1835; Holland to Granville, 4 July 1837, Granville MSS, PRO 30/29/424; Greville, *Journal*, II, p. 266.
9. *Ibid.*, III, pp. 284, 287–9; *The Times*, 25 July 1837; B.L. Add. MS 40424, ff. 166–72; Newcastle MSS, Nottingham University Library, 5325 (30 October 1837).
10. Greville, *Journal*, III, pp. 363 (Aug. 1836), 290; *The Greville Diary* ed. P.W. Wilson (1927), I, p. 521 (21 Aug. 1835).
11. D.C. Large, 'The House of Lords and Ireland in the age of Peel, 1832–50', in Jones and Jones, *Peers, Politics, and Power*, pp. 373–405.
12. Ashley to Russell, 24 June 1850, Clarendon 1 July: *Later Correspondence of Lord John Russell* ed. G.P. Gooch (1925), pp. 77, 79.
13. *Campbell*, 24 Feb. 1852: II, p. 302.
14. Hansard; CLVIII, 1504–7: for the full debate, 1439–548.
15. *Autobiography and Memoirs of George Douglas, 8th Duke of Argyll* ed. Dowager Duchess of Argyll (1906), pp. 159–62; *Diaries of John Bright*, ed. R.A.J. Walling (1930), pp. 249–50.
16. Lady Gwendolen Cecil, *Life of Robert Marquis of Salisbury* (1921), II, p. 23; Hansard, CXCIII, 36, 89–90; Argyll, II, pp. 247–51.
17. *Life and Letters of George William Frederick, 4th Earl of Clarendon*, ed. Sir H. Maxwell (1913), II, pp. 359–60; Cecil, *Salisbury*, II, pp. 24–5; Hansard, CXCVII, 83–4.
18. *Ibid.*, CXCVI, 1655–8 (14 July 1869); Lord Edmond Fitzmaurice, *Life of . . . second Earl Granville* (1905), II, pp. 10–11.
19. Hansard; CCVIII, 454–542; Maxwell, *Clarendon*, II, pp. 298–301.
20. Salisbury to Carnarvon, 20 Feb 1872, Cecil, *Salisbury*, II, pp. 25–6, 27–8; Hansard; CCVII, 1256–307; CCXI, 1493; G.H.L. le May, *The Victorian Constitution* (1979), pp. 134–8.
21. *Ibid.*, pp. 139–45.
22. D. Cannadine, *The Decline and Fall of the British Aristocracy* (1990).

CHAPTER SEVEN

The House of Lords and the Public

The survival of the House of Lords through an era of advancing democracy has often been thought to require explanation. Why, after the reform of 1832 or in the years of conflict between the two Houses that followed, or after the second instalment of reform in 1867, was not the Upper House swept away by the tide of middle-class and radical opinion? Why did an age which increasingly prided itself on its advanced ideas and practices in the economic sphere, in the 'march of intellect' and moral improvement, and in rationality in politics, not abolish this relic of the medieval and feudal past? The answers are to be found, first, in the continued acceptance of the peerage itself in society, deriving from the maintenance of social distinctions and hierarchy which made the peerage a target for socially ambitious families benefiting from the increased wealth of the commercial, industrial and professional classes; second, in the restraint which the House of Lords came to exercise in voluntarily limiting its own capability to obstruct the will of the Commons and their constituents; third, in the Victorian respect for tradition and continuity of English historical development which was theoretically embodied in their 'Whig interpretation of history' and in practice symbolized by the Gothic structure of the new Houses of Parliament; and, finally, in the role which the peerage continued to fill in the performance of social and political duties in the country as well as in national government.[1]

THE LORDS AND REFORM

The Reform Act of 1832 was, paradoxically, to be the instrument by which the mid-nineteenth century acceptance of the House of Lords was to be achieved. Before 1830, the Upper House was seen as an instrument of aristocratic dominance and for the repression of reform. The influence of the peerage over elections to the Lower House, and the presence of so many of their sons and other close relatives in it, provided the major target for critics of the unreformed constitution.[2] The attitude of the Lords reinforced this feeling. Since the arousal of fear of revolution in the 1790s, the Lords had backed Pitt's 'repressive' policies towards liberal or radical movements and this had continued after the end of the French wars in 1815. During Liverpool's postwar administration the Lords were generally willing to acquiesce in the government's measures. The Corn Laws of 1815 passed the Lords with no difficulty, even the Whig opposition failing to make capital out of it because many of its members shared the view, expressed by Grey himself, that the landed interest, and the price of corn, should be kept up. His opposition was halfhearted, and procedural rather than substantive. The Lords likewise gave enthusiastic support to such repressive measures as the suspension of habeas corpus in 1817, the Seditious Meetings Bill of 1817 and the 'Six Acts' of 1819, all of which restricted popular liberties in some degree. By 1820 the radicals were in full spate against the Lords: John Wade, author and compiler of the radical *Black Book*, not only listed prominently the total of public money bestowed on members of the peerage by patronage and office, but declared the Corn Laws to be a tax on the people for the benefit of the aristocracy,[3] and in 1820 the fact that the government introduced the Bill of Pains and Penalties against Queen Caroline into the Lords, so that the committee stage took on the character of, and became known as, 'the Queen's trial', further increased the rage of the radicals against it.

In all these measures, the House of Lords did not necessarily show itself to be more reactionary or repressive than the majority in the Commons; but the Lords were neither elected by popular approval, nor did they contain many individuals of 'advanced' liberal or reformist views to give the appearance of some support for the people. The Whig aristocracy, as represented by Grey, Lansdowne, Holland, or the Cavendish family, were mild reformers at best, concerned more to use reform as a means to improve their chances of office than to crusade for social changes to benefit the 'lower orders'. Only slightly eccentric individuals such as the 3rd earl of Radnor, or the 1st Lord Durham, expressed radical sympathies in the House of Lords, and they found little support. Durham, indeed, justified his acceptance of a peerage from Goderich in 1828 on the grounds that it would place one voice favourable to reform in the Upper House.

The radical assertion that under the influence of Lord Eldon, the Duke of Wellington and the Duke of Cumberland, the Lords had become a totally repressive body, if not 'terrified out of their wits', as Cobbett said they were of Henry Hunt, seemed to carry conviction.[4] The Lords certainly provided a graveyard for non-governmental but important measures such as the bills prohibiting the use of climbing boys as chimney sweeps, and for the attempts of Mackintosh, Romilly and others to reduce the apparent severity of criminal punishments.

Yet in many respects the Lords were not entirely hostile to change and were at least prepared to be pragmatic. Their well-known resistance to the Catholic relief bills of the 1820s was more a reflection of their wish to support the king and his government than of reactionary conservatism. Emancipation was an 'open' question in Liverpool's Cabinet, but the majority of the peers in the Cabinet were opposed to it. It was also strongly believed that public opinion was against it. The Lords' opposition was at least in part a response to the lead given by the government front bench and when in 1829 Wellington accepted the inevitable and introduced emancipation as a government measure the peers dutifully followed him. 'It is very ridiculous to see the faces many of these Tory Lords make at swallowing the bitter pill', wrote Greville:[5]

> All this has given a blow to the aristocracy, which men only laugh at now, but of which the effects will be felt some day or other . . . I am glad to see them dragged through the mire, as far as the individuals are concerned, but I am sorry for the effect that such conduct is likely to produce.

Yet, as Gash has remarked, the Lords were merely showing themselves again to be 'peculiarly amenable to executive influence', as often during the period from 1815 to 1830.[6]

However, this did not mean that the House of Lords became the mere tool of successive governments. In 1831–2 they showed that they were prepared to bring down a government, virtually elected by the people, with whose measures they disagreed. They claimed in this respect to have as much right as the Commons to represent the interests of the country and to be justified in blocking hasty or ill-considered legislation from the Lower House. This claim became progressively less tenable as the process of electoral reform linked the Commons more closely with the will of the people. In the 1830s, however, the Lords were prepared to face out the radical demand that they defer to the House of Commons, or be 'mended or ended'. They persisted in opposing the Whig Reform Bill in 1831–2 despite the overwhelming mandate of the general election of 1831. When in

May 1831 William IV expressed the hope that Grey's Cabinet would modify the Reform Bill in order to make it more acceptable to the Lords, Grey replied that the verdict of the country had been so decisive that it would be impossible for the government to propose a less extensive measure. The Cabinet met in June to examine the possibility of introducing such modifications, but concluded that it was not possible to do so. The Lords could only be coerced, however, by the creation, or threat of creation, of sufficient additional peers in favour of the bill to outweigh the expected majority against it. This, William IV protested in October, was a step 'no government could propose and no Sovereign consent' to, and Grey was equally reluctant to take what he called such 'a measure of extreme violence', although he pointed out in the chamber that the Crown's prerogative of making peers was an essential device to prevent the House of Lords frustrating the will of the government and becoming 'an uncontrollable oligarchy'. In his eyes, to force the Lords to bow to the will of the people was against the main purpose of the bill, which was to restore and make acceptable aristocratic dominance and to preserve the ancient institutions of the country.[7] The refusal of the majority of the Lords to accept the Reform Bill as it stood ultimately compelled Grey to face and resolve that dilemma.

The Lords also had to face the anger of the people. In September 1831, two weeks before the introduction of the Reform Bill into the Upper House, T.B. Macaulay forecast that

> Three weeks . . . will probably . . . bring to an issue the question, Reform or Revolution. One or the other I am certain that we must and shall have. I assure you that the violence of the people, the bigotry of the Lords, and the stupidity and weakness of the ministers, alarm me so much that even my rest is disturbed by vexation and uneasy forebodings . . . for this noble country.

The contest, he added, was between 'an insolent oligarchy on the one side and infuriated people on the other'.[8]

The rejection of the second reading of the bill by 41 votes in the Lords at 7a.m. on 8 October after five nights of debate[9] sparked off the anticipated popular demonstrations, not only in London, where the Duke of Wellington's windows at Apsley House were broken again in an attack lasting nearly an hour, but in several parts of the country, most notably at Derby, Nottingham and Bristol, where mobs created havoc and, at Bristol, burnt large areas of the city. *The Times* remarked on 10 October of the 'just indignation' of the people, directed above all against the bishops who provided 21 of the 41 majority. A placard in Bond Street proclaimed '199 versus 22,000,000!', red caps of liberty were seen in St Pancras, and a line of police and Horse Guards was drawn across the Mall to keep the crowd away from the royal palace. Detachments of foot and Horse Guards, artillery and marines were placed at strategic points in and around London.[10] The immediate threat subsided during the winter while the country waited to see whether the government would force the bill through the Lords by the creation of additional peers, but it revived when the peers, after passing the second reading of the reintroduced bill in March 1832, carried a wrecking amendment in committee in May. When the king refused to create a sufficient number of peers to force the bill through, the ministers resigned and William called on Wellington to form a new administration.

The country erupted in fury. At Birmingham a meeting of 200,000 persons, led by the radical banker Thomas Attwood, resolved to pay no taxes until reform was passed and threatened to march on London to force the Lords to do so.[11] In London a run on the banks was organized, and *The Times* alleged that over £1 million pounds was withdrawn in less than a week.[12] Sir Denis Le Marchant noted in his diary that a Birmingham manufacturer was offering to supply the local Political Union with 10,000 muskets, and on 19 May Lord Lyttelton wrote to his wife 'There is no House of Lords today. It has occurred to me that it may not be long ere the *today* may be omitted.'[13]

Wellington, however, failed to form a new Cabinet, largely because of Peel's refusal to serve, and the Whigs resumed their offices, fortified by the king's reluctant pledge to create sufficient peers to pass the bill. Under this threat, Wellington and the majority of his followers withdrew from the House and allowed the bill to pass. Wellington 'has destroyed himself and his Tory high-flying association for ever', exulted Thomas Creevey.[14]

Grey's attitude to the creation of new peers was significant. He made it clear to his Cabinet colleagues, some of whom were very reluctant to force the Lords in this way, that he too was averse to the step unless he was forced to take it, and he risked alienating those who were in favour of additional creations by attempting to delay proceedings for as long as possible. In the end, Grey was swayed by his view of the opinion of the country at large. He had quoted to William IV the significance of the 1831 election results, and he pointed out that the loss of the bill would arouse hostility towards the House of Lords itself, and that the mutilation of the bill in the Upper House would revive the agitation for more radical and dangerous reforms such as universal suffrage and the ballot. In the end, Grey was prepared to force the king and the Lords in order to save the country, as he believed, from revolution; but after the Reform Act was passed he made it clear on several occasions that he was determined that it should be the end, and not the beginning, of constitutional change. The lesson which was ultimately to be learnt from the episode was that the Lords would, in the last resort, have to give way to the clearly expressed opinion of the electorate as represented by the majority of the House of Commons.

THE THREAT TO THE LORDS

The Reform Bill crisis nevertheless confirmed the radicals in their dislike of the Upper House. Francis Place had forecast in 1827 that the aristocracy 'would not govern this nation much longer, for the great moral and intellectual improvement of the masses has prepared them for assuming charge of the nation'. When the Lords rejected the Reform Bill in October 1831, *The Times* foretold the destruction of their power:

> They have done what they can never undo. They can never replace the House of Peers on its old foundations in the respect and confidence of the people. A gulf has been opened by the Peers between them and the British nation.

The successful coercion of the Lords and the passage of the bill thus seemed at first to herald the march of democracy. Tocqueville in 1833 saw it coming 'like a rising tide'. Under the stress of the events of 1831 even some Whig MPs joined in the radical demand that the Upper House should be reformed: Colonel Torrens suggested putting it into Schedule A, to be abolished along with the 'close' boroughs, and Charles Western declared the need for a large 'infusion of fresh blood' into the peerage to balance the Tory creations of sixty years. Radicals were even more outspoken. Daniel O'Connell wrote that

> They are mad, stark mad, to dare to fly in the face of popular
> sentiment and popular indignation. I do think we shall live to see the
> hereditary peerage abolished in England . . . If the English be true to
> themselves they must trample over the scoundrel Aristocracy.

In 1834 John Wade, editor of *The Black Book*, declared that the work of reform was unfinished until the Lords were dealt with, and a popular pamphlet declared that the next election would be fought on the question of whether the country should be governed by the House of Lords or on the principles of the Reform Act. As the Lords showed themselves even more hostile to the Liberal government's measures after Melbourne's return to office in 1835, popular anger was fanned by O'Connell on a speaking tour to Scotland and the north of England in 1837. He advocated the substitution of a second chamber of 150 peers chosen by constituencies of 200,000 electors. J.A. Roebuck, the radical MP, proposed depriving the Lords of the power to reject bills approved by the people's representatives and Francis Place demanded that they be reformed or abolished.[15]

Nevertheless, the radical campaign for reform of the Lords lacked wide popular support. The objection to them, as Gash pointed out, was not the hereditary basis of the chamber, but the fact that they opposed Liberal reforms passed by the Commons. Alexis de Tocqueville wrote perceptively in 1833 that people 'will complain of such-and-such a Lord, or the course which the House of Lords has adopted' but 'you will only very rarely notice . . . that violent feeling, full of hatred and envy, which incites the lower classes in France against all who are above them'. The middle classes hate 'some aristocrats, but not the aristocracy' and are themselves 'full of aristocratic prejudices'.[16] The general feeling was averse to interference with the Upper House, provided the peers would behave sensibly and not flout public opinion too often or too directly. Lord Morley assured George Villiers in July 1836 that 'the House of Lords is supported by the great mass of the property and intelligence of the country'; he believed that it was only 'the newspaper writers – *The Times*, the *Morning Herald*, the *Morning Post* brawl on one side, and the *Chronicle, Spectator*, and *Examiner* on the other, but without producing the slightest effect . . . There is nothing better ascertained than the entire impotence of the Press at this time in England.' Charles Villiers remarked that the aristocracy exaggerated the threat of popular violence towards them, but that they were in a 'humiliating and unsatisfactory position':[17]

> From their constitution nobody feels that they ought to be entrusted
> with the powers they have; but fearing the disturbance which a change
> might occasion by their resistance, most people are unwilling to make
> the attempt to effect it; and, while some abuse them and call for reform
> by bringing them in closer relation to the rest of the community,
> others defend their existence as they are, trusting to their yielding to
> fear upon every occasion when their judgement is opposed.

His wish, he wrote, would be for a reformed second chamber, possibly by extending the Scottish and Irish system of representation to the English peers, but there was as little support for any general reform of the Upper House as there was for the removal of the bishops from it. Speaker Abercromby wrote to Melbourne in 1835 that

> Everywhere I find that the House of Lords is a general topic of
> discussion. Their present safety consists in the absence of any
> practicable plan capable of being carried out without a violent struggle.

As Carlyle wrote in *Shooting Niagara – and After*,

> Our Aristocracy are not hated or disliked by any Class of the People –
> but on the contrary are looked up to – with a certain vulgarly human
> admiration and spontaneous recognition of their good qualities and
> good fortune, which is by no means wholly envious or wholly servile
> – by all classes, lower and lowest class included.[18]

Proposals for reform of the Upper House to make it more of
a representative assembly were, in any case, likely to be counter-
productive. The experience of the existing system of representative
peers for Scotland and Ireland suggested that such members were even
more likely to be conservative than the existing House in general,
while a reform that would create a second chamber which merely
mirrored the majority in the Commons would be pointless. The
real solution lay in the realization and acceptance by the leading
members of both the Lords and the administration of the need for
moderation and pragmatism in the joint task of carrying on the
government, broadly in accordance with the will of the electorate
but with a recognition of the need for restraint and compromise.
It was the English genius for pragmatic solutions which prevailed.
After 1837, the Lords' majority allowed itself to be guided by Peel
and Wellington, who were fully conscious of the need to keep the
Lords in touch with public feeling and not to put themselves again in
the position of 1834–5 when a Conservative administration lacked the
power to control the House of Commons, and had to give way despite
a majority in the Lords. The Liberals under Melbourne were equally
anxious not to become embroiled in any repeat of 1831–2, especially
as successive general elections since 1835 were eroding their position
in the Commons, and they were anxious not to play into the hands
of the Radicals.

As a result, the House of Lords lost its former high political profile
and demands for its reform consequently languished. When Russell
proposed, after the division on the Navigation Bill in 1849, the
admission of a limited number of life peers selected from distinguished
men in various walks of life who would contribute to the work of the
House without permanently increasing its numbers, the Cabinet was
unreceptive, failing to see the necessity of raising a controversial issue
and perhaps realizing that such a step might be regarded as an attack
on the independence of the House.[19] Later attempts to introduce life

peerages, in 1856 and 1869, were presented in the context of the difficulties over the judicial rather than the legislative role of the Lords, but they too were rejected, largely on the grounds that they might lead to the 'packing' of the House with government nominees, or the literary and scientific intellectuals favoured by Prince Albert.[20] There was, in truth, no widespread enthusiasm for reform of a House which, with all its theoretical deficiencies, worked well enough in practice and gave little real trouble.

The march of progress nevertheless demanded a further instalment of parliamentary reform and Disraeli's act of 1867 not only greatly extended the borough electorate but, in Bright's view, ended the era of aristocratic dominance. In his Edinburgh speech on 5 November 1868 he compared the act with the Glorious Revolution of 1688: the latter had stripped absolute power from the monarchy only to confer it on the aristocracy, but 1867 marked the abdication of the nobility and power 'has been given henceforth and for ever to the people'. He added:

> In every country the possessors of great wealth are likely to have
> power. I am not complaining of this. . . . But although the influence
> of wealth is great, the spirit of the country has changed, and the centre
> of power has been moved. . . . There is no longer a contest between
> us and the House of Lords; we need no longer bring charges against
> a selfish oligarchy; we no longer dread the power of the territorial
> magnates; we no longer feel ourselves domineered over by a class; . . .
> the power which hitherto has ruled over us is shifted.[21]

ARISTOCRATIC RECOVERY

The Lords were not done for, however, nor had Disraeli intended that they should be. His purpose in passing the Reform Act was not to advance democracy but to increase the Conservative Party's power in Parliament. As the bill was a Conservative measure, the House of Lords offered no strong opposition to it, only one of their number speaking against it and the Liberal peers supporting it, both sides showing an impressive degree of party discipline. What was advancing in the mid- and later nineteenth century was not in fact 'democracy', if that is defined as 'government by the people', but *parliamentary* government – the transfer of sovereign authority to a Parliament which was not yet, and perhaps never has been the instrument of popular power, but the body through which the dominant classes in society exercise their control of the executive. As the peerage remained part of that dominant class until the end of the nineteenth century, the House of Lords did not fade away, though its power and prestige derived from the continued power of its members as individuals rather than from its own authority as an institution.

The aristocracy also maintained its hold on the institutions of local, especially county, government, its sons staffed the army and Civil Service and administered the empire, and the public schools to which the sons of the wealthier middle classes were increasingly sent inculcated aristocratic rather than bourgeois values and ideals. Matthew Arnold wrote in 1861 that 'The aristocracy still . . . administers public affairs; and it is a great error to suppose, as many persons in England suppose, that it administers but does not govern'.[22] The rule of a wealthy, leisured class who were motivated by a tradition of public service rather than by personal ambition was widely accepted as preferable to the growth of a professionalized bureaucracy; here, as in the eighteenth century, Englishmen compared themselves favourably with continental practices.

The aristocracy also showed wisdom in conforming to the values of Victorian society. *Blackwood's Edinburgh Magazine* printed in 1834 some 'Hints to the Aristocracy', warning that social exclusiveness and aloofness from the gentry and middle classes would isolate them and engender hostility: 'support must be won by condescension: affection can only be secured by good deeds'. It recommended greater attention to social inferiors, greater 'seriousness' of conduct and participation in the recreations and amusements of the people.[23] These old-fashioned aristocratic virtues were indeed reflected in the nineteenth-century peerage and helped them to retain the respect of the country. Adam Badeau, an American consul, wrote in 1885 that the English aristocracy was still the pivot of social and political life, and T.H.S. Escott in 1879 that 'the aristocratic principle is still paramount, form[ing] the foundations of our social structure'.[24] Public opinion continued to ape aristocratic fashions, and men who made new fortunes in trade, industry and the professions aspired to join those coveted upper echelons of society rather than to form their own. Even the majority of the 'new' peers of the last twenty years of the century whose wealth came from industry had passed through a period of acclimatization by purchasing land, mingling in aristocratic circles and acquiring aristocratic manners.

Thus, not only did the aristocracy as a class retain its connections with many areas of Victorian social life, but the House of Lords retained its prestige as the assembly in which so many men of weight and influence sat. As the 12th duke of Somerset wrote at the end of this period:[25]

> In every civilized country there will arise a class of men, who, having inherited wealth, are released from the necessity of manual labour and from the drudgery of professional employment. Even under Republican institutions, this class will gradually assume many of the characteristics of a social aristocracy. They attach importance to inherited names, to family connections, and they like to trace out an ancestral history. . . .
>
> A form of government which repudiates and ostracises this class is defective. It loses the benefit of abilities which run to waste, and drives men, who are not unfit for public employment, to pass their lives in enforced idleness. . . . Political affairs, meanwhile, being entirely relinquished to the industrial classes, are lowered to a trade, and pursued in a sordid spirit as a profitable employment.

This argument possibly exaggerated the disinterestedness of the Victorian peerage. A different view, of the value of the House of Lords as a body widely representative of the major interests in the nation, was put by the earl of Rosebery in 1884, speaking to propose setting up a select committee on improving the efficiency of the House of Lords. He asserted that the House was 'neither so popular as its friends assert, nor so unpopular as its enemies make out', and that though its members 'have not, and they cannot have, the constant compulsory connection with the nation that adds so much to the strength of the House of Commons', the House had a claim to be representative of 'a great variety of many complex interests'. He instanced the Churches, both through the Anglican episcopate and by the presence of several Roman Catholic laymen, and some Presbyterians; the professions, notably the army, navy and the law, though defective in the sciences, literature and medicine; and the 'commercial and mercantile interests of the community', including 'four or five noble Lords connected with the banking and railway interests'. The decrease in the value of and income derived from land, and the absolute as well as relative increase in fortunes made in commerce, should be reflected in the House by the introduction of life peerages for suitably representative individuals. He concluded, 'I firmly believe what the people of England want is no abolition and no violent reform of this House, but simply to have as efficient a Second Chamber as can be furnished.'[26] The earl of Onslow who followed Rosebery agreed that more life peers, especially from the colonies, and admirals and generals not rich enough to receive hereditary peerages, would improve the House, and he suggested that there should be a power to resign membership when peers were not politically active, whether through old age or lack of interest. Of the 516 peers then extant, he declared, 8 were minors, 6 permanently employed abroad, and 132 (over 25 per cent) over 70 years of age. Only 332 of the 516 had spoken or voted during the last session, against an average of 345 over the whole Parliament (1874–80).[27]

Lord Granville agreed with many of the points Rosebery had made, and further declared it scandalous that on ordinary occasions so few Lords bothered to attend, whereas on party questions they flooded in in crowds. Salisbury, however, for the government, pointed out that this was not unknown in the Commons. He doubted whether a select committee would be an effective way of dealing with the problems, and the motion was defeated by 38 to 77.[28]

Discussions about the effectiveness or acceptability of the House of Lords surfaced occasionally throughout the Victorian period, but in truth no one proposed any scheme that received general support, and governments of both parties shied away from the constitutional and political crisis that would surely result from any attempt at reform. In the absence of overwhelming public demand for change or for abolition, no politician would burn his fingers with the question until absolute necessity required it: that occasion was not to arise until 1909. In the meantime, the House and the peerage continued to function as an organic part of government and society. The peerage was not a separate caste, it had no legal or financial privileges, and as great landowners and local dignitaries the Lords saw themselves and were seen as having an acceptable and valuable role in society at every level. Only when the threat of discriminatory taxation of land values in the 'People's Budget' to finance social welfare benefits seemed to sound the knell of a landed class already under pressure from falling incomes and rising expenditure did its representatives try to assert rights which they had long allowed to sleep, and in the context of the party struggle of the Edwardian period that was to prove fatal. The Duke of Wellington's warnings in the 1830s[29] were vindicated when his successors at the head of the Conservative Party neglected the lesson experience had taught him.

THE ELYSIAN FIELDS

'I am dead; dead, but in the Elysian fields.' So Disraeli described his elevation to the House of Lords in 1876.[30] Ill health demanded a respite from the pressure of business and attendance as Prime Minister in the House of Commons. The choice lay between complete retirement, or a peerage and continuing in office. Either path, he asserted, led to political oblivion. He consulted Salisbury, who advised that it was

> a choice of evils. You would be very heartily welcomed in the House
> of Lords: and you would give life to the dullest assembly in the world.
> But the command of the House of Lords would be a poor exchange
> for the singular influence you now exercise in the Commons.[31]

Disraeli had often written in terms of contempt for the House of Lords, as fit for old men and grandees without talent. He admired aristocratic pedigree and believed that the aristocracy had an essential place in English society and in the maintenance of those traditions which he saw as central in his conception of Conservatism. But the House of Lords seemed to him to be so inferior in power to the Commons that since 1832 it had become a political anachronism, a mere court of registration for the decrees of the Lower House. Even as a revising chamber he saw no use for it: it was absurd, he wrote in *Coningsby*, to suppose that the weak could restrain the strong. A political realist, the English Bismarck in this respect at least, he was interested in power and not in outward show. Peerages were sops to vanity rather than rewards for service: as Prime Minister he gave them as favours, but he had a high regard for the importance of their being attached to respectable birth and wealth. He thought an income of at least £10,000 necessary to maintain its dignity, a sum five times that considered essential by *Burke's Peerage*.

Yet Disraeli's cynicism was often a pose. His apparent preference for retirement, one commentator has suggested, was affected in order to induce his friends to persuade him to take the peerage, and though he certainly did so only because his health was not up to further attendance in the Commons, he revelled in his title and status as an earl. Lord Selborne, Gladstone's Lord Chancellor in 1872–4, remarked that Disraeli

> began political life as an adventurer; and his social position was
> for a long time ambiguous. Not even the romance of success in an
> extraordinary self-made career, and the great office of Prime Minister
> . . . went so far to overcome these drawbacks, as the acquisition
> of high rank, and of a place in the most aristocratic assembly of
> the realm. This was the crowning conquest of a wonderful personal
> history; it gratified his innate taste for prestige and splendour, without
> any abatement of real power.[32]

The House of Lords may have seemed an anachronism in the materialistic money-making age of later Victorian England, to be dismissed along with the artificial 'Gothic' of the palace of Westminster as a frippery in an earnest age: Gathorne Hardy, on becoming Lord Cranbrook in 1878, noted that he 'went through the quaint and somewhat absurd ceremony of taking my seat in the House of Lords'.[33] Wellington had once remarked that 'the House of Commons is everything in this country, and the House of Lords nothing'. But its life was not extinct. The general lack of contentiousness in the relations between the two Houses in the 1870s did not signify that the Lords was a mere ornamental survival of a past age. Bagehot remarked in 1868 that the House of Lords was not a bulwark against revolution, but its existence signified that revolution was unlikely to happen.[34] In the interlude of the 'age of equipoise' which mid-Victorian England enjoyed after the turbulence of the 'age of reform' and before the age of social conflict in the decade before the First World War, the House of Lords and the peerage basked in the general approval, or at least indifference, of the public. Social harmony and the acceptance of social distinctions gave the Lords a recognized place in English life, and if agricultural depression, Irish bankruptcies and falling English land values robbed the old aristocracy of its security, new men were reaching upwards to take their places. From the 1880s, the influx of wealth from trade, industry and the supply of the mass market greatly increased the numbers of the peerage, and perhaps led to the more assertive tone which the Lords adopted towards reformist legislation in the Edwardian era. The 1870s marked the end of one era and the start of another, in which the Lords had to be taught again the lessons which their older and wiser predecessors had learnt more willingly in the 1830s. The new earl of Beaconsfield correctly foretold in 1880 that 'the politics of this country will probably for the next few years mainly consist in an assault upon the constitutional position of the landed interest'.[35] For the moment, however, the peerage and the House of Lords enjoyed an indian summer in which his vision of the Elysian Fields seemed altogether appropriate.

REFERENCES

1. W.L. Arnstein, 'The Survival of the Victorian Aristocracy', in *The Rich, the Well-Born and the Powerful*, ed. F.C. Jaher (Urbana, Ill., 1973).
2. See above, Chapter 6.
3. (J. Wade), *The Extraordinary Black Book* (1832 edn), pp. 245–85.
4. S.J. Reid, *Life and Letters of the first Earl of Durham 1792–1840*, (1906), I, pp. 341–2; *The Creevey Papers*, ed. Sir H. Maxwell (1903), II,

p. 55 (12 Nov. 1822).

5. *The Greville Diary*, ed. P.W. Wilson (1927), I, p. 190.

6. N. Gash, *Reaction and Reconstruction in English Politics, 1832–52* (Oxford, 1965), pp. 30–1.

7. *Correspondence of Earl Grey with H.M. King William IV and with Sir Herbert Taylor from Nov. 1830 to June 1832*, ed. Henry. Earl Grey (1867), I, pp. 276–81, 360–8; D. Le Marchant, *Memoir of John Charles, Viscount Althorp, Third Earl Spencer* (1876), pp. 407–13; E.A. Smith, *Lord Grey 1764–1845* (Oxford, 1990), pp. 268–78; Hansard, 3rd Ser. XII, 1005–6.

8. Macaulay to Hannah Macaulay, 13 Sept. 1831: *Letters of T.B. Macaulay*, ed. T. Pinney (Cambridge, 1974), II, p. 99.

9. The debate, wrote Greville, was 'a magnificent display, and incomparably superior to that in the House of Commons': *Journal of the Reign of George IV and William IV*, ed. H. Reeve (1874), 10 Oct. 1831; II, p. 202.

10. Wellington to Mrs Arbuthnot, 12 Oct.: *Wellington and his Friends*, ed. The Duke of Wellington (1965), p. 99. J.C. Hobhouse, 1st Baron Broughton, *Recollections of a Long Life* ed. Lady Dorchester (1909), 12 Oct. For anger against the Bishops, see above p. 84–6.

11. [Alexander Somerville], *Autobiography of a Working Man* (1848), 243.

12. 15 May 1822.

13. Le Marchant, Diary, in *Memoir of . . . Althorp*, p. 433; Lyttelton to Lady Lyttelton, 19 May: *Correspondence of Sarah Spencer, Lady Lyttelton 1782–1870*, ed. Mrs Hugh Wyndham (1912), p. 271.

14. Creevey to Miss Ord, 26 [May]: *Creevey Papers*, II, p. 247.

15. Place to J.C. Hobhouse, 19 Dec. 1827. B.L. Add. MS 35148, f8; *The Times*, 10 Oct. 1831; Arnstein, 'The Survival of the Victorian Aristocracy', pp. 205–6; O'Connell to R. Barrett, 5 and 8 Oct. 1831, *The Correspondence of Daniel O'Connell*, ed. M.R. O'Connell (Dublin, 1977), IV, pp. 354, 356; C.S. Parker, *Life and Letters of Sir James Graham 1792–1861* (1907), I, pp. 125–7; *Appendix to the Black Book* (1834); E. Lytton Bulwer, *Letter to a Late Cabinet Minister* (1834); *Annual Register* (1835), 367 ff; R.E. Leader, *Life of J.A. Roebuck* (1897), p. 69; G. Wallas, *Life of Francis Place* (1918), p. 346; quoted in Gash, *Reaction and Reconstruction*, pp. 35–6.

16. A. de Tocqueville, *Journeys to England and Ireland*, ed. J.P. Mayer (1968), p. 70.

17. *Life and Letters of George William Frederick, 4th Earl of Clarendon*, ed. Sir H. Maxwell (1913) I, pp. 123–7.

18. *Lord Melbourne's Papers*, ed. L.C. Sanders (1890), p. 291; T. Carlyle, *Critical and Historical Essays*, in *Works* (1869), XI, pp. 339–92.

19. Gash, *Reaction and Reconstruction*, pp. 52–8.

20. W.D. Jones, *Lord Derby and Victorian Conservatism*, (Oxford, 1956), p. 210.

21. *Public Addresses by John Bright, MP*, ed. J.E. Thorold Rogers (1879), pp. 122–5.

22. Arnstein, 'Survival of the Victorian Aristocracy', pp. 212–21.

23. *Blackwood's Edinburgh Magazine*, XXXV (1834), 68–80.

24. A. Badeau, *Aristocracy in England* (New York, 1885), p. 5; T.H.S. Escott, *England, her People, Polity, and Pursuits* (1879), quoted in Arnstein, 'The Survival of the Victorian Aristocracy', p. 207.

25. *Monarchy and Democracy* (1880), quoted in *Letters, Remains, and Memoirs of Edward 12th Duke of Somerset* ed. W.H. Mallock and Lady Gwendolen Ramsden (1893), p. 493.
26. Hansard, CCLXXIX, 937–58, 20 June 1884.
27. *Ibid.*, 958–60.
28. *Ibid.*, 961, 963–7.
29. See Chapter 5, pp. 100–1.
30. D. Slater, 'Beaconsfield: or, Disraeli in the Elysian Fields', in *Parliamentary History, Libraries, & Records: Essays presented to Maurice Bond*, ed. H.S. Cobb, House of Lords Record Office (1981), pp. 66–76.
31. Salisbury to Disraeli, 27 July 1876: W.F. Monypenny and G.E. Buckle, *Life of Benjamin Disraeli* (1929 edn), II, p. 834.
32. *Memorials, Personal and Political, 1869–95 by Roundell Palmer, Earl of Selborne*, ed. S.M. Palmer (1898), I, pp. 447–8.
33. *The Diary of Gathorne Hardy, First Lord Cranbrook* ed. N. Johnson (Oxford, 1981), p. 371.
34. J.R.M. Butler, *The Passing of the Great Reform Bill* (1914), p. 286; W. Bagehot, *The English Constitution* (1963 edn), pp. 132–3.
35. D. Cannadine, *The Decline and Fall of the British Aristocracy*, (1990) p. 35.

PART THREE

Decline, but not Fall, 1880–1911

CHAPTER EIGHT
The Pattern of Change

The mid-nineteenth century peerage was still a predominantly landed aristocracy. Of men ennobled between 1837 and 1851, 90 per cent had come from families already established as owners of substantial estates and they joined a pre-Victorian peerage which overwhelmingly represented the 'landed interest'.[1] Even in the 1880s Lord Rosebery, speaking in the House to propose a select committee to consider improving the efficiency and acceptability of the Lords, admitted that 'there is too much receiving of rent in this House and too little paying of rent. We represent too much one class.'[2] Newcomers to the peerage were still expected to draw substantial incomes from rents and other forms of revenue deriving from the land, to be men of independent means and of sufficient leisure to give their time to political pursuits, and to be acceptable as members of a homogeneous social elite.

By the turn of the century, the pattern was beginning to change as 'new men' entered that wealthy elite. That was partly because there were now few families of great landed property who were not already possessors of titles, so that new creations had perforce to come from elsewhere, and partly because the long process of commercial and industrial change had bred a new class of plutocratic businessmen who felt that their interests ought to be more prominently represented in the corridors of power, and their wives and daughters eligible for inclusion in the highest layer of society. Between 1882 and 1896, 35 per cent of new peerages were conferred on men of other than predominantly landed background, and between 1897 and 1911 the numbers rose to 43 per cent.[3] Even so, less than 50 out of 100 new creations between 1885 and 1911 lacked landed estate altogether. The House of Lords on the eve of the First World War was still predominantly a landowning assembly, and in so far as its membership coincided with the 'elite' in British society that elite can hardly be described as 'open'. The great majority of new creations before the 1890s came from the baronetcy, the Scots and Irish peerages and the wealthy landed gentry. The House of Lords did not create the aristocracy, but was merely the upper layer of it.

The changing composition of the House of Lords and its attitudes towards the political issues of the day which have been noted by some commentators thus reflected external changes in the nature of society and politics. The weakening of the Lords as a barrier against threats to aristocratic dominance did not arise from within the chamber, but from the weakening of the landed sector of the economy and of the aristocracy as a governing elite. That weakening occurred not so much in absolute terms but relative to the commercial and industrial sectors, and from the challenge to aristocratic governance from the growth of democratic ideas and institutions. The relative fall in rental incomes and the value of land, most notably in Ireland but felt sensibly in Britain too, might be compensated in some cases by more profitable investment in urban property, in the funds, and in mining and other industrial pursuits. The peerage was still a wealthy class. The tide, however, had set in nationally against the old order in which the possession of land of itself conferred social and political authority. Nor was the possession of land now so much regarded as a social responsibility to tenants and dependants, but rather as an economic asset or a status symbol, as a private benefit rather than a public responsibility. The 'abdication of the governors' described by one historian as a critical factor in the displacement of eighteenth-century paternalism by Victorian class-consciousness was in fact more strongly characteristic of the last two decades of the nineteenth century.[4] As the rising claims of democracy, particularly in the towns, were directed against aristocratic dominance, so the aristocracy retreated to defensive positions, ready to resist attacks, real or fancied, rather than continue to give orders. The resistance of the Conservative peers in the Upper House to Liberal 'social' reforms in the decade before the First World War was part of this process, translated into party political terms. The House of Lords was conscious of the threat to its own constitutional and political authority which arose from this conflict, but the conflict itself was a party battle rather than a constitutional one.

CHANGING MEMBERSHIP

Between 1882 and 1911, 242 individuals received peerages of first creation or promotions to a higher rank, bringing the total size of the House, including representative peers and bishops, to 630. Of the 200 or so newcomers to the peerage, about one third had risen from the professions, the armed forces and the Civil and Diplomatic Services, and a quarter came from old-established landed families. The remainder, nearly 39 per cent of the total, represented the influx of 'new' families, mainly from industrial and commercial backgrounds, the new plutocracy of bankers, brewers, iron, steel and shipping magnates, manufacturers and members of the stock exchange.[5] The proportion of new peers from these categories continued to rise during the period. The consequent change in the balance of membership did not represent a deliberate attempt to widen the social or economic basis of the peerage. It was still the case that most peerages, even many in the 'new' categories, were bestowed on men who had been MPs, in return for political services either in the Commons or in the country, perhaps by contributing to party funds or local party organization.

Two thirds of those ennobled between 1885 and 1914 had served in the Lower House, some as high-ranking ministers of the Crown:[6] Gathorne Hardy, Conservative MP 1856–78, for example, had served in a number of departments and was Home Secretary in 1867–8 and Secretary for War in 1874–8.[7] He went to the Lords as 1st Baron Cranbrook in 1878 and subsequently served in Cabinet as Secretary for India 1878–80 and Lord President of the Council 1885–6 and 1886–92. Other distinguished ex-ministers included G.J. Goschen, a director of the Bank of England and MP for the City and other constituencies, who held several offices between 1865 and 1900 including that of Chancellor of the Exchequer 1887–92. He became Viscount Goschen in 1900. Stafford Northcote, MP 1855–85, also rose to be Chancellor of the Exchequer 1874–80 and leader of the House of Commons after 1876; he was created earl of Iddesleigh in 1885 and was Foreign Secretary in 1886–7. Other ex-ministers received peerages in compensation when they were 'shelved' on their party's return to office: Robert Lowe, W.F.C. Temple and Edward Hugesson Knatchbull-Hugesson received such peerages from Gladstone in 1880, Sir Lyon Playfair in 1892 and the Conservative H. Matthews in 1895.[8] A different kind of 'consolation' peerage perhaps was the viscountcy conferred a month after his death in 1891 on the widow of W.H. Smith, the newsagent and bookseller who had become First Lord of the Admiralty, Secretary for War and leader of the Commons between 1887 and 1891.

Apart from senior ministerial figures, men who gave long service to their parties in lesser offices also sometimes reached the Lords.

These included William Hood Walrond who was a junior Lord of the Treasury 1885–6 and 1886–92, Conservative chief whip and Patronage Secretary to the Treasury 1895–1902, and Chancellor of the Duchy of Lancaster 1902–5, who became Baron Waleran, and George John Shaw-Lefevre who held a string of junior ministerial posts during thirty-two years as an MP and was created Baron Eversley in 1906. In 1887 George Sclater-Booth, Conservative MP 1857–87 who had been Secretary to the Poor Law Board, Financial Secretary to the Treasury and President of the Local Government Board in Disraeli's administrations was created Baron Basing as one of eight peers to mark the queen's golden jubilee. Lord Randolph Churchill described him as 'mediocrity distinguished by a double-barrelled name', though he was more objectively to be considered a rather dull but competent and painstaking public servant. Others who rose to high position and a peerage included Thomas Brassey, son of a millionaire railway contractor, who became a barrister and was a Liberal MP from 1868 to 1886, serving as a Lord of Admiralty and Secretary to the Admiralty before he was defeated in two constituencies in 1886 and was given a 'consolation peerage' as Baron Brassey. He became Governor of Victoria, 1895–1901. Augustus Hare remarked that he grew 'from nothing to a peerage, with only boundless money and commonsense as his aides-de-camp'.

Parliamentary service in other capacities was also rewarded, usually to mark retirement. Thomas Erskine May, Clerk to the House of Commons 1871–86, was created Baron Farnborough on his retirement, only to die six days later. Ex-Speakers could expect a peerage: examples here include Henry Brand, Speaker 1872–84 (Viscount Hampden) and Arthur Wellesley Peel, fifth son of Sir Robert the Prime Minister, 1884–95 (Viscount Peel). Another instance was that of Edmund Beckett, a lawyer and leader of the parliamentary bar who became Baron Grimthorpe in 1886.

Distinguished public service in the armed forces and the colonial and diplomatic service of the Crown was rewarded with peerages. Henry Brougham Loch served in the Royal Navy in 1840–2 but made his name commanding the Third Bengal Cavalry in 1844 and Skinner's Horse in 1850–2, and went on to serve as attaché to Lord Elgin on missions to China and Japan 1857–60, and as Governor of Victoria 1884–9 and the Cape of Good Hope 1889–95. He became Baron Loch in 1895. More famous still were Garnet Wolseley, whose exploits in Egypt and elsewhere were recognized by a barony and a grant of £30,000 in 1892 and a viscountcy in 1895, and Field Marshals Roberts and Kitchener and Admiral of the Fleet Lord Fisher. Frederick

Seymour, a career naval officer who served in Burma and the Crimea in the 1850s and commanded the channel squadron 1874–7 and the Mediterranean fleet 1880–3, where he served alongside Wolseley in Egypt, became Baron Alcester in 1882 with a parliamentary grant of £25,000.

Imperial proconsuls such as Cromer and Milner, and others who served the empire also reached the peerage. Arthur Hamilton-Gordon, youngest son of the 4th earl of Aberdeen, the Prime Minister, was Governor in turn of New Brunswick, Trinidad, Mauritius, Fiji, New Zealand and Ceylon, the last after the grant of the title of Baron Stanmore in 1893. Donald Alexander Smith started as a clerk in the Hudson Bay Company in 1838, became governor in 1869 and held a number of important offices in Canada. He was partly responsible for the building of the Canadian Pacific Railway, and became High Commissioner for Canada 1896–1914, being created Baron Strathcona and Mount Royal in 1887. He raised and equipped Strathcona's Horse in the Boer War and died worth £4 million.

The Diplomatic Service was represented in the new peerages after 1880. Thomas Henry Sanderson became a junior clerk in the Foreign Office in 1859 and served missions in Denmark 1863–4, attended the Black Sea Conference in 1871, the Alabama claims conference in 1871–2, and became private secretary to both Derby and Granville at the Foreign Office between 1866 and 1885. He ended as Permanent Under-Secretary for Foreign Affairs 1894–1906 and Baron Sanderson in 1905. His successor in the last named office, Charles Hardinge, who had previously been ambassador to St Petersburg, also received a peerage on his retirement in 1910.

Ex-civil servants began to appear in the Lords during this period. In 1871 Frederick Rogers, who had been Registrar of Joint Stock Companies, Emigration Commissioner, and Permanent Under-Secretary for the Colonies, was given a peerage as Baron Blachford. Eight others from the 'meritorious ranks of the civil service' were ennobled between 1874 and 1894, all but one on Gladstone's recommendation. Blachford, wrote J.H. Newman, was 'the most gifted, the most talented, and of the most wonderful grasp of mind of any of his contemporaries' at Oriel in the 1830s; he was also a 'thoroughly earnest churchman' of the Gladstonian type. Other representatives of the Civil Service included Arthur Hobhouse, who served as an Endowed Schools Commissioner 1868–72, a law member of the Council of the Governor-General of India 1872–7, and a member of the Judicial Committee of the Privy Council 1877–1904, during which time he became Baron Hobhouse (1885), and Reginald Earle

Welby, who served in the Treasury from 1856 to 1894, becoming Permanent Secretary in 1885, and was created Baron Welby in 1894. Public service in other spheres included men such as Francis Knollys, Private Secretary to King Edward VII from 1870 and to George V from 1910 to 1913, who was created a baron in 1902 and viscount in 1911. Robert James Loyd-Lindsay who won the VC in the Crimea, became Equerry to the Prince of Wales 1858–9, retired from the army, became a Conservative MP for twenty years, was Financial Secretary to the War Office 1877–80, and became Baron Wantage in 1885. He devoted the later part of his life to public service in Berkshire and to the volunteer movement in particular.

The most noticeable change in the composition of the peerage was the increasing ennoblement of men who had made fortunes in business. Starting with the creation of Edward Strutt, cotton manufacturer, as Lord Belper in 1856, there followed in 1880 Gladstone's creations of Sir Ivor Bertie Guest, the South Wales ironmaster, as Baron Wimborne and Sir Arthur Edmond Guinness, the brewer, as Baron Ardilaun. Of these three, Strutt was the only one who had no previous aristocratic connections, though his ennoblement was as much the reward for his political and public service as MP for Nottingham as a recognition of the importance of commerce and industry. Nevertheless, *The Times* saluted his elevation as 'a graceful and prudent act', showing 'a wise appreciation of the signs of the times . . . for . . . the descendants of the mailed barons of England to admit into their order a man who not only has made but is making his fortunes by spindles and looms'. Guest and Guinness were also eminent businessmen but both had already inherited baronetcies and their wives were daughters of a duke and an earl respectively.[9]

It was Salisbury who set the trend in full swing during his ministry of 1886–92. His advancement of Henry Allsop, the brewer of Burton-on-Trent, to the Lords as Baron Hindlip in 1886 was followed by those of a governor of the Bank of England, a textile manufacturer, an armaments manufacturer, a second Guinness peerage and several others. The pace accelerated after 1905, when the Liberals ennobled more businessmen in eight years than had the Conservatives in seventeen. Between 1901 and 1910, 24 out of 70 new peers came from business, and by 1913, 59 of the 104 peers on the Liberal benches had been created since 1892.[10]

Among the 'businessmen' peers were men such as Michael Arthur Bass, head of the family brewery at Burton-on-Trent, who was created Baron Burton by Gladstone in 1886 after serving as a Liberal MP since 1865. He then deserted the Liberals, partly because of Irish Home Rule but also because of the party's growing dependence on the nonconformist temperance lobby. His obituary in *The Times* in 1909 spoke of his 'princely generosity, business acumen, public spirit, patriotism, and kindness of heart', which in this case gained him a coronet. Another eminent businessman with claims for public service was Henry Hucks Gibbs, partner in the family firm of Antony Gibbs & Sons, London merchants, who was a director and sometime governor of the Bank of England and Conservative MP for the City. He was created Baron Aldenham in 1896 and on his death in 1907 left over £700,000 gross and estates totalling 4,472 acres in four counties. The less respectable side of self-made peers from trade was perhaps illustrated by the case of James Williamson of Ashton, Lancashire, who was educated at Lancaster Grammar School and carried on a successful business as a linoleum manufacturer at Ashton. He was Liberal MP 1886–95 when he was the recipient as Baron Ashton of one of the four peerages created on Rosebery's retirement from the premiership. The editor of the *Complete Peerage* caustically remarked that

> There would seem at first sight little to justify two out of these four creations, *viz* this and 'Wandsworth', but as the bad days of jobbery are gone by, and it is impossible that a Minister desirous of mending the House of Lords should recommend anyone for a peerage except on the ground of merit and public service, it is clear that the grantees must have privately advanced solid reasons for their promotion, though these have not been, and are not likely to be, revealed to the outside world.

The case of Sydney James Stern, the head of the London firm of Stern Brothers, was even more shocking. He had been an MP for only four years and had never held any public office when Rosebery included him in his list in 1895 as Baron Wandsworth. The magazine *Truth* baldly remarked that 'he knew well what he wanted – it was a Peerage. He did not waste his time in studying politics or in making speeches, being a *practical* man, *he used the most practical means* to attain the object of his ambition.'

Many other businessmen ennobled in the last thirty years of this period were men of great wealth. John Mulholland, Baron Dunleath (1892) was a Belfast linen manufacturer and Conservative MP who left over £500,000 personal estate as well as large landed property in Northern Ireland. Sir Charles Henry Mills, a partner in Glyn, Mills Bank (also a Conservative MP) left nearly £1,500,000. Allsopp the brewer, Baron Hindlip, left over £500,000 and Nathan Rothschild, the first Jewish peer (1885) who was the son of the first practising Jew to sit in the House of Commons, hardly depleted his immense fortune by his expenditure on Liberal party causes and the same might be said of Samuel Montagu, head of the banking firm of the same name, who became Baron Swaythling in 1907. Other wealthy provincial businessmen included Edmund Beckett Faber, senior partner in Beckett's Bank of Leeds, a director of the London County Westminster and Parr's Bank, of the London and North Western Railway and the Sun Insurance Company, William Henry Wills, of the Bristol tobacco company and a director of the Great Western Railway, and William James Pirrie, partner in the Belfast shipbuilders Harland & Wolff.

In addition to those peers who were genuinely involved in, or had been directly managing businesses, many of the landed peerage in the later nineteenth century became company directors. This, however, does not indicate the scale of the connection between the peerage and the world of business. The *Complete Peerage* lists 167 in 1896,[11] but the editor, while acknowledging the presence of 'magnates in coal, shipping, and other industries . . . of late . . . raised to the peerage', made caustic reference to 'peers in search of fees allowing themselves to be put forward as figureheads of commercial enterprises of which they have no special knowledge, and for which they have had no special training'.

Many of the new peers from the world of business lacked landed estates of any significant size though they might acquire a country house for social reasons. They were 'a moneyed nobility, of men who did not have a stake in the country'.[12] Nevertheless, the peerage as a whole was still predominantly a landed aristocracy. It has been calculated that between 1886 and 1893, 324 peers held landed estates in England and Scotland of over 10,000 acres, 70 of them with over 50,000 acres. Wealthy country gentlemen were still being added to the peerage also: John Allan Rolls (Baron Llangattock 1892) was a Conservative knight of the shire and a leading landowner and figure in Monmouthshire, Master of the Monmouth Hunt, a generous contributor to local charities and breeder of shire horses and shorthorn cattle. The Ridleys, whose peerage in 1900 rewarded the 1st viscount's public and political services (he was Home Secretary 1895–1900), were great landowners in Northumberland, and Cromer's wife inherited the Grey family estates in the same county. Wentworth Beaumont, said to be 'among the last truly great landowners to have been ennobled', was created Baron Allendale in 1906 after forty years as a back-bench Liberal MP. His fortune of over £3 million was based on lead and coal mines on his property in Northumberland and Durham. The richest men in the country at the end of the nineteenth century were still, mainly, the great landowners, and they predominated in the House of Lords.[13]

However, the lavish creations of the years 1885–1911 were beginning to change the balance. If in some ways this broadened the experience of the House of Lords and gave it a more plausible claim to represent the major interests of the country, it also diminished the respect in which it had been held when it was seen as a combination of the old aristocracy and of the distinguished public servants of the time. Plutocracy was displacing aristocracy, and material wealth rather than lineage was becoming the hallmark of the social elite. Walter Bagehot had written in 1867 that one major use of the order of nobility in England was to 'prevent the rule of wealth – the religion of gold' and to preserve 'the *style* of society' from 'the worship of money' for its own sake.[14] By the 1880s the ability of the old aristocracy to withstand the infiltration of new wealth had weakened, and the prestige of the House of Lords in turn diminished. As Bagehot noted even in the 1860s,

> The social prestige of the aristocracy is, as every one knows, immensely less than it was a hundred years or even fifty years ago. . . . The rise of industrial wealth in countless forms has brought in a competitor. . . . Every day our companies, our railways, our debentures, and our shares, tend more and more to multiply these *surroundings* of the aristocracy, and in time they will hide it.

Token ennoblement of a few distinguished scientists, artists and men of letters such as William Thomson the physicist, Sir Frederick Leighton, P.R.A. (who died the day after the conferment of his peerage), Joseph Lister the surgeon and Alfred Tennyson hardly achieved Salisbury's avowed wish 'to give the feeling that the House of Lords contained something besides rich men and politicians', though it did give a nod of recognition towards other forms of merit in an increasingly democratic age.

PEERS IN POLITICS

The House of Lords remained a partisan assembly in the period 1880–1911, as it had predominantly been since 1832. Few of its members who attended at all regularly were not committed to a political party, and even on the relatively rare occasions when the 'backwoodsmen' were induced to attend a debate and vote they did so because they wanted to strengthen one (usually the conservative) side on a particular issue that affected their interests. 'Really,' wrote Lord Carnarvon in a memorandum on 'The House of Lords' in 1875, 'cross-benchers play less part than is supposed. On the whole there are two broad divisions: government and opposition.'. Genuine independents were rare: most cross-benchers were men disaffected with their former party rather than true independents. Even the great majority of the law lords, ennobled supposedly for their contribution to the judicial business of the House, were party men: ten of the sixteen created between 1885 and 1914 were party politicians from the Commons and they played a full part in political debates; four of the five Lord Chancellors of the period were ex-MPs. Even archbishops and bishops were political appointees and the majority took party whips. In 1880, 280 peers described themselves as 'Conservative' and 203 as 'Liberal', against only thirteen of no party, six of whom were non-attenders. In 1906 there were 354 'Conservatives', 107 'Liberal Unionists' (who combined with the Conservatives in 1912), 98 'Liberals', and 43 of no party among the lay peers. Respectively, 20 and 19 of the 26 prelates of the Church similarly professed party support.[15]

The major change in the balance of parties during this period was the consequence of Gladstone's commitment to Irish Home Rule, which divided the former Liberal Party, the bulk of the old 'Whig' element in the Lords, together with some more radical Liberals, moving towards the Conservatives. The change took effect gradually in the Upper House since the Lords did not have to vote on Home Rule until 1893, the 1886 bill being defeated in the Commons. Until 1893 in fact the Liberal Unionists, as they came to be called, maintained an independent stance, voting more often with the Liberals than with the Conservatives, particularly on English and Irish land questions and matters concerning local government and franchise reform. It was the apprehensions of the old Whig magnates over Chamberlain's radicalism and the 'unauthorized programme' as well as their dislike of Irish Home Rule that led to their gradual realignment with the Conservatives. The latter in turn after the 1884–5 enfranchisement of the urban middle and lower classes and the increase in urban representation moved towards the Liberal Unionists in an attempt to attach suburban England to their party cause.

The secession of the Liberal Unionists was completed by the Home Rule Bill of 1893, when a rump of only forty-one Liberals voted for the Home Rule Bill, and in 1897 only twenty-five could be scraped together to vote in a leadership election to succeed Rosebery. Barely a dozen attended the eve-of-session dinners given by Lord Kimberley for the next few years. After their electoral victory in 1906 the Liberals had to rebuild their party in the Upper House, and they created 102 peerages between 1906 and 1916. In 1909, only seventy-five could be whipped in to vote for Lloyd George's 'People's Budget' but even that included a handful of renegade Unionists and cross-benchers.[16]

The Unionist section of the former Liberal Party numbered between 95 and 130 until the formal merger with the Conservatives in 1912, but their attendance was lax and they were badly organized, if at all. Their leaders, Devonshire and Lansdowne, were active, but when they entered the Cabinet in 1895 they became in effect Conservatives and they succeeded Salisbury in turn as leaders of the House for the Conservative government until 1905 and then of the party in opposition. The Conservative peers themselves were equally poor attenders and their whips not very effective, but as the opposition in the Lords was so feeble they had little incentive to do better. Most of their work dealt with patronage and fund-raising for the party rather than mustering support in the chamber.[17]

Party leadership in the Lords was more important than the size of active membership. Salisbury, for the Conservatives, dominated the chamber from 1881 until 1902, and despite his aloofness and his occasional rashness he was respected on both sides for his commitment to the aristocratic order and its interests. He possessed, one writer has remarked, 'a strong will, an intense emotional commitment to the House of Lords extending over a long career in politics, a combativeness of temperament approaching recklessness, . . . and a high intelligence, critical and questioning in its nature'. Lord Blake has described him as 'the most formidable intellectual figure that the Conservative party has ever produced'.[18] His successors, Devonshire and Lansdowne, both ex-Whigs, were men of prestige and experience, but Lansdowne was aloof and frigid and seemed unapproachable to his followers. At the same time he was inclined to be hesitant and reluctant to discipline his troops, which contributed to the débâcle of 1909–11. Lansdowne, as his colleague Lord Selborne later remarked, was the 'most perfect gentleman in the world, of great experience, ability, and good sense; but ridiculously diffident, and a nature too cautious, almost timid . . . he has some vision, but little initiative, and no driving power'.[19] He did well enough as leader in his first years of opposition after 1906 and by restraining his hot-heads over some of the Liberals' social reforms postponed the clash which, however, he failed to avert in 1909–11.

The Liberals were still led by Granville until 1891. He had considerable authority over his followers, who greatly respected him. His biographer remarked that 'He was by nature a diplomatist' and he carried this quality into his management of the party and, in government, of the House. He lacked, however, constructive abilities of the order of Russell or Gladstone. He was 'a born fighter', at his best in 'masterly retreats before overwhelming forces' and tactical sallies 'by which he tried to encourage his never numerous and frequently divided and dispirited followers'. Being leader of the House of Lords in a government headed by Gladstone was never likely to be an easy task, but Granville achieved a great deal in keeping the two Houses as much in harmony as was possible. 'His immense experience', said Derby in paying tribute to him after his death, 'had taught him tolerance', and his 'thorough knowledge of individual character was combined with a knowledge of the wants and ideas of society as a whole'. Lord Cranbrook, speaking on behalf of Salisbury, declared that during all his forty years in the House Granville never made a personal enemy there, 'very largely because he was a true friend to the House in which he sat . . . and on all occasions watched with jealous watchfulness over its interests, its dignity, and its honour'.[20]

Granville was succeeded by Kimberley. He was not formally elected, but a meeting of the Liberal peers on 14 April 1891 agreed that Kimberley should act as leader for the time being. In 1892 he was formally designated as leader by Gladstone, serving until 1894 when Rosebery was appointed. Rosebery resigned after two years and Kimberley was elected in January 1897 until 1902 when Spencer took the post for three years, also by election. Ripon (1905–8) was appointed by the Prime Minister Campbell-Bannerman and Crewe (1908–22) by Asquith. They could make little impact in view of the weakness of their following, and though one peer remarked that Ripon was 'gaga' and Crewe 'like a mute at a funeral', the latter at any rate was an effective debater and business manager.[21]

The party leaders in the Lords were generally men of importance in the Cabinet and senior office holders. Granville combined the Liberal leadership with the Foreign Office between 1870 and 1874 and in 1880–5, but in Gladstone's Cabinet in 1886 he held the Colonial Secretaryship because he considered the Foreign Secretaryship too onerous to combine with the Lords. Salisbury, however, combined the two offices with that of Prime Minister as well until 1900 and then gave up the Foreign Office for the less burdensome post of Lord Privy Seal. On the Liberal side, Kimberley, Rosebery and Devonshire held the Lord Presidency of the Council while leaders of the House and Crewe was Colonial Secretary (1908–10), Secretary of State for India

(1910–11) and Lord Privy Seal (1908–11). Lansdowne, Conservative leader after 1903, was also Foreign Secretary.

'Absenteeism is the first great recognized blot of the Upper Chamber', wrote Curzon in the *National Review* in 1888.[22] Average attendance per session between 1887 and 1909 has been calculated as between 15 and 20 per cent of the total number of peers on the roll, while the total number of speakers in debate varied between 69 in 1906 and only 18 – 3 per cent of the membership – in 1897. Sittings were correspondingly short: the average length varied between 182 minutes (1906) and 62 minutes (1890 – when only on eight occasions did the House rise later than 7 p.m.). Before the last eight weeks or so of the sessions, the House rarely met for longer than 20 minutes. After 1905 attendances became more numerous and sittings rather longer, though rarely over three hours. Debates, though on routine days little more than conversations between the two front benches, were not always dull.[23] The presence of men of experience and of a number of ministerial office holders meant that set-piece debates could be authoritative and of high quality, and Salisbury's biographer remarked that the 1880s were a brilliant period in the oratorical history of the House, with Salisbury, Cairns and Cranbrook leading for the Conservatives and Argyll, Selborne, Derby and Granville for the Liberals:[24]

> On field-days in the Lords – which the pertinacious challenge of
> the Opposition made sufficiently frequent – the galleries, the Bar,
> and the steps of the Throne, would be thronged with Commons'
> members taking refuge from the dreary loquacity of mediocrities or the
> interminable interludes of Parnellite obstruction. The superiority of the
> Lords' debates, both in form and substance, became a commonplace of
> newspaper criticism.

Morley remarked that the debate on the India Bill in the Commons in April 1909 was far inferior to that in the Lords for strength and knowledge, and he himself was a thoroughly competent speaker. He found the Lords, he wrote, 'a thoroughly reasonable and civil audience, but then,' he added, 'you know I have never talked to them about Land, Church, or Sport'.[25] The House of Lords nevertheless was a forum for considered argument only among a very small proportion of politically active members of the peerage, the great majority of whom lacked the interest or the time to participate in its business.

The period after 1880 was not, on the whole, one in which the Lords contributed much to policy or legislation. The problem still remained that most of the important bills of each session did not complete their passage through the Commons and reach the Lords until the last few weeks, when the majority even of politically active peers were itching to get away to the country in time for the country-house round of shooting parties. The House therefore failed to perform its role in revising and scrutinizing legislation to any great effect, and the series of Liberal reforms after 1906 aroused little response in the Lords. The exception lay in the field of private bills, which formed the bulk of its legislative output and where the pressure of time was less. Here the role of the Chairman of Committees remained vital, in managing and scrutinizing a multitude of bills, most of which concerned the public interest in such fields as railways, public utilities and local authority powers and business. The House and its committees were better attended when these matters were being dealt with, reflecting the continued concern of the peerage with the management of local affairs which touched their private interests. The volume of private bill legislation diminished towards the end of the period, however, as the new County and County Borough Councils set up in the late 1880s took more responsibility for local affairs.

THE LORDS AND GOVERNMENT

Peers continued after 1880 to fill a significant number of government offices. A seat in the Lords was attractive to the head of a busy department since it relieved him of the pressures of House of Commons business and questioning. It was conventional in the nineteenth century for the Foreign Secretary to be in the Upper House, since foreign affairs were traditionally the business of the Lords, where a number of diplomats and ex-ambassadors were often to be found. Foreign affairs, however, were rarely debated. All Foreign Secretaries between 1868 and 1905 were peers, as were all Lords Lieutenant of Ireland and Lord Chancellors. The honorific offices of Lord President of the Council and Lord Privy Seal were always reserved for peers, with the exception of the elderly Gladstone who combined the Privy Seal with the premiership in his last two ministries and Balfour similarly in 1902–3. Offices such as First Lord of the Admiralty, Chancellor of the Duchy of Lancaster and Secretary of State for India or for the Colonies were shared roughly equally between peers and commoners during the period, while the Home Office and departments concerned with finance, trade and war were wholly or predominantly reserved for the House of Commons.

The Conservative and Unionist governments tended to be top-heavy with peers and even Gladstone's Cabinet in 1880–5 was criticized as being unduly aristocratic, half its members and most of the leading offices being in the Lords. Hartington complained in 1886 that 'the Peers, who never do a day's work out of office, can't expect half the places in another Liberal Cabinet'.[26] The departure of the Liberal Unionists after 1886 threw the Liberals back on the House of Commons, though there were still several peers in the Liberal governments before 1906. Gladstone's Cabinet in 1886 contained six Lords out of fourteen members, in 1892 five out of seventeen, and Rosebery in 1894 six out of sixteen. Sir William Harcourt protested to Gladstone in 1892 that

> the proposed distribution of the principal offices in the Cabinet as between the House of Lords and the House of Commons is one which will not meet with the approval or support of the Liberal party. More than half of what are considered the places of greatest emolument and dignity are assigned to the Peers. . . . Tory governments in the last forty years have set a much better example in this matter than recent Liberal administrations.

He warned that this circumstance 'carries with it what I cannot but regard as the recognition of undue claims of predominance for the House of Lords, which must have for the future serious bearing on the great struggle that lies before us'. Gladstone took the view that the weakness of the Liberals in the Upper House made it necessary to place important office holders there, to which Harcourt replied that 'You might as well try to strengthen the ocean by pouring into it a *petit verre* of cognac'.[27]

The Conservatives, as might be expected, were more evenly balanced, Salisbury in 1885–6, 1886 and 1900 having equal numbers, and in 1895 nine out of nineteen peers in the Cabinet. Balfour in 1902 had nine out of twenty. The Liberals after 1905 reduced the aristocratic element to six out of nineteen (1905–8) or twenty (1908).[28]

The premiership was not yet conventionally restricted to a member of the House of Commons, and between 1880 and 1902 peers occupied the post for a total of thirteen years against seven for Commoners. After 1902 the office has always been held by a commoner, though this was not recognized as a constitutional convention until 1922. The Liberal Party was averse after 1894 to the premier being in the Lords, as Harcourt warned Gladstone, but on the latter's retirement in 1894 the Cabinet imposed Rosebery against the opposition of the radical wing in the House of Commons, who would have preferred Harcourt, so depriving him of his last chance to occupy the highest office.[29]

Gladstone, Balfour and Asquith among the commoners had landed or aristocratic connections, and Campbell-Bannerman (1905–8) inherited an estate from his mother's family although he himself was the son of a Glasgow businessman and never mingled in aristocratic society. Gladstone, despite his territorial status, was the son of a Liverpool merchant and hardly an aristocrat by inclination. Asquith, though well connected by marriage, was a nonconformist self-made lawyer and never possessed a landed estate. The day of the old governing families was over and the rejection of Curzon (whose title in any case was a recent one) as a candidate for the premiership in 1922 in favour of Bonar Law, a Glasgow iron-merchant born in Canada, confirmed the fact. The end of the era in which the Prime Minister was as likely to be found in the Lords as in the Commons coincided with and reflected the retreat of the Upper House from a claim to a position of equality with the Lower. It also marked the acceptance of the fact that political power had passed from the Lords, not to the Commons, but to the electorate. The head of the government was increasingly seen as the embodiment of the people's will, accountable to their representatives who were elected primarily in order to support or oppose him. These trends were confirmed in the second half of the twentieth century but they were under way by the end of the nineteenth. In this respect, as in others, the advance of democracy required a readjustment of the role and functions of the House of Lords, which was to be the theme of its history in the first decade of the twentieth century.

REFERENCES

1. R.E. Pumphrey, 'The Introduction of Industrialists into the British Peerage', *American Historical Review* LXV (1959), 1–16.
2. Hansard, CCLXXIX, 937–58, 20 June 1884.
3. Pumphrey, 'The Introduction of Industrialists', 7.
4. H. Perkin, *The Origins of Modern English Society* (1969), pp. 184–5.
5. A. Adonis, 'The political role of the British peerage in the third Reform Act system', unpublished D. Phil. thesis (Oxford, 1988), 5–6; J.V. Beckett, *The Aristocracy in England, 1660–1914* (Oxford, 1986), p. 487; F.M.L. Thompson, *English Landed Society in the Nineteenth Century* (1963), p. 204; Pumphrey, 'The Introduction of Industrialists', 7–12; D. Cannadine, *The Decline and Fall of the British Aristocracy* (1990), pp. 196–206.
6. *Ibid.*; Thompson, *English Landed Society*.
7. *The Diary of Gathorne Hardy, First Lord Cranbrook* ed. Nancy Johnson (Oxford, 1981) *passim*.

8. For these examples see G.E.C., *The Complete Peerage* (1910–59).
9. Pumphrey, 'The Introduction of Industrialists', 10–11.
10. W.L. Guttsman, *The British Political Elite* (1963), pp. 87, 126.
11. G.E.C., *Complete Peerage*, V, Appendix C. G.D. Phillips, 'The Whig Lords and Liberalism, 1886–1893', *Historical Journal* XXIV (1981), 167–73, counts 138 directors of public companies in the peerage in 1886.
12. Cannadine, *Decline and Fall*, p. 202.
13. Phillips, 'Whig Lords and Liberalism', 172; W.D. Rubinstein, *Men of Property* (1981), pp. 194–6, 201–2, 211.
14. W. Bagehot, *The English Constitution* (1963 edn.), pp. 121–3.
15. Adonis, 'The political role of the British peerage', 5–8.
16. *Ibid.*, 14; D. Southgate, *The Passing of the Whigs (1832–1886)* (1962), pp. 383–416; Phillips, 'Whig Lords and Liberalism', *passim*.
17. Adonis, 'The political role of the British peerage', 17–21.
18. C.C. Weston, 'Salisbury and the Lords, 1868–1895', *Historical Journal* XXV (1982), 107; R. Blake, *Disraeli* (1966), p. 499.
19. Quoted in Adonis, 'The political role of the British peerage', 27–8.
20. Lord Edmond Fitzmaurice, *Life of . . . second Earl Granville* (1905), II, pp. 501–4.
21. Quoted in Adonis, 'The political role of the British peerage', 16.
22. *The National Review* II (1888), 125.
23. Adonis, 'The political role of the British peerage', 34–6.
24. Lady Gwendolen Cecil, *The Life of Robert Marquis of Salisbury* (1921), III, p. 2.
25. John, Viscount Morley, *Recollections* (1917), II, pp. 305, 311.
26. Harcourt to Granville, 3 Oct. 1886; Bernard Holland, *The Life of Spencer Compton, 8th Duke of Devonshire* (1911), II, p. 73.
27. A.G. Gardiner, *The Life of Sir William Harcourt* (1923), II, pp. 182–3.
28. Figures from *Handbook of British Chronology* ed. E.B. Fryde, D.E. Greenway, S. Porter and I. Roy (1986), Adonis, 'The political role of the British peerage', 121–4, and Cannadine, *Decline and Fall*, pp. 206 ff.
29. Gardiner, *Harcourt*, II, pp. 188, 262–3, 271–2.

CHAPTER NINE

Challenge and Response

Despite its growth in size and the widening of its social and economic composition, the later nineteenth-century House of Lords was beginning to seem an even greater anachronism in an age of rapidly advancing democracy. The political control and influence of the peerage in the country was diminishing with the widening of the electoral franchise, while the secret ballot of 1872, the Corrupt Practices Act of 1883 and the development of central party organizations further reduced the ability of the rich and powerful to enforce deference or deploy their wealth to win political control. Gladstone's 'Midlothian campaign' against Disraeli in the general election of 1880 set the tone for future electoral contests, in which the voters would be wooed by public oratory and presented with a choice between national party leaders and manifestoes, rather than marshalled by the stewards and agents of local notables. Members of the House of Commons, too, were no longer individually responsible to electoral patrons but subordinated to the discipline of party whips and accountable to the electorate. In 1868 Disraeli resigned the premiership after the defeat of the Conservatives at the polls, without first meeting the House of Commons, so in effect conceding sovereignty to the electorate rather than to Parliament.[1] At the local level, the setting up of democratically elected councils in the 1880s and 1890s removed control of county affairs from the aristocratic houses, despite the (largely honorific) presence of members of the peerage on many of the county councils and as mayors of several towns. Queen Victoria's private secretary told Sir William Harcourt in March 1894 that the queen was much distressed at the defeat of the government on Labouchère's amendment to the address which demanded the abolition of the Lords' veto on legislation:[2]

> She considers a Second House to be a necessity in a free country, and
> the presence in Parliament of an independent body of men who have
> no need of being afraid of the clamour of a noisy set of constituents
> who represent no party but only a temporary excitement is a most
> valuable and important body in a state.

Unfortunately, the 'noisy set of constituents' who now chose the
House of Commons were less inclined to accept that their wishes
could be thwarted by an assembly whose political power derived from
hereditary rank and wealth rather than from utility and responsibility
to the public. Class-consciousness did not form the basis of party
divisions at Westminster but its spread in the country made the
Lords seem less like a necessary constitutional safeguard and more
like the instrument of an outdated and narrow governing class, or,
even worse, of the Conservative Party in or out of office. It offended
both democratic political instincts and feelings of equality and justice.
Bagehot perceptively warned in 1867[3] that

> the danger of the House of Lords . . . is, that it may never be
> reformed. Nobody asks that it should be so; it is quite safe against
> rough destruction but it is not safe against inward decay. It may lose
> its veto as the Crown has lost its veto. If most of its members neglect
> their duties, if all its members continue to be of one class, and that not
> quite the best; if its doors are shut against genius that cannot found a
> family, and ability which has not £5,000 a year, its power will be less
> year by year, and at last be gone, as so much Kingly power is gone –
> no one knows how. Its danger is not in assassination, but atrophy; not
> abolition, but decline.

The Lords had to steer their course in the last thirty years of this
period with one eye on public opinion and one on the jealousy of
their own members in face of challenges to their right to independent
authority. Their pilots were generally men of wisdom and caution,
but the crews could be mutinous and the storm was not easy to
weather.

THE LORDS AND THEIR ROLE

The Bryce Commission of 1917 identified four functions of a second
chamber: as a revising body, to modify in the public interest bills sent
up from the House of Commons that may not have had adequate and
thorough examination; to initiate legislation on non-controversial (and
non-financial) issues; to interpose, where necessary, sufficient delay on
the passing of a bill to allow the opinion of the nation to be expressed

and the Commons to reflect; and to be a forum for 'full and free discussion of large and important questions' on which legislation was not proposed, for example foreign policy.

These views reflected the actuality of politics since 1832, when, as Bagehot remarked, the Lords had ceased to be a 'directing' chamber and became a 'revising and suspending house' with 'a veto of delay' and 'a power of revision', but no more.[4] The revising function was more necessary than ever from the 1880s, when Irish Nationalist obstructionist tactics forced the House of Commons to adopt restrictions on their debates and prevented full discussion of all the clauses of bills to which the 'guillotine' and other measures were applied. In practice, however, the Lords were not well equipped for the role because of their lack of expertise in the complex details of legislation on a multitude of economic matters in particular, and in any case they were still hampered by the shortage of time left in the session after bills came up from the Commons.[5] The initiation of legislation in the Lords really applied only to relatively unimportant matters. The delaying function was thus the one which the Lords sought to exercise through the use of Salisbury's theory of the 'referral or referendal role' of the House, sometimes referred to as 'the doctrine of the mandate'.[6] It was, therefore, on the referral role that attention was focused after 1880.

Salisbury's doctrine, as has been seen, arose from the Lords' actions on the Irish Church in 1868 and 1869, when they rejected the Suspensory Bill on the grounds that the question of Irish Church disestablishment had not been put before the electorate, and that a general election was in any case imminent. The issue was put to the electorate in 1868, and the Liberals received the mandate they asked for. In 1869 some Conservative peers nevertheless threatened to reject the Disestablishment Bill because it was regarded as an attack on property, but Salisbury accepted the implications of his theory and persuaded enough of them to vote for the bill to allow it to pass its second reading, though reserving the right to perform the revising function by amendments in committee. If the House of Commons refused to agree to the Lords' amendments, he further accepted that the bill should be allowed to pass in its original form.

This doctrine, as subsequently developed in the 1870s, was designed to give the House of Lords a democratically acceptable basis for the use of its remaining power, by presenting it as a safeguard for the country against extreme measures which might otherwise be imposed by a government secure in the control of a party majority in the Commons. Ironically, it was the coming of (virtually) universal male suffrage that provided the Lords with the opportunity to revive its power. It adapted the long-established claim of the House to act in the interests of the whole nation against a partisan government or House of Commons. The drawback in practice was that the House of Lords was just as much a partisan assembly as the Commons and that, especially after the 1880s, the inbuilt permanent Conservative majority used the doctrine against Liberal measures while remaining passive against Conservative ones. The doctrine, therefore, failed to find general acceptance in the country or to provide an effective justification for the continued existence of a merely hereditary second chamber.

Before 1906, the most effective use of the doctrine was on the Irish Home Rule Bill of 1893, when Salisbury added a further refinement, that of the 'predominant partner'. It was argued that Gladstone's bill had passed the Commons only because his government was dependent on Irish votes, and that the electorate in England – the 'predominant partner' in the United Kingdom – had not given it their approval, but had given a majority to the Conservatives. Rightly judging that public opinion in England was strongly opposed to Home Rule, the Lords were secure in rejecting the bill by an overwhelming majority, 41 to 419 (the largest division ever recorded in the House), 'almost without protest or murmur from the greater part of this country', as the duke of Devonshire said in the Lords.[7] At the next general election in 1895 they were vindicated, the electorate giving the Conservatives a majority of 150 seats.

Nevertheless, the doctrine was not always so successfully applied. In 1882 the Conservative leaders opposed the Irish Arrears Bill, which was considered too favourable towards tenants against their landlords, but many of their party declined to follow, the English peers because they doubted if the Conservatives would win an election if they forced one by defeating the government at that time, and their Irish supporters because they feared the consequences of rejection in Ireland.[8] In 1884 there was a crisis between the two Houses when the Conservatives in the Lords refused to pass the Franchise Bill, extending virtual manhood suffrage to all constituencies, unless it was accompanied by provisions to redistribute seats. The Conservatives feared that extension of the franchise in the present constituencies, particularly in Ireland, would be against their party interests and that Gladstone might call a general election before introducing a Redistribution Bill in order to increase his majority. Salisbury feared the loss of forty-seven seats would result. The Conservatives sought, therefore, either to force the government to pass the Redistribution Bill at the same time as the Franchise Bill, or, by rejecting the latter, to force a general election on the existing franchise, which they thought they could win.

The Cabinet was indignant, Gladstone declaring in a letter to the queen that to dissolve the House of Commons at the bidding of the House of Lords would make the Commons inferior to the Lords, and threatening that any attempt to establish such a principle would end in 'organic changes, detrimental to the dignity and authority of the House of Lords'.[9] Other ministers made threatening noises, Morley declaring that the Upper House should be 'mended or ended', and Bright advocated the abolition or restriction of the Lords' veto which was 'a constant insult to the House of Commons'. The public also responded: it was said that the two parties held a total of 700 meetings in ten weeks, and there was a 'monster demonstration' in London. The crisis was resolved by the queen's personal intervention and a compromise was agreed, the Lords passing the Franchise Bill after the Redistribution Bill had been introduced in the Commons.[10]

The episode had generated a great deal of controversy over the use of the Lords' veto and a flood of pamphlets and articles in the political journals.[11] Lord Bryce, a Liberal MP, asked whether a second chamber was necessary and asserted that in any case 'The House of Lords cannot go on as it is'.[12] When the question of reform of the Lords was raised, however, difficulties arose: the Conservatives favoured reform in order to make the position of the House stronger and more acceptable; Liberals and Radicals preferred to concentrate on removing or modifying the Lords' independent power of veto, without altering its composition. These were the alternatives which dominated discussion of the power of the House of Lords for the next twenty-five years.

MENDED OR ENDED?

As Lord Newton, a member of the Unionist majority in the Lords admitted, the House of Lords in the early twentieth century was 'overgrown, unrepresentative, and unwieldy, when the Unionists were in office it was expected merely to act as a kind of registry office, and to pass without amendment, and occasionally without discussion, any measure sent up to it', but when the Liberals were in power 'it was expected to come to the rescue of a discomfited Opposition'. Although the Lords could on occasion 'be a more correct interpreter of public feeling than the House of Commons, its gigantic and permanent Conservative majority deprived it of any appearance of impartiality', while it had shown no sign of independence by rejecting any Conservative measure.[13] In these circumstances, proposals for reform of the House of Lords were considered on several occasions, starting with the controversy over their interference with the Franchise and Redistribution Bills in 1884. In that year Rosebery moved for a select committee to consider 'the best means of promoting the efficiency of the House',[14] suggesting the introduction of life peerages to broaden the range of its membership and in particular to bring in 'a larger infusion from those large classes among whom is to be found much of the wealth and power of the country'. His proposal was defeated, both front bench leaders speaking against it. In 1888 he returned to the subject, suggesting a more elaborate scheme. In addition to the introduction of life peerages, there should be an end to the automatic right of any male possessor of a hereditary peerage to a seat in the House. Instead, a limited number should be elected by the whole body to serve for a limited period, with peers not elected being eligible to seek election to the House of Commons. Municipalities and county councils should also elect delegates to membership of the Lords and the colonies should be represented by their Agents General. Finally, disputes between the Lords and the Commons should be resolved by joint sittings of the two Houses.

Rosebery's scheme attracted more support than his 1884 motion, particularly from Conservative peers, but he was again unsuccessful. The notion that not all hereditary peers should sit of right in the Upper House was taken up by Curzon, who had been given an Irish peerage in order not to remove him from the Commons, together with a number of heirs to peerages in the Lower House. They suggested that hereditary peers should sit only if they qualified by public service, and that the other members of the Lords should be life peers, nominated by the government of the day, and a non-hereditary group elected for a fixed period by the House of Commons. In 1894 Curzon proposed that an MP who inherited a peerage should be allowed to continue to sit in the Commons, and in the following year Lord Wolmer, a close colleague of Curzon's, attempted to remain in the Commons when he succeeded to his father's earldom, but the House of Commons refused to agree.

The year 1894 saw the Lords again using their power to mutilate Liberal legislation. They amended the Employers' Liability Bill to allow individual workmen to contract out of the provisions designed to ensure their right to compensation, in the name of individual freedom of contract, and mutilated the Parish Councils Bill. Harcourt demanded that the Lords must now be dealt with. The House, he declared in a speech to the National Liberal Federation, 'is the champion of all abuses and the enemy of all reform', and he repeated Russell's famous phrase about the Tory resistance to the Reform Bill in 1831–2, threatening that the electorate 'shall determine once for all whether the whisper of faction is to prevail over the will of the people'. However, when Gladstone urged his colleagues to make the House of Lords question the central issue at the general election of 1895 they refused, sensing that it was not a question on which the public felt strongly enough. Harcourt commented that 'There are two things that you can neither mend nor end: the House of Lords is one, the other is the Pope of Rome.'[15]

The election of 1895 marked the end of the Gladstonian era and inaugurated ten years of Conservative supremacy, during which the controversies over the power of the Lords died down as the majority did not wish to hamper a Conservative government: indeed, under Salisbury's firm control, the Conservative peers were usually conspicuous by their indifference to attendance. They saw no reason to attempt reform of the House, and Salisbury applied his authority to keep the political temperature down. When a group of Irish landowners, who were among the Conservative majority, tried in 1896 to oppose a government bill to assist Irish tenants, Balfour and Salisbury used the majority in the Commons to reject the Lords' amendments, while the Liberals and Liberal Unionists supported the government in the Lords. Similarly, in 1898 the passing of the Irish Local Government Bill, an important element in Salisbury's policy of 'killing Home Rule by kindness', showed that the Conservatives would sacrifice the interests of the Irish peers to preserve the power of the House of Lords. That power was only safe, however, so long as the Conservatives were in office or so long as the Lords refrained from using it to support a Conservative opposition and prevent a Liberal government from carrying out its measures. This the Lords did not do in the years following the Liberal victory in 1906. Their partisanship, which earned them the nickname 'Mr Balfour's poodle', made it inevitable that their right to continue as an independent branch of the legislature would be challenged.

There were those who would have 'ended' rather than 'mended' the House of Lords. In 1882 Henry Labouchère moved, in the words of the resolution of the Long Parliament in 1649, that the House was 'useless, dangerous, and ought to be abolished'. No vote was taken, but he introduced motions to end the hereditary element in the Upper House in 1884, 1886 and 1888, the vote in favour increasing from 74 to 162. The Labour Party proposed abolition of the Lords in 1907, but the Commons preferred to vote for a Liberal motion

> That, in order to give effect to the will of the people as expressed by
> their elected representatives, it is necessary that the power of the other
> House should be so restricted by law as to secure that within the limits
> of a single Parliament the final decision of the Commons shall prevail.

It became the policy of the Liberals to remove or modify the Lords'
veto on legislation rather than abolish or reform the House; as Sir
William Harcourt wrote to Morley in December 1889, 'If you are to
have a second chamber, you had better have one which is moderately
stupid and tolerably timid, which is what you have now'.[16] It was the
Conservatives who persisted with proposals for reform in the hope
of making the Lords a more effective and acceptable second chamber
with its full independent power.

In 1907 Lord Newton proposed a bill to restrict the number of
peers sitting in the House. He took up Curzon's idea that only
peers qualified by public service should sit by hereditary right alone.
Others, as in Rosebery's earlier proposals, would be elected by the
remaining peers or be life peers appointed by the government of
the day, with a limited number of spiritual peers elected by the
bishops. Peers excluded from the Lords would be eligible for election
to the Commons. A select committee, chaired by Rosebery, was
appointed to consider the question and though Newton's scheme was
withdrawn the committee's report in 1908 endorsed the principle that
the possession of a peerage should not of itself confer the right to sit
in the House of Lords. It suggested that 200 'Lords of Parliament'
should be elected by the whole body of hereditary peers for the
lifetime of each Parliament and that to these should be added 130
hereditary peers qualified by past or present public service or who
succeeded to peerages after at least ten years as members of the
Commons, ten prelates of the Church of England, and law lords
and life peers. The number of life peers should be subject to an
annual limit of four creations. However, the committee's report was
considered, especially by the Liberal peers, as an irrelevance to the
major problems of the relationship between the Lords and Commons,
the imbalance of parties in the Lords and the representation of wider
interests, and it was not even discussed by the House.[17]

In 1910 Rosebery returned to the subject, proposing three resolutions: that a strong and efficient second chamber was necessary; that
it would best be achieved through reform of the present House of
Lords; and that the possession of a hereditary peerage should no
longer confer an automatic right to sit in the House. The Liberals
again dismissed these ideas as irrelevant and no more was heard of
them. In 1911, after the second general election over the 'People's

Budget', the Conservatives came up with a final set of proposals. The House should consist of 350 'Lords of Parliament', of whom 100 who had held high offices should be elected by the peers from amongst themselves, 120 elected by electoral colleges of MPs on a regional basis, 100 appointed by the government in proportion to the size of parties in the Commons, and the remainder to be prelates, law lords and members of the royal family. The Lords of Parliament were to serve for a maximum of twelve years, one third retiring every four years. Peers not sitting as Lords of Parliament would be eligible for election to the Commons. Finally, the number of new hereditary peerages should not exceed five per year. The bill passed a second reading but it was not proceeded with, Morley, for the government, having made it clear that even such a reformed assembly would be subject to the restrictions on its power proposed in the Parliament Bill, so making the reform pointless.

This was the end, for the time being, of proposals to tackle the problem of the House of Lords by reform of its membership. Liberals, Radicals and Socialists, angered by the partisan attitude of the Conservative majority in the Lords, preferred to restrict the House's power to block legislation from the Commons rather than to make that power more acceptable by reform. The resolution of 1907, setting out this principle, was the consequence of the Lords' action in the first session of the 1906 Parliament in rejecting two major bills which had been part of the Liberals' programme in the election, namely, the Education Bill and the Plural Voting Bill. The former had aroused violent opposition from the Unionists and Irish Nationalists, partly on the grounds of its provisions affecting religious instruction, and the Lords proposed amendments which would have made fundamental changes. A conference between representatives of each party and the archbishop of Canterbury failed to agree on a solution and the bill was lost, to a 'prodigious outcry' from the country. Campbell-Bannerman, the Prime Minister, declared that 'the resources of the House of Commons were not exhausted, and that a way would be found by which the will of the people could be made to prevail'.[18]

Conflict was intensified by the Lords' rejection of the Land Valuation Bill in 1907 and 1908, and the Licensing Bill of 1908. The latter was considered on the Conservative side to be vindictive, confiscatory and deliberately intended to provoke a trial of strength between the Houses. Despite the intervention of King Edward VII who called Lord Lansdowne, leader of the Conservative peers, for an interview, a party meeting in November decided by an overwhelming majority to reject the bill, in the full realization that this course would make a collision between the Houses unavoidable. The second reading was lost by 272 to 96 and bitterness was increased by the rejection of another education bill. For the time being, the Cabinet, which was not fully united on the matter and which was aware that it might not have the public wholly on its side, held its fire; but it was from these circumstances that the 'People's Budget' of 1909, which brought the whole question to a crisis, was born.

THE PEOPLE'S BUDGET

After 1908, with Asquith now Prime Minister and Lloyd George as Chancellor of the Exchequer, the Liberals embarked on a more radical programme of social reform, known as the 'new Liberalism'. The Lords did not oppose the great majority of the Liberals' social legislation between 1906 and 1911, reserving its obstruction for bills for which it believed the public was not enthusiastic such as the Education and Licensing Bills. Balfour believed that the House had strengthened its position by rejecting Home Rule in 1893 and that judicious opposition to other controversial measures would have the same result.[19] One junior minister pointed out that the Lords had killed only seven bills in four years, although three of them were major government measures.[20] The public reaction was muted; the country was inclined to be suspicious of 'nonconformist fads' and the Licensing Bill was widely unpopular. The decision to introduce a 'People's Budget' in 1909 to finance further and more radical social reforms was taken mainly to recover the initiative for a Liberal government which was beginning to lose popularity, as measured in by-election results, and only partly to focus popular resentment against the House of Lords as the tool of the Conservative Party if the Lords rejected the budget. The new taxes proposed in the budget might, to some extent, be considered discriminatory against landed wealth, and though the extension of the estate inheritance duty, the increased income tax and the tax on the 'unearned increment' of land values were modest compared to what was to come later in the century, they seemed to embody socialist principles.

Lansdowne and Balfour decided that the Lords should oppose the budget not only because it was alleged to discriminate against property but because they asserted that the government had included in it licensing and land valuation provisions which were not really financial and which the Lords had previously rejected. They stood on the principle that the Commons should not misuse their power over finance bills to 'tack' on to them other measures which the Lords could not reject. They also calculated that rejection by the Lords would force a general election from which the Liberals would emerge dependent on the Irish. The consequence would be a Home Rule Bill which the Lords would throw out, and a general election which the Conservatives would win.

The budget also raised the issue of free trade or tariff reform. Its provisions were seen as an attempt to raise the extra £16 million of revenue needed for social reforms and for rearmament without reimposing tariffs, which Chamberlain and the Conservatives favoured. In this respect it could be argued that the budget involved questions of general policy and not merely revenue-raising considerations.

The debates in the Lords lasted for six days. Lansdowne favoured rejection rather than amendment, because the latter might be constitutionally beyond the competence of the Lords, whereas they had never formally acquiesced in the abolition of their powers of rejection.[21] On 10 November, Lansdowne gave notice that he would move, not outright rejection, but that the Lords would not assent to the budget until it had been 'submitted to the judgment of the country'.[22] On 1 December Lansdowne's amendment was passed by 350 to 75. On the following day the Commons passed Asquith's resolution that the Lords' action was a breach of the constitution and Parliament was dissolved. At the election in January 1910 the Conservatives and their allies gained about 100 seats, making their numbers almost equal to the Liberals. As expected, the Irish and the Labour members held the balance: the price for Irish support for the Liberals was the abolition of the Lords' veto on Home Rule. 'We regarded the abolition or limitation of the veto of the House of Lords as tantamount to the granting of Home Rule', declared Redmond, the leader of the Irish Nationalists, and the Labour Party also stipulated for reform of the veto as the price for their support for the budget.[23]

In March, Asquith moved resolutions in the Commons to set up a committee on relations between the Houses, to abolish the Lords' veto on money bills, to impose a time limit on their veto on other legislation and to limit the maximum duration of Parliaments to five years instead of seven. On 14 April the committee's proposals were passed by a majority of 100 and on the same night Asquith introduced the Parliament Bill, saying that if the Lords rejected it he would advise the Crown as to the steps necessary to ensure its passage. On 18 April the budget was reintroduced and passed, the

Lords accepting the verdict of the general election in conformity with the 'mandate' doctrine. The government nevertheless persisted with the plan to restrict the veto in future.

The death of Edward VII on 7 May and the desire to spare the new king a constitutional crisis led to the calling of a Constitutional Conference, whose discussions were prolonged through the summer and autumn but without final agreement. Towards the end of November the government again presented the Parliament Bill to the House of Lords, declaring it would accept no amendments, and Asquith announced a general election. Lansdowne put forward alternative proposals for the reform of the House of Lords so that the electorate could decide between them. The preamble of the Parliament Bill promised reform of the Lords to provide a second chamber elected on a popular basis, but only after the bill itself, which dealt only with the Lords' veto and the duration of Parliament, had been passed and brought into effect.

The general election was not held on the single issue of the House of Lords. Tariff reform, Home Rule and female suffrage in fact aroused greater public interest and the result was to leave the strengths of the parties very much the same. The Irish still held the balance, however, and their major concern was the removal of the Lords' veto. The Parliament Bill was therefore reintroduced, while Lansdowne proposed an alternative bill, to reconstitute the House of Lords as an effective second chamber.[24] After three further months of debate, and under the threat that the king had agreed to create enough new peers to pass the bill if necessary, the Lords gave way as they had done in 1832: 300 Unionists abstained, Lansdowne and his leading colleagues watching the final stages of the debate from the gallery over the throne. Only 114 'die-hards' persisted in voting against the bill at the final stage; even so the government won by a majority of only 17 votes.

So, after a struggle as long and as bitter as that over the first Reform Act in 1831–2, the House of Lords lost its status as a full, independent and equal branch of the legislature to the House of Commons. The warnings of Wellington in the 1830s, that confrontation with the Commons would result in the loss of the powers of the Lords, were at least partly fulfilled. The Conservative peers in the early twentieth century had ignored the constraints which their predecessors had accepted on their right to act independently and to interpret the people's will and interests as much as the Commons; but the House of Lords still existed and, as in 1832, emerged from the crisis with a substantial degree of power and influence intact.

REFERENCES

1. The precedent was not universally followed; Salisbury did not resign before meeting the Commons in 1892 and it did not become a convention for a defeated Prime Minister to do so until 1929: C.S. Emden, *The People and the Constitution* (Oxford, 2nd edn. 1956), p. 165.
2. A.G. Gardiner, *The Life of William Harcourt* (1923), II, p. 278.
3. W. Bagehot, *The English Constitution* (1963 edn.), p. 149.
4. *Ibid*, pp. 128, 131. For the Bryce Commission see P. Ford and G. Ford, *A Breviate of Parliamentary Papers, 1917–1939* (Oxford, 1951), pp. 4–5.
5. C.C. Weston, 'Salisbury and the Lords, 1868–1895', *Historical Journal* XXV (1982), 105; Le May, *Constitutional History, passim.*
6. Bagehot, *The English Constitution*, p. 141.
7. Lady Gwendolen Cecil, *Life of Robert Marquis of Salisbury*, (1921) III, pp. 50–7.
8. Bernard Holland, *The Life of Spencer Compton, 8th Duke of Devonshire* (1911), II, p. 396 (22 Feb. 1906).
9. E. Allyn, *Lords versus Commons: a Century of Conflict and Compromise, 1830–1930* (New York, 1931), pp. 116–21; *Letters of Queen Victoria* ed. A.C. Benson and Viscount Esher, 2nd ser. (1926), III, p. 158.
10. The Redistribution Bill was passed in the following session.
11. Listed in Allyn, *Lords versus Commons*, pp. 249–55. On the queen's action see C.C. Weston, 'The royal mediation in 1884', *English Historical Review* LXXXII (1967), 296–322.
12. Cecil, *Salisbury*, III, p. 109.
13. Lord Newton, *Lord Lansdowne, a Biography* (1929), p. 360.
14. See Chapter 7, p. 141.
15. *Autobiography and Memoirs of George Douglas, 8th Duke of Argyll* ed. Duchess of Argyll (1906), II, pp. 466–8; Gardiner, *Harcourt*, II, p. 256; John, Viscount Morley, *Recollections* (1917), II, p. 97.
16. Hansard, 4th ser. CLXXVI, 909, quoted in Allyn, *Lords versus Commons*, p. 174; Gardiner, *Harcourt*, II, pp. 130–1.
17. For the proceedings and report of the committee see Newton, *Lansdowne*, pp. 362–5.
18. *Ibid.*, pp. 355–7.
19. *Ibid*, pp. 353–5.
20. Allyn, *Lords versus Commons*, pp. 185–6.
21. B.K. Murray, *The People's Budget, 1909–10* (Oxford, 1980), p. 210; A. Adonis, 'The political role of the British peerage in the third Reform Act system unpublished Ph.D. thesis (Oxford, 1988),' 108–9. There is a full account of the constitutional crisis in G.H.L. Le May, *The Victorian Constitution*, (1979) ch. 7, pp. 189–219.
22. Newton, *Lansdowne*, p. 380.
23. Allyn, *Lords versus Commons*, p. 188.
24. See p. 173 above.

Conclusion: The Parliament Act and Beyond

The Parliament Act[1] divided bills into two categories. 'Money bills', defined as those so designated by the Speaker of the House of Commons according to criteria specified in the act, were to be presented for the royal assent one month after being sent to the Lords, whether agreed to or not, without amendment. All other bills, if rejected by the Lords, were to be presented for the royal assent provided they were passed by the House of Commons in three successive sessions over a period of at least two years. The act also reduced the maximum length of a Parliament from seven to five years, to ensure that the government would not act against the wishes of the electorate at such a long distance from the last general election.

The power of the Lords was not destroyed, however. In many ways the Parliament Act merely put into statutory form the conventions which the Lords had tacitly adopted since 1832, in that they had to all intents and purposes accepted that if the House of Commons, supported by the people, was determined on a measure the Lords would accept it. It removed the basis of the doctrine of the 'mandate' by not requiring that a contentious measure should be submitted to the electorate, but it contained certain safeguards for the Lords which ensured that the House of Commons would not rule unchecked. Thus, the veto remained in effect for a period of two years, during which time the Commons had to debate and pass the bill three times. When the Irish Home Rule and Welsh Church Disestablishment Bills were rejected by the Lords in 1912, the work of the Commons was seriously hampered for the next two years by the need to reintroduce and pass them. It was also laid down that the bill finally submitted to the royal assent after two years must be identical with that originally sent up from the Commons, save only for any amendments agreed by both Houses, or minor changes certified by the Speaker as being necessary merely owing to the lapse of time. These provisions made it difficult and cumbersome to invoke the Parliament Act save on matters of fundamental importance. In practice, legislation has been little influenced by its existence since the passing under its provisions of the Irish Home Rule Act and Welsh Disestablishment Act in 1914. Only on one other occasion has the act been invoked, in 1949 to pass a new Parliament Act further restricting the power of veto, and in 1991 that act was used in order to pass the bill permitting the prosecution of individuals for war crimes committed during the Second World War to which the Lords objected on grounds of principle. The provisions regarding money bills have never had to be invoked.

Even at the time of its passage, opponents of the Lords claimed that the Parliament Act was more significantly a limitation on the powers of the Commons and a confirmation of those of the Lords. Ramsay Macdonald voiced that criticism in 1914, and the Labour Party since then has continued to advocate the abolition of the second chamber, while others have brought forward schemes to replace the Lords by some other form of representative house.[2] None of these schemes has commanded much support. The Parliament Act itself was intended only as a temporary expedient, pending the working out of a scheme, in the words of the preamble to the act, 'to substitute for the House of Lords as it at present exists a second chamber constituted on a popular instead of a hereditary basis'. In fact the Conservatives have always been reluctant to embark on any comprehensive reform, while the other parties, less favourable to the House of Lords as it exists, have never found it so obstructive as to make it worth while to try to overcome the practical difficulties involved in setting up an alternative system. A Cabinet committee, set up after the passing of the act by the Liberal government to consider how to carry into effect the pledge in the preamble, quickly ran into the sand over such questions as the nature and size of constituencies, the role of party organizations in elections to a second chamber and the type of member who might be elected. In the final analysis, a second chamber which merely mirrored the balance of parties in the Commons would be superfluous, and one which conflicted with it would be even more obstructive, because it could plead a popular mandate of a real kind. In truth, it was the development and persistence in the United Kingdom of a two-party political system which has made it impossible to resolve this dilemma.

In 1917 the Bryce Commission, appointed to consider reform of the second chamber, failed to reach agreement across their party lines of division. They proposed a combination of some members from the hereditary peerage, chosen by a committee of Lords and Commons in equal numbers, constituting a quarter of the new chamber, and the other three quarters directly elected by members of the House of Commons, divided into thirteen districts according to their constituencies. Members were to serve for twelve years, one third retiring every four years. There were other provisions regarding the limited powers of the new body, but action was repeatedly postponed by the coalition government on various pretexts, and after 1922 the Conservatives showed no willingness to jeopardise their position by attempting such controversial legislation. Delay followed postponement, and nothing was done, despite the perennial raising of the question during the interwar years.

When a Labour government came to power in 1945, it set about fulfilling the party's pledge to reform or abolish the House of Lords, but after two years' argument the act of 1949, which had to be passed without the Lords' agreement by invoking the Parliament Act of 1911, only reduced the period of delay to one year and the number of sessions in which the Commons had to pass the bills from three to two. The question was reopened in 1968, when a government bill proposed to abolish the right of hereditary peers to sit in the Lords and to restrict the right to speak and vote to a limited number – about 230 – of holders of life peerages (for which hereditary peers might be eligible). Voting peers would be paid, be expected to attend and be subject to a retirement age. The bill was generally welcomed by the House of Lords but was defeated in the Commons, when it was feared that such a reformed second chamber would have far greater power to interfere with the will of the Commons than the existing House. So the House of Lords has remained unreformed, and the smooth working of Parliament still depends upon the 'sensible' behaviour of the peers and their leaders, conditioned by the knowledge that, as Lord Carrington remarked in 1964, 'once we start using our veto, we're damaging the object of a Second Chamber. If the House of Lords is to work, we must show forbearance and common sense'.[3]

Nevertheless, there have been significant changes in the composition and role of the House of Lords since the Second World War. These have come about through the large increase in the number of life peerages and the virtual abandonment (except for the earldoms customarily bestowed on retired Prime Ministers) of the creation of hereditary titles. The introduction of life peerages since 1958 has enabled governments to place in the Lords men and women who might contribute usefully to political discussion or to the work of committees but who were reluctant to embark on a career as an MP or to stand for popular election, and also others who do not profess allegiance to one political party. Appointments to life peerages have for the most part been partisan, but several distinguished people in various spheres of life who are politically independent have been introduced into the Lords and they make a considerable contribution to the experience and balance of debates.

Among other changes has been the act of 1963 which allowed holders of hereditary titles to renounce their peerages for their own lives only, and to seek election as commoners to the Lower House: in a number of cases this has allowed peers who were seen, or saw themselves, as potential Prime Ministers to pursue that ambition and in one case, that of Lord Home in 1963, immediately to be elected as Conservative Party leader and therefore Prime Minister without disturbing the convention that the office must be in the House of Commons. In two cases, that of Home himself and that of Quintin Hogg, Viscount Hailsham, renunciation of the peerage was later followed by the grant of another title (for life) allowing the holder to return to the Lords, the former on retirement, the latter after being unsuccessful in attaining the premiership, to become Lord Chancellor. In total eleven peers resigned their seats in the House between 1963 and 1971.[4]

Again, the introduction of attendance allowances in 1957 has enabled individuals who are not possessed of great wealth to accept membership of the Lords without undue financial loss, or even with financial gain, and has quite considerably improved the attendance at the House, if not always throughout its debates. The House has also greatly increased the number of its committees on a wide range of public affairs, and their reports are often non-partisan and influential.

The introduction of life peerages greatly increased the size of the House of Lords. By 1980, their lordships (and ladyships – peeresses by succession, and all remaining Scots peers, were admitted in 1963) numbered 1,200.[5] The Irish peers lost their representation in 1922. Life peers and peeresses were generally regular in attendance at the chamber, though holders of hereditary titles were also more inclined to attend in the 1960s: it was calculated that 138 hereditary peers and 153 created peers (that is, life peers or hereditary peers of first creation) attended more than one third of all sittings in 1967–8.[6] A distinction has tended to grow up between 'honorific' and 'working' life peerages: they have been conferred as a mark of distinction on individuals who have given public service, or on their spouses, or to strengthen the front benches and to make debates more authoritative. Prime Ministers customarily consult leaders of other parties when making recommendations in the second category. Life peerages have thus re-vitalised the House of Lords as an effective part of the legislature.

The twentieth-century House of Lords has consequently in many ways fulfilled better than the other chamber the historic function of Parliament since the seventeenth century, to check and criticize the government of the day in the national interest. Many observers noted about the time of the first Parliament Act that the act had tended, along with other developments, to increase the power of the executive over the House of Commons. Changes in Commons' procedures since the 1880s and the hardening of the two-party system have meant that the House of Commons, supposedly the source of the government's authority, has become the tool of governments, buttressed by the party whips, impregnable in their possession of a majority for five years at a time. The Lords, not so dependent as the Commons on the favour, patronage, or discipline of the executive, have been able and willing to exercise their constitutional function as a revising chamber, which the complexity and volume of modern legislation and the use of 'guillotine' procedures have made it impossible for the Lower House to do. The increased need for this kind of check on government legislation, which has often been exposed as badly drafted, is a further reason why the Lords, though they may still be criticized in public as irresponsible, are in private largely accepted as fulfilling a necessary role. During the First World War, the Lords were even described by the Labour politician J.H. Thomas as 'the real guardians of the people's liberties' – it was the Lords who amended the 1914 Defence of the Realm Bill to preserve the right to trial by jury. Sidney and Beatrice Webb conceded in 1917 that the case for a second chamber, in this respect was 'irresistible'.[7]

Thus the British constitution has again shown itself to be responsive, by a process of evolution and adaptation rather than by confrontation and legislation, to the changing needs of time. The British parliamentary system may be no longer, as it was thought in the past to be, the model for imitation throughout the developing world in the period after decolonization, but it retains the support and allegiance of all parties and of most people in the nation itself, and the reluctance of many Britons to see their country merged into some kind of European federal system is largely the result of this loyalty to traditional institutions which have managed to adapt to circumstances without the need for revolutions. That may certainly be said of the House of Lords, whose prestige and authority probably stand higher in public estimation today than ever before in this period, and the quality of whose contribution to political affairs was made apparent when it became the first of the two Houses to allow television coverage of its debates. In those showings, the somnolent peers scattered along the red benches in the nineteenth century might have recognized their successors, yet they would be astonished not only at the survival of 'their Lordships' House' but at its still secure place in the affections of their countrymen.

REFERENCES

1. 1 & 2 Geo.V cap. 13.
2. E. Allyn, *Lords versus Commons: a Century of Conflict and Compromises, 1830–1930* (New York, 1931), pp. 216–7.
3. J.P. Morgan, *The House of Lords and the Labour Government 1964–70* (Oxford, 1975), p. 5.
4. *Ibid.*, p. 21.
5. M.L. Bush, *The English Aristocracy. A Comparative Synthesis* (Manchester, 1984), p. 37. For analysis of new peerages, 1911–54, see P.A. Bromhead, *The House of Lords and Contemporary Politics 1911–57* (1958), pp. 22–30.
6. Morgan, *House of Lords and Labour Government*, p. 11.
7. Allyn, *Lords versus Commons*, p. 221.

Bibliography

MANUSCRIPT SOURCES

Add. MSS, British Library.
Chatsworth MSS
Granville MSS, Public Record Office
Grey MSS, Durham
Hatherton MSS, Staffordshire Record Office
Newcastle MSS, Nottingham University Library
Sutherland MSS, Staffordshire Record Office

PRINTED SOURCES
Unless otherwise stated, the place of publication is London.

Works of Reference

Contemporary
Annual Register.
Blackwood's Edinburgh Magazine XXIX, 1831, and XXXV, 1834.
The Builder V. 1847.
Dublin Almanac. 1839.
General Almanac of Scotland, and British Register. 1813.
Gentleman's and Citizen's Almanac. Dublin, 1815.
Gentleman's Magazine XXVII. 1847.
The Parliamentary History of England III and IV. 1808.
Hansard, *Parliamentary Debates* XXIX–XLI (1815–20).

Hansard, *Parliamentary Debates*, new series I–XXV (1821–30).

Hansard, *Parliamentary Debates* 3rd ser., I–CCXXVI (1831–75).

Journals of the House of Lords L–CVII (1815–75).

Journals of the House of Commons, IX (1678).

A Key to Both Houses of Parliament. 1832.

The National Review. new series. 1888.

New Edinburgh Almanac. 1875, 1880.

T.H.B. Oldfield, *Representative History of Great Britain and Ireland*. 1816.

Poor Man's Guardian.

The Times.

Secondary

J. Bateman, *The Great Landowners of Great Britain and Ireland*. 1883.

G.E.C[ockayne], *The Complete Peerage* 13 vols. 1910–59.

G.E.C[ockayne], 'The peerage of Ireland', *Genealogist* N. S. V, 1889, 1–16, 82–9, 145–52, 180–205.

Sir James Balfour Paul, *The Scots Peerage* 9 vols. Edinburgh, 1904–14.

W. Carpenter, *A Peerage for the People*. 1837.

C.R.R. Dod, *Electoral Facts, 1832–52* ed. H.J. Hanham. 1972.

English Historical Documents, 1783–1832, XI, ed. A. Aspinall and E.A. Smith. 1959.

[J. Wade], *The Extraordinary Black Book*. 1832. chap. 6, pp. 254–85.

Appendix to the Black Book. 1834.

P. Ford and G. Ford, *A Breviate of Parliamentary Papers 1917–1939*. Oxford, 1951.

J. Grant, *Random Recollections of the House of Lords* 2nd edn. 1836.

The House of Commons 1790–1820 ed. R. Thorne, 5 vols. 1986.

Dictionary of National Biography (*DNB*).

Handbook of British Chronology ed. E.B. Fryde, D.E. Greenway, S. Porter and I. Roy. 3rd edn. 1986.

38th Annual Report of the Deputy Keeper of the Public Records. 1877.

J.E. Thorold Rogers, *A Complete Collection of the Protests of the Lords* 3 vols. 1875.

Official Publications of the House of Lords

Handlist of Articles in Periodicals relating to the History of Parliament comp. H.S. Cobb. 1973.

Officers of the House of Lords 1485–1971. House of Lords Record Office Memorandum no. 45. ed. J.C. Sainty. 1971.

J.C. Sainty, *The Origin of the Office of Chairman of Committees in the House of Lords*. House of Lords Record Office Memorandum no. 52. 1974.

J.C. Sainty, *Representative Peers for Scotland, 1707–1963, and for Ireland, 1800–1961*. House of Lords Record Office Memorandum no. 39. 1968.

Private Bill Records of the House of Lords, House of Lords Record Office Memorandum 16.

Leaders and Whips in the House of Lords 1783–1964. House of Lords Record Office Memorandum no. 31. 1964.

Guide to the Records of Parliament ed. M.F. Bond. House of Lords Record Office. 1971.

Contemporary diaries, memoirs, correspondence and other publications (in alphabetical order of the subject or author, by name or title)

Sir Denis Le Marchant, *Memoir of John Charles Viscount Althorp, Third Earl Spencer*. 1876.

Correspondence of Charles Arbuthnot ed. A. Aspinall. Camden 3rd ser., LXV. 1941.

The Journal of Mrs Arbuthnot 1820–1832 ed. F. Bamford and the Duke of Wellington. 2 vols. 1950.

Autobiography and Memoirs of George Douglas, 8th Duke of Argyll, ed. Dowager Duchess of Argyll. 2 vols. 1906.

W. Bagehot, *The English Constitution*, 1963 edn.

Memoir of Charles James Blomfield, D.D. Bishop of London, ed. A. Blomfield. 2 vols. 1863.

Diaries of John Bright ed. R.A.J. Walling. 1930.

Diary of Lord Hatherton, Hatherton MSS.

Life and Speeches of the Rt. Hon. John Bright MP ed. G.B. Smith. 1881.

Public Addresses by John Bright, MP ed. J.E. Thorold Rogers. 1879.

The Life and Times of Henry, Lord Brougham, written by himself. 3 vols. 1871.

J.C. Hobhouse, 1st Baron Broughton, *Recollections of a Long Life* ed. Lady Dorchester. 6 vols. 1909–11.

Memoirs of the Courts and Cabinets of William IV and Queen Victoria ed. Duke of Buckingham and Chandos. 2 vols. 1861.

E. Lytton Bulwer, *Letter to a Late Cabinet Minister*. 1834.

Life of John, Lord Campbell ed. Mrs M.S. Hardcastle. 2 vols. 1881.

T. Carlyle, *Works*, XI. 1869.

Memoirs and Correspondence of Viscount Castlereagh ed. marquess of Londonderry. 4 vols. 1849.

Life and Letters of George William Frederick, 4th Earl of Clarendon, ed. Sir H. Maxwell. 2 vols. 1913.

Journal of Henry Cockburn, 1831–54. 2 vols. 1874.

Diary and Correspondence of Charles Abbot, Lord Colchester, ed. Lord Colchester. 3 vols. 1861.

The Creevey Papers ed. Sir H. Maxwell. 1903.

The Croker Papers ed. L.J. Jennings. 3 vols. 1884.

B. Disraeli, *Vindication of the English Constitution in a letter to a noble and learned lord.* 1835. Reprinted in W. Hutcheon (ed.) *Whigs and Whiggism: Political Writings by Benjamin Disraeli.* New York, 1913.

S.J. Reid, *Life and Letters of the First Earl of Durham 1792–1840.* 2 vols. 1906.

A Political Diary, 1828–30, by Edward Law, Lord Ellenborough ed. Lord Silchester. 2 vols. 1881.

Lord Forbes, *The House of Lords, 1874–1891. A Sketch.* Edinburgh, 1891.

Letters of King George IV ed. A. Aspinall. 3 vols. Cambridge, 1938.

C.S.Parker, *Life and Letters of Sir James Graham 1792–1861.* 2 vols. 1907.

C.C.F. Greville, *Journal of the Reigns of George IV and William IV* ed. H. Reeve. 3 vols. 1874.

C.C.F. Greville, *Journal of the Reign of Queen Victoria, 1837–52* ed. H.Reeve. 3 vols. 1885.

The Greville Diary ed. P.W. Wilson. 2 vols. 1927.

Correspondence of Earl Grey with H.M. King William IV and with Sir Herbert Taylor from Nov. 1830 to June 1832 ed. Henry, Earl Grey. 2 vols. 1867.

The Diary of Gathorne Hardy, First Lord Cranbrook ed. Nancy Johnson. Oxford, 1981.

Autobiography and Memoirs of Benjamin Robert Haydon 1786–1846 ed. A.P.D. Penrose. 1927.

Three Howard Sisters ed. Lady Leconfield and John Gore. 1955.

Correspondence of Sarah Spencer, Lady Lyttelton, 1782–1870 ed. Mrs Hugh Wyndham. 1912.

Letters of T.B. Macaulay ed. T. Pinney. 6 vols. Cambridge, 1974–81.

Lord Melbourne's Papers, ed. L.C. Sanders. 2nd edn. 1890.

John, Viscount Morley, *Recollections.* 1917.

Diary of Philipp von Neumann ed. E. Beresford Chancellor. 1928.

The Correspondence of Daniel O'Connell, ed. M.R. O'Connell. 3 vols. Dublin, 1972–80.

Lady Palmerston and her Times ed. Mabell, Countess Airlie. 1922.

Memories, by Lord Redesdale (1867–76), ed. Lord Redesdale, 2 vols. 1915.

Later Correspondence of Lord John Russell 1840–78 ed. G.P. Gooch. 1925.

Memorials, Personal and Political, 1869–95 by Roundell Palmer, Earl of Selborne, ed. S.M. Palmer. 1898.

Diary of Frances Lady Shelley 1818–1873 ed. R. Edgecumbe. 1913.

Letters, Remains, and Memoirs of Edward . . . 12th Duke of Somerset ed. W.H. Mallock and Lady Gwendolen Ramsden. 1893.

[Alexander Somerville], *Autobiography of a Working Man.* 1848.

Letterbag of Elizabeth Spencer Stanhope, 1806–73 ed. A.M.W. Stirling. 2 vols. 1913.

A. de Tocqueville, *Journeys to England and Ireland* ed. J.P. Mayer. 1968.

Letters of Queen Victoria ed. A.C. Benson and Viscount Esher. 1st ser. 1907, ed. G.E. Buckle; II ser. 1926.

Correspondence of Lady Burghersh with the Duke of Wellington ed. Lady Rose Weigall. 1903.

Despatches, Correspondence and Memoranda of Field Marshal Arthur, Duke of Wellington, K.G. 1819–32 ed. by his son. 8 vols. 1867–80.

Wellington and his Friends ed. 7th Duke of Wellington. 1965.

The Prime Minister's Papers: Wellington, Political Correspondence ed. J. Brooke and J.Gandy. 2 vols 1833–4, 1834–5. 1975–86.

Correspondence of Charlotte Grenville, Lady Williams Wynn ed. Rachel Leighton. 1920.

Autobiographies and Biographies (in alphabetical order of subject)

Marquess of Anglesey, *One Leg: The Life and Letters of Henry William Paget, First Marquess of Anglesey.* 1961.

G.M. Trevelyan, *The Life of John Bright.* 1925.

J.J. Bagley, *The Earls of Derby, 1485–1985.* 1985.

Bernard Holland, *The Life of Spencer Compton, 8th Duke of Devonshire* 2nd edn. 2 vols. 1911.

W.F. Monypenny and G.E. Buckle, *Life of Benjamin Disraeli.* 2 vols. rev.edn. 1929.

R. Blake, *Disraeli.* 1966.

Holden Furber, *Henry Dundas.* Oxford, 1931.

Anita Leslie, *Mrs Fitzherbert.* 1960.

Lord Edmond Fitzmaurice, *Life of . . . second Earl Granville.* 2 vols. 1905.

E.A. Smith, *Lord Grey, 1764–1845.* Oxford, 1990.

A.G. Gardiner, *The Life of Sir William Harcourt.* 1923.

Lord Newton, *Lord Lansdowne, a Biography.* 1929.

Lord Malmesbury, *Memoirs of an Ex-Minister.* 1854.

Mary Soames, *The Profligate Duke* [Marlborough]. 1987.

W.M. Torrens, *Memoirs of William Lamb, second Viscount Melbourne.* 1890.

P. Ziegler, *Melbourne.* 1976 and 1978 edn.

G. Wallas, *Life of Francis Place.* 1918.

A Regency Visitor: the English Tour of Prince Pückler-Muskau ed. E.M. Butler. 1957.

R.E. Leader, *Life of J.A. Roebuck.* 1897.

G.W.E. Russell, *Collections and Recollections.* 1903.

Spencer Walpole, *Life of Lord John Russell.* 2 vols. 1889.

Lady Gwendolen Cecil, *Life of Robert Marquis of Salisbury.* 4 vols. 1921–32.

Sir Sydney Lee, *Queen Victoria.* 1904.

E. Longford, *Victoria R.I.* 1964.

Sir H. Maxwell, *The Life of Wellington.* 2 vols. 1900.

Gervas Huxley, *Victorian Duke: the Life of Hugh Lupus Grosvenor, 1st Duke of Westminster.* Oxford, 1967.

Other Secondary Works

D.H. Akenson, *The Church of Ireland, 1800–85.* New Haven, Conn., 1971.

E. Allyn, *Lords versus Commons: a Century of Conflict and Compromise, 1830–1930.* New York, 1931.

A. Aspinall, *Three Early-Nineteenth Century Diaries.* 1952.

A. Badeau, *Aristocracy in England.* New York, 1885.

W. Bagehot, *The English Constitution.* 1963 edn.

D.G. Barnes, *George III and William Pitt.* New York, 1965.

J.V. Beckett, *The Aristocracy in England, 1660–1914.* Oxford, 1986.

P.A. Bromhead, *The House of Lords and Contemporary Politics 1911–57.* 1958.

C.K. Francis Brown, *A History of the English Clergy 1800–1900.* 1953.

M.L. Bush, *The English Aristocracy. A Comparative Synthesis.* Manchester, 1984.

J.R.M. Butler, *The Passing of the Great Reform Bill.* 1914.

D. Cannadine, *The Decline and Fall of the British Aristocracy.* 1990.

D. Cannadine, *Lords and Landlords: the Aristocracy and the Towns. 1774–1967.* Leicester, 1980.

J. Cannon, *Aristocratic Century.* Cambridge, 1984.

J. Mordaunt Crook and M.H. Port, *The King's Works* VI, 1782–1851. 1973.

C.S. Emden, *The People and the Constitution.* 2nd edn. Oxford, 1956.

R.C.K. Ensor, *England, 1870–1914.* Oxford, 1936.

T.H.S. Escott, *England, her People, Polity, and Pursuits.* 1879.

Sir James Fergusson, *The Sixteen Peers of Scotland*. Oxford, 1960.

N. Gash, *Aristocracy and People: Britain 1815–1865*. 1979.

N. Gash, *Politics in the Age of Peel*. 1953.

N. Gash, *Reaction and Reconstruction in English Politics, 1832–52*. Oxford, 1965.

M. Girouard, *A Country House Companion*. 1987.

W.L. Guttsman, *The British Political Elite*. 1963.

W.L. Guttsman, *The English Ruling Class*. 1969.

C. Jones and D.L. Jones (eds), *Peers, Politics, and Power, 1603–1911*. 1986.

W.D. Jones, *Lord Derby and Victorian Conservatism*. Oxford, 1956.

Anita Leslie Mrs Fitzherbert (1960).

G.H.L. le May, *The Victorian Constitution*. 1979.

M.W. McCahill, *Order and Equipoise: the Peerage and the House of Lords, 1783–1806*. 1978.

P. Mandler, *Aristocratic Government in the Age of Reform*. Oxford, 1990.

W.L. Mathieson, *English Church Reform 1815–1840*. 1923.

J.P. Morgan, *The House of Lords and the Labour Government, 1964–70*. Oxford, 1975.

B.K. Murray, *The People's Budget, 1909–10*. Oxford, 1980.

L.B. Namier, *Crossroads of Power*. 1962.

H. Perkin, *The Origins of Modern English Society*. 1969.

Sir Charles Petrie, *The Carlton Club*. 1955.

N.C. Phillips, *Yorkshire and English National Politics*. Christchurch N.Z. 1961.

L.G. Pine, *Constitutional History of the House of Lords*. 1894.

The Houses of Parliament ed. M.H. Port. 1976.

N. Ravitch, *Sword and Mitre*. The Hague, 1966.

W.D. Rubinstein, *Men of Property*. 1981.

R.D.H. Seaman, *The Reform of the Lords*. 1971.

D. Southgate, *The Passing of the Whigs, 1832–1886*. 1962.

D. Spring, *The English Landed Estate in the 19th Century: Its Administration*. Baltimore, Md. 1963.

R.B. Stevens, *Law and Politics: the House of Lords as a Judicial Body 1800–1976*. 1979.

F.M.L. Thompson, *English Landed Society in the Nineteenth Century*. 1963.

A.S. Turberville, *The House of Lords in the Age of Reform 1784–1837*. 1958.

E.L. Woodward, *The Age of Reform 1815–70*, 2nd edn. Oxford, 1939.

A. Wright and R. Smith, *Parliament Past and Present*. 1902.

Articles and Essays

O. Anderson, 'The Wensleydale peerage case and the position of the House of Lords in the mid-nineteenth century', *English Historical Review* LXXXII, 1967. 486–502.

W.L. Arnstein, 'The survival of the Victorian aristocracy', in *The Rich, the Well-Born and the Powerful*, ed. F.C. Jaher (Urbana, Ill., 1973).

A. Aspinall, 'The Grand Cabinet, 1800–1837', *Politica*, Dec. 1938.

A. Aspinall, 'The Cabinet Council 1783–1835', *Proceedings of the British Academy* XXXVIII, 1953.

T.W. Bamford, 'Public schools and social class, 1801–50', *British Journal of Sociology* XII, 1961. 224–35.

T. Beven, 'The appellate jurisdiction of the House of Lords', *Law Quarterly Review* XVII, 1901; part II; 357–71.

T.S.R. Boase, 'The decoration of the new palace of Westminster 1841–63', *Journal of the Warburg and Courtauld Institutes* XVII, 1954. 319–58.

H. Colvin, 'Views of the old palace of Westminster', *Architectural History* IX, 1966. 13–184.

P. Tudor-Craig, 'The Painted Chamber at Westminster', *Archaeological Journal* CXIV, 1957. 92–105.

R.W. Davis, 'Deference and Aristocracy in the time of the Reform Bill', *American Historical Review* LXXXI, 1976, 532–9.

T. Edwards, 'Barry and his Gothic palace', *Contemporary Review*, July 1960. 386–8.

T. Edwards, 'Charles Barry and the palace of Westminster', *History Today*, May 1960. 302–12.

V.M.R. Goodman, 'Appellate jurisdiction', *Parliamentary Affairs* VII, no. 1, 1953. 77–87.

F.J. Grady, 'The exclusion of Catholics from the Lord Chancellorship, 1673–1954', *Recusant History* VIII, 1965. 166–74.

W.J.J. Gun, 'The succession to baronies by writ of summons', *Genealogists' Magazine* V, no. 2, 1929: part 2, 34–7.

S.M. Hardy and R.C. Baily, 'The downfall of the Gower interest in the Staffordshire boroughs, 1800–30', *Historical Collections, Staffordshire*. 1950–1.

T.H. Hollingsworth, 'A demographic study of British ducal families', *Journal of Population Studies*. 1957, 4–26.

T.H. Hollingsworth, 'The demography of the British peerage', *Population Studies* suppt. XVIII, 1964.

D. Large, 'The decline of the "party of the Crown" and the rise of parties in the House of Lords, 1783–1837', *English Historical Review* LXXVIII, 1963. 669–95.

D. Large, 'The House of Lords and Ireland in the age of Peel, 1832–50', in *Peers, Politics and Power* (qv), pp. 373–405.

M.W. McCahill, 'Peerage creations and the changing character of the British nobility 1750–1850', in *Peers, Politics, and Power* (qv), pp. 407–32.

M.W. McCahill, 'Peers, patronage and the Industrial Revolution, 1760–1800' in *Peers, Politics and Power* (qv), pp. 433–56.

W.B. Perkins, 'The English Judicature Act of 1873', *Michigan Law Review* XII, 1914. 277–92.

G.D. Phillips, 'The Whig Lords and Liberalism, 1886–1893', *Historical Journal* XXIV, 1981. 167–73.

J. Enoch Powell, 'Proxy voting in the House of Lords', *Parliamentary Affairs* IX, 2, 1955–6. 203.

R.E. Pumphrey, 'The Introduction of Industrialists into the British Peerage', *American Historical Review* LXV, 1959. 1–16.

J.J. Sack, 'The House of Lords and parliamentary patronage in Great Britain, 1802–32' in *Peers, Politics, and Power* (qv), pp. 347–71.

D. Slater, 'Beaconsfield: or Disraeli in the Elysian Fields', in *Parliamentary History, Libraries and Records: Essays presented to Maurice Bond* ed. H.S. Cobb. House of Lords Record Office, 1981.

E.A. Smith, 'Earl Fitzwilliam and Malton', *English Historical Review* LXXX. 1965. 51–69.

E.A. Smith 'The Pageant of Monarchy', *The Historian*, 31, 1991, 13–16.

R. Stevens, 'The final appeal: reform of the House of Lords and the Privy Council 1867–76', *Law Quarterly Review* LXXX, 1964. 343–69.

A.S. Turberville, 'The episcopal bench 1783–1837', *Church Quarterly Review* CXXIII, Jan.–March 1937. 261–285.

A.S. Turberville, 'The House of Lords and the advent of democracy, 1837–67', *History* XXIX, 1944. 152–83.

C.C. Weston, 'The royal mediation in 1884', *English Historical Review* LXXXII, 1967. 296–322.

C.C. Weston, 'The Liberal leadership and the Lords' veto 1907–11', *Historical Journal* XI, 1968. 508–37.

C.C. Weston, 'Salisbury and the Lords, 1868–1895', *Historical Journal* XXV, 1982. 103–29.

Unpublished Ph.D. theses

A. Adonis, 'The political role of the British peerage in the third Reform Act system', Oxford D. Phil. 1988.

R.S. Fraser, 'The House of Lords in the first Parliament of Queen Victoria, 1837–41', Cornell Ph.D. 1967.

J.M. Sweeney, 'The House of Lords in British politics, 1830–41', Oxford D. Phil. 1973.

P.B. Zaring, 'In Defense of the Past: The House of Lords, 1860–86', Yale Ph.D. 1966.

Index